PACIFIC
OCEAN

RUS

DEN

KENYA

SEYCHELLES

ZANZIBAR
YASALAND

MAURITIUS

ZILAND
LAND

INDIAN OCEAN

HONG KONG

SINGAPORE

FEDERATION
OF MALAYA

NORTH BORNEO
BRUNEI
SARAWAK

BRITISH
SOLOMON
ISLANDS

GILBERT
AND
ELLICE IS

NEW
HEBRIDES

FIJI IS

TONGA

Colonies, Protectorates, Protected States and Trust
Territories, the affairs of which are dealt with in
the Colonial Office

South Africa High Commission Territories

Other countries of the Commonwealth

The Colonial Office

The Colonial Office

SIR CHARLES JEFFRIES

K.C.M.G., O.B.E.

Deputy Under-Secretary of State
for the Colonies

With a Foreword by
SIR THOMAS LLOYD

G.C.M.G., K.C.B.

Permanent Under-Secretary of State
for the Colonies

GREENWOOD PRESS, PUBLISHERS
WESTPORT, CONNECTICUT

Library of Congress Cataloging in Publication Data

Jeffries, Charles Joseph, Sir, 1896-
  The Colonial Office.

    Reprint. Originally published: London ; New York :
Allen & Unwin, 1956.
    Includes index.
    1. Great Britain. Colonial Office. 2. Great
Britain--Colonies--Administration. I. Title.
JV1043.J4 1983   325'.31'41   83-10876
ISBN 0-313-24122-8 (lib. bdg.)

Other books by Sir Charles Jeffries

THE COLONIAL EMPIRE AND ITS CIVIL SERVICE

PARTNERS FOR PROGRESS

THE COLONIAL POLICE

etc.

First published by George Allen & Unwin in 1956

Reprinted with the permission of George Allen & Unwin, Ltd.

Reprinted in 1983 by Greenwood Press
A division of Congressional Information Service, Inc.
88 Post Road West, Westport, Connecticut 06881

Printed in the United States of America

10 9 8 7 6 5 4 3 2 1

Foreword

THE other volumes already published in the *New Whitehall Series* were the work of teams from within the organisations which they covered. Sir Charles Jeffries has acknowledged his debt to his colleagues in the Colonial Office, both past and present, for their assistance, without which his task could not have been accomplished, but the book as it stands is his production and to him goes the credit, as well as the responsibility, for what is contained in it. His long experience of the Office, which he has served continuously since 1917, and the gifts as an author which he had shown in a number of published works, made him an obvious choice for this undertaking. That choice he has more than justified by the comprehensive account which he has here given both of the ways in which the organisation and work of the Office have altered and expanded with the rapid constitutional development in the Colonial territories, and of the change of relationships, through that cause and others, between their Governments and Her Majesty's Government in the United Kingdom. I am particularly glad that he has chosen to pay tribute both to the loyal and enthusiastic spirit which, throughout this time of stress and change, has animated the staff of the Colonial Office, and to the personal friendliness which, both within the Office and between its members and those of Her Majesty's Oversea Colonial Service is, to my mind, one of our distinctive and most agreeable features.

The Colonial Office was, I believe, once likened to a grandmother burdened with the care and rearing of a brood of young children. I doubt whether the simile was ever really sound, and certainly it no longer holds. In some places and in some respects our role is still that of a guardian but for the most part it has now evolved into that of counsellor and friend. I can confidently recommend this book to all who are interested in the story of that process of evolution and in the practical working of the machinery by which Her Majesty's Secretary of State for the Colonies carries out his responsibilities.

T. I. K. LLOYD

Author's Preface

LET me face it at the start. This book will be dubbed complacent by those in whom the very sight or sound of the word 'Colonial' awakens angry passions, and also by those who conceive of 'Colonial Office rule' as something negative, damping and frustrating.

No charge of complacency, however, shall deter me from writing with affection, admiration and enthusiasm about the Office in which I have had the honour to spend my working life, or from maintaining that the Colonial Office is a good place in which to serve and that its work is continuously, and on the whole successfully, directed towards the realisation of worthy ideals. What I have put in this book is of my own knowledge and belief, and I have been under no official inhibition or compulsion to state a case.

Of course the Colonial Office has made mistakes. It is, after all, a body of imperfect human beings, dealing with problems of immense complexity in which a straight choice between the good cause and the bad is rarely possible. There have been occasions when the Civil Servants have given unwise advice or failed to give wise advice to Ministers. There have been occasions when Ministers, for reasons that seemed good at the time, have taken decisions which proved to have been unwise. What else could be expected?

But when I came into the Office as a very young man, I received an impression which time and experience have only strengthened and confirmed. Though more innocent in those days than now, I was even then a little surprised to discover that, in considering every question which came up to them for decision, my superiors asked themselves not what was expedient or fashionable or convenient or economical but what, in all the circumstances of the given case, was 'right'. And in judging of what was 'right' they were guided by a code which was no less compulsive for being unwritten and taken for granted. It was indeed the common code of our British Christian cultural inheritance, and amongst its rules were such as these—that an undertaking once given must be honoured at whatever cost; that every person has an equal title to have his case heard and to receive impartial justice; that the rights of the individual against the state are as important as the rights of the state against the individual; that in case of doubt, judgment should err, if err it must, in the direction of charity.

If, then, mistakes were made, they were ascribable to insufficient knowledge or appreciation of the factors which should have been

7

taken into account, rather than to any unworthy element in the approach of the Office to a problem.

In its internal working, too, the Office code stood firmly against self-seeking, intrigue and personal rivalry. I cannot compare the Colonial Office with other institutions in which I have not lived and worked, but I doubt whether any other official or unofficial organisation can be more free from these evils than the Colonial Office as I have known it. Here again, it would be absurd to claim perfection, but there is undoubtedly a corporate spirit in the Office which keeps such tendencies firmly in check.

Most of us, quite frankly, have come into the Office with the simple purpose of earning our livings, and perhaps with the thought of work here as 'a job in the Civil Service'. The Office is indeed part of the Home Civil Service, but, like the other oversea departments of State (the Foreign Office and the Commonwealth Relations Office), by the nature of its work and functions it stands a little apart from the complex organisation of interrelated departments which collectively carries on the government of the United Kingdom. It has an intense life of its own, and inspires in its members a special kind of loyalty which, without being pretentious or sentimental about it, I can fairly describe as a sense of vocation. The Colonial Office is not quite like any other institution, inside or outside the Civil Service. There are few men or women privileged to serve in the Office for many years in any capacity who, when the time has come for them to take their leave, have not testified with complete sincerity that they would not have exchanged this service for any other. That is the inheritance which has been handed down, and the same spirit lives on in spite of all changes, expansions and developments.

To those of the past who have built up this goodly heritage and to those who carry the torch to-day, this contemporary portrait is affectionately dedicated.

I have in general refrained from referring by name to living members of the Office, whether serving or retired, and I have named only a random few of the many distinguished figures in the Office's history. To list here all those of my present colleagues who have helped with advice, material, criticisms and suggestions in the writing of this book would be impossible; it must suffice to acknowledge collectively the generous assistance without which my task could not have been discharged.

I may perhaps, however, be allowed to single out for personal thanks Sir Cosmo Parkinson, who has encouraged me in the writing and permitted me to use published and unpublished material; and also my wife, who has done a large part of the typing.

Colonial Office,
January, 1955.

Contents

A•

Introduction

AN author beginning a book about the Colonial Office might fairly claim to invoke the patronage of some at least of the Muses: of Clio, certainly, who has charge of history, and of Urania who oversees the globe; of Calliope, noblest of the Nine, the epic Muse; of Thalia, too, and of Melpomene, for comedy and tragedy both have their places in the story.

But perhaps a Christian writer would do better to call in humility upon the Saints to whose protection devout discoverers committed the islands of the as yet uncharted seas: upon St. Vincent and St. Lucia, St. Christopher and St. Helena, St. Ursula and her virgin train; above all upon St. Michael and St. George, joint patrons of that Order of chivalry whose Chancery is housed in the Colonial Office. For, though a government department is not commonly a theme of romance, the dingiest Colonial Office window is a magic casement. Here the great names, charged with ancient mystery, are mere household words, the copper currency of daily business— Zanzibar and Sierra Leone, Seychelles and Fiji, Ashanti and Jamaica, Tonga and Trinidad and Tristan, Kano and Calabar and a hundred more. Here, too, strange fruits and spices for the sake of which men of old time ventured their lives to circumnavigate the world—pineapple and banana, lime and mango, coconut and clove, cinnamon and pepper—are but matters for prosaic minuting in an Economic Department file. In and out of these dull London office rooms pass men and women, rulers and statesmen, officials and students, of a vast diversity of races, tongues and creeds; strangely and unsuitably garbed, sometimes, for English weather, yet all familiar visitors and colleagues whose presence here, though they have come five thousand miles since yesterday, is so natural as to pass without comment.

THE OFFICE TRADITION

During the years from 1875 to 1947, while the Colonial Office occupied the building on the south-east corner of Downing Street, there hung in the room of the Permanent Under-Secretary of State an ever growing portrait gallery of all those who had held the seals of the Office of Secretary of State with charge over the Colonies since the Earl of Hilsborough (afterwards Marquess of Downshire) became the first Secretary of State in 1768. Some day the line of portraits will be properly displayed in a new building, worthy of the Office and its great tradition. To-day the pictures are disposed along the corridor leading to the Conference Room in the Colonial Office's temporary quarters in the Church House. This series of likenesses, from the Earl of Hilsborough to the last incumbent of the Office, is a reminder that the Colonial Office is not, properly speaking, an institution at all. It is the Secretary of State who is the institution. The Colonial Office is a name signifying the place where he does his work or, alternatively, the staff which helps him to do his work.

But the portrait gallery is a reminder, also, that Secretaries of State come and go, sometimes with disconcerting frequency, according to the dispositions of Providence, of Prime Ministers or of the electorate, but the Office goes on. The staff are there, preserving continuity and placing their experience and knowledge at the disposal of each new Minister without respect to Party or person. Whoever holds the seals of office, it is their unceasing task to provide him with the material which he needs in order to come to decisions; to translate his decisions into action; and to carry out on his behalf and under his general authority, a mass of duties for which he is responsible but which—being but one human being—he could not possibly deal with in person. In handling this mass of work the staff must largely rely upon a corporate tradition, built up through many decades, by which the attitude of each official towards the matter in hand is determined, and by which the principles behind whatever practical action he may take are firmly established. Even Secretaries of State may not lightly set aside the garnered and matured experience of their Office. To expound this tradition will be one of the main purposes of this book. But the principles themselves have been stated in words that cannot be improved upon by a former Permanent Under-Secretary of State, Sir Cosmo Parkinson:

On 10th April, 1942, I said good-bye to my colleagues in the Colonial Office, and I made to them my confession of faith after thirty-three years of administrative work in Government service. I gave them my favourite words from all English literature, words that come from the Bible: 'Stand ye in the ways, and see, and ask for the old paths, where is the good way, and walk therein, and ye shall find rest for your souls.'

The old paths where is the good way, signify for me certain unchangeable principles of action; they were true when the world was made, they are true to-day, and they will be true to the end of time. Unhappily, it is possible to depart from them: but whatever the apparent immediate advantage, nothing would ever convince me that good can ultimately come of it. These principles can be stated quite simply; they are—just dealing, honesty of purpose, and humanity. 'And for my part,' I said, 'I would not quarrel with any who should hold that the greatest of these is humanity.'[1]

The Colonial Office from Within.

SOME MAKERS OF THE TRADITION

In spite of all constitutional niceties, the Colonial Office is then, after all, an institution *de facto* if not *de jure*. Its tradition is a live thing, created and developed by people. Every Secretary of State makes some mark upon the Office, some contribution to the tradition. There have been great Secretaries of State who have altered the course not merely of Office history. It would be improper to discuss the living, but, amongst the dead, few if any could challenge the claim to pre-eminence of Joseph Chamberlain who held the seals of the Colonial Department from 1895 to 1903, by far the longest tenure of this office in modern times. But the average length of time during which a Secretary of State is in office is two years, and it is no reflection upon these great men to suggest that it is chiefly to the successive generations of permanent staff that the formation and growth of tradition must be ascribed. Since 1825 there have been no more than eighteen holders of the office of Permanent Under-Secretary of State. There have been fifteen Secretaries of State since 1925. Five of these, however, had previously served in the Office as Parliamentary Under-Secretary or Minister of State.

The Colonial Office has never lacked civil servants of outstanding, and often of extremely individual, character, whose influence upon their colleagues has been decisive. An agreeable book could be written on 'Colonial Office Worthies'. It would include, no doubt, the young Henry Edward Manning, a Supernumerary Clerk from 1830 to 1832, whose portrait in Cardinal's vestments now hangs in an Office room; but it must be confessed that in fact no record of any notable work done by him in the Office has been traced. It would certainly include the 'estimable but crotchety old baronet, who had no sympathy with holidays himself and was unable to understand any necessity for them in the case of others', under whom Sir William Baillie-Hamilton served when he entered the Office in 1864. Even this martinet was satisfied if his juniors

appeared punctually at 12 and remained till 5.30, at which hour, without fail, he himself would be tucked carefully into his brougham and driven home to West Kensington. And while enforcing strict discipline on his subordinates, the good old gentleman was careful not to impair his own constitution by overwork. It was his daily habit, after luncheon, to ensconce himself in a cunningly designed rocking-chair, and for exactly one hour to devote himself, ostensibly, to the perusal of old *Quarterly Reviews*, to which it was understood that bygone members of his family had been extensive contributors, and from which he doubtless derived much edification and support. During this period he was very properly altogether inaccessible; and it would in fact have been dangerous to disturb him.[1]

[1] 'Forty-four Years at the Colonial Office', in *The Nineteenth Century*, April, 1909.

A catalogue of 'worthies' could not omit Sir Henry Taylor, poet, dramatist and author of *The Statesman*, who joined the Office in 1824, and in 1847 was offered and refused the post of Permanent Under-Secretary. In 1859 he tendered his resignation on account of ill-health 'but his services were too valuable to lose, and accordingly he was allowed to live at Bournemouth, was sent the despatches by mail, and got £200 a year extra'.[1]

Taylor was not only an enviable but a great civil servant, yet himself confessed that his senior, Sir James Stephen, Permanent Under-Secretary from 1836 to 1847, was 'one of the largest intellects of his day and generation'. Often violently attacked as 'Mr. Over-Secretary' and 'Mr. Mother-Country', Stephen was in fact a liberal and humble-minded man with the good of humanity, and especially of the newly liberated slaves, very close to his heart.

The coming of competitive examination as the method of entry into the Colonial Office, in common with other government departments, in 1877, did not dry up the supply of 'worthies'. It may even have stimulated the flow. The recollections of Sir Cosmo Parkinson, and of others now alive, go back to days when the first generations of examination entrants were still in active service. One indisputable claimant to 'worthiness' amongst the earlier members of the new civil service was Sidney Webb. He joined the Office as a Second Class Clerk (Assistant Principal, we should say nowadays) in 1881 and left in 1891 to take up the social and economic work for which he and Mrs. Webb became famous. In 1929 he returned to his old Office as Secretary of State, was created Lord Passfield, and remained until the change of government in 1931. His fellow-Fabian and fellow-junior in the Colonial Office, Sydney Olivier, eventually became Governor of Jamaica, and afterwards, as Lord Olivier, served as Secretary of State for India in the same government.

If Office legend can be trusted, there has never been a lack of 'characters' amongst the staff. There was the man who, tired of having the files over which he procrastinated removed from his room, took the top paper from each bundle home, so that his mature cogitation could not be disturbed. Large quantities of Office papers were recovered from his house after his death. His settled habit was only· temporarily disturbed even by the explosion which took place when an urgent troop movement in Africa could not be carried out because the soldiers had no trousers; the reason being that the indent for these necessary garments was still, after many months, awaiting his consideration.

Readers of Sir Arthur Grimble's *A Pattern of Islands* will recall the portrait there given of the departmental head who interviewed

[1] Henry L. Hall, *The Colonial Office*.

the young Grimble on his first appointment to a Cadetship, and will not deny his title to 'worthiness'. A near-contemporary of this man, whose great ability carried him to the top of the Service, gathered about him a collection of legends illustrating an outward show of cynicism which probably, as is so often found, concealed an essential kindliness. One story relates that, on leaving his office one Christmas Eve he went out, then looked back into the room and said to his colleagues: 'Oh, by the way, Merry Christmas, if you believe in that sort of thing'. It was possibly he of whom Sir Cosmo Parkinson tells the tale that, on being interrupted by a colleague, he looked up and said: 'You might shut the door . . . on the other side, please'.

To attempt to assess the claims of the living to inclusion in the list of 'worthies' would be impertinent, but the curious may find some hints in the intimate pages of Sir Cosmo Parkinson's *The Colonial Office from Within*. Amongst those who have but lately died, however, it is permissible to suggest some candidates. One, certainly, would be Sir Edward ('Eddie') Marsh, patron of art and poetry, inveterate first-nighter, translator of Horace and of La Fontaine, and prince of Private Secretaries. Beginning in 1896 as an ordinary civil servant, he became an Assistant Private Secretary four years later, and spent practically the whole of his remaining official life as Private Secretary to one Minister or another—either to Sir Winston Churchill in whatever office he happened to occupy or to the Secretary of State for the Colonies if Sir Winston was not in office. Eddie Marsh lent the Colonial Office a touch of elegance matched in a different way by Sir John Shuckburgh, a prose stylist who published all too little, but who touched no official file without adorning it: Lord Curzon declared him to be the best draftsman he had ever known. Shuckburgh joined the Office in 1921 as head of the newly formed Middle East Division, one of the more exotic members of which was a certain Colonel T. E. Lawrence, styled Adviser on Arabian Affairs.

Indeed, most of the men who entered the Office between 1877 and 1914—to go no farther backwards or forwards in time—were men of character, and examples could be multiplied almost indefinitely. Many of these men remained bachelors, and this circumstance, along with the generally leisurely and gentlemanly atmosphere in which business was conducted before the first world war, gave the Office the air of a club—one of those comfortable West-End clubs to which the civil servants repaired for luncheon and dinner—or of an Oxford or Cambridge Senior Common Room. The very furnishings, with their solid, dark mahogany and deep leather upholstery, and the smoky coal fires, so much more comforting than the soulless radiator, contributed to the illusion.

One of the pleasant features of the Office has always been the scope which it has given to members of the staff to make their work a hobby. Sir Herbert Read, who served in the Office from 1889 to 1924, and then became Governor of Mauritius, was the chief originator of the great drive against tropical disease which marked the first quarter of this century. E. R. Darnley, for many years head of the West Indian Department, took a single-minded interest in the problems of whaling and set in motion the great oceanic research organisation based on the Royal Research ships *Discovery* and *Discovery II*. J. F. N. Green, who served from 1896 to 1934, was a geologist of renown and was always consulted when any geological question arose on Office files. Others took up entomology, currency, survey, forestry and other abstruse subjects which they came across in their official duties, and acquired if not a professional at any rate a respectable amateur status. This was of great benefit to the Office in the days when life was simpler and the need for expert, whole-time Advisers had not made itself felt.

These observations have related more especially to the Administrative or what used to be called the 'First Division' Staff, but they apply also to the old 'Second Division'. There was only a small establishment of Second Division men in the old days, much of the routine and clerical work being done by the apprentice administrators; and although in Civil Service theory there was a firm line drawn between the two Divisions, in the Office itself all were included in the same family. Many of the old Second Division civil servants were men of parts who could write you a guide to Westminster Abbey or compose devastating lampoons upon their official superiors, run a correspondence college for aspiring youth, or even keep a public house, in their not too restricted spare time. For, unlike the First Division, whose whole time was theoretically at the disposal of the Secretary of State and who therefore worked for no fixed hours, the Second Division were engaged for so many hours a day, and were free outside those hours to work or play as they wished—or so it was popularly supposed.

The temptation to dwell over-long on the good—or perhaps the bad—old days must be resisted. But these random comments have had a purpose, and that purpose is to establish in the reader's mind a conception of the Colonial Office as a living community with a pronounced characteristic flavour, or rather a peculiar blend of a number of strongly individual flavours.

FAMILY SPIRIT

For the greater part of its long history the Colonial Office was comparatively small, predominantly administrative (and also almost exclusively masculine) in character; and it was concentrated under a single roof. In these conditions, as has already been observed in this Introduction, it partook somewhat of the nature of a club. Everyone knew everyone else, there were no marked hierarchic distinctions and the atmosphere of the place was friendly, informal and even cosy. Except for Ministers and the Permanent Under-Secretary of State, who were conscientiously guarded by their Private Secretaries, anyone could be visited by anyone without the formality of making an appointment or even of knocking at the door,[1] and no one was addressed by his colleagues as 'sir'.

This well-rooted tradition has been maintained in spite of the expansions and changes of recent years. Though so much larger a family than it used to be, the Office is still a family. Admittedly it is more difficult than it was for everyone to know everyone else. The Office is too big and too much scattered for newcomers to be taken round (as was always done in the old days) and personally introduced to all their colleagues—a procedure which could indeed be embarrassing, as on one occasion long ago when the great man to whom the neophyte was to be presented was discovered fast asleep.

But the growth of the Office has had its compensations. It has made possible the creation of a number of flourishing social, cultural and sporting clubs. The fact that considerable numbers of women now serve in all grades from the Administrative downwards has no doubt had a civilising effect. (It has certainly produced more than one Office 'romance'.) The presence of many officers of H.M. Oversea Service and of members of the local public services in the Colonies, seconded for duty in the Office, has ensured that the home staff are kept in constant remembrance of the facts of life overseas. The social and economic changes which have led to the creation of an Office Refreshment Club (in the vulgar tongue canteen), where all ranks take meals together on strictly democratic lines instead of scattering to clubs and restaurants, have thus helped greatly to preserve the family spirit and to prevent disintegration. To the present writer, at least, one of the most inspiring and encouraging manifestations of that spirit is the monthly corporate service of Holy Communion which was started experimentally in November, 1952, for Anglican members of the staff. Held at 8.30 a.m. on the first Tuesday in each month, and followed by breakfast, these services have been regularly attended by a quite substantial number of staff of all grades from all parts of the Office. In December, 1953, and again in December, 1954, the Archbishop of Canterbury was the celebrant. Carol services, led by the Colonial Office choir, at Christmas time, and Passiontide

---

[1] An exception was the Copying Department, where the lady typists were kept in strict purdah, and all business had to be transacted with the (male) Superintendent.

services in Holy Week are held in the parish church of St. Stephen's, Rochester Row.

AN OLD OFFICE, YET A YOUNG ONE

The Colonial Office has gone through many vicissitudes, but although the office of Secretary of State goes back to 1768, and although the term 'Colonial Office' has been in use since early in the nineteenth century, it is still to-day a young Office, not merely because in its present form it goes back only to 1925, but because the average age of the staff in relation to rank is low. This is due to the progressive expansion of the Office during the last thirty years. At the time of writing (1955) the oldest of the Assistant Under-Secretaries of State is but 50 years of age, and the youngest only 40. Many of the Assistant Secretaries (heads of departments) are naturally younger still. Some of them, and practically all the Principals, have joined the Office since the end of the second world war.

The Office can hardly go on expanding for ever, and indeed the indications are that in size it has passed its peak. There may therefore be some prospect of promotion blocks in the future, though the experience of old hands is that promotion prospects are never so bad (or so good) as they look. For the present, however, it is probably a fortunate circumstance that the Office is equipped with youth and the vigour and enthusiasm of youth to deal imaginatively with challenges which are surely more exacting and exciting than at any previous time. By its very nature, the Colonial Office lives in a perpetual state of transition. But there are periods when the tide flows more or less smoothly and there are also moments when the accumulated effect of small and gradual changes builds up the wave to breaking point. To-day the Office approaches such a moment in good heart.

The purpose of this book is to describe, if only in bare outline, the historical forces and accidents which have made the Colonial Office what it is, and the builders who have added fresh storeys to the edifice. I shall try to indicate generally the function of the Office in the complex, informal and constantly shifting pattern of British and Commonwealth constitutional evolution, and the method and spirit in which this function has been and is discharged. And I shall attempt to survey, in all too few pages, the field of the Office's work—the immensely varied and intensely individual countries and islands with which the Secretary of State for the Colonies is concerned.

The duties and responsibilities of the various departments and sections of the Office will be considered against this background. The task is baffling, for if the Colonial Office is not precisely all things to all men, it does deal in some measure with every aspect of the art and practice of government. Other Departments of State necessarily specialise in one or another aspect of administration or social organisation. Even the Treasury, though concerned with all Departments, is primarily concerned with them from the point of view of finance and staffing. The Colonial Office is concerned with the Secretary of State's responsibility for the good government of oversea territories, each of which possesses a complete and self-contained administrative organisation, simple or complex as the case may be. Even in the most primitive territory the administration has to carry out all the activities which current political thought regards as proper to the government of a modern State. Even the most advanced territory calls for advice and assistance in all kinds of matters.

It is this unequalled variety and range of work which make the Colonial Office surely the most fascinating of government departments.

PART ONE

The Secretary of State and his Functions

CHAPTER I

The Office of Secretary of State for the Colonies

HISTORY OF OFFICE

THE arrangements made in London for dealing with the affairs of the oversea territories of the Crown may be divided historically into four phases.

The first phase covers the period from 1660 to 1782. Before the former date there was no organised machinery for handling business concerned with the colonial settlements of North America and the West Indies. Everything was novel and experimental, and there were no precedents on which to rest. In 1660, however, the need for a separate central organisation for the administration of colonial affairs was recognised by the creation first of a Committee of the Privy Council 'for the Plantaçons', and shortly afterwards of a separate 'Council of Foreign Plantations'. John Evelyn was appointed as a member of this Council in 1671, with 'a salary of £500 per annum to encourage me'. In the following year the Council was amalgamated with the Council for Trade, and was called the 'Council of Trade and Plantations'. It was not a very active body, and in 1677 it was suppressed and its functions transferred back to the Privy Council. It was, however, reconstituted in 1695.

The office of Secretary to the Sovereign had originally been held by a single person. In 1539 a second Principal Secretary was appointed; from 1708 to 1746 there was a third, who dealt only with the affairs of Scotland. In 1768 an office of Secretary of State for the American, or Colonial, Department was created in addition to the two Secretaryships then existing; but the Council of Trade and Plantations remained in being until 1782, the affairs of India having been added to its charge in 1748.

The second phase covers the period from 1782 to 1854. This was the age of the 'Second British Empire', during which by settlement, conquest or cession, Australia, New Zealand, Cape Colony, Ceylon, Mauritius, Trinidad, Malta, Sierra Leone, Seychelles, the Straits Settlements and many more islands and territories were brought under the expanding wings of what soon came to be known as the Colonial Office.

In the reconstruction of government machinery following the loss of the United States, both the new office of Secretary of State and the Council of Trade and Plantations were at first abolished;

Colonial affairs reverted to the Privy Council, and were dealt with temporarily in a branch of the Home Department called the Plantations Branch. The work of this branch was transferred in 1784 to a new 'Committee for Trade and Foreign Plantations'. During the next few years, however, this Committee became increasingly concerned with general trade questions and less concerned with colonial affairs; eventually, the latter became firmly recognised as the proper concern of a Secretary of State, while the Committee itself developed into the Board of Trade. The turning point was the year 1801, when the creation of an office of 'Secretary of State for the War and Colonial Department' formally confirmed an arrangement which already existed in practice. With the end of the wars in Europe, this Secretary of State was increasingly occupied with the colonial side of his work, and from 1812 onwards the 'Colonial Office' became a firmly established institution. When the Crimean War broke out in the middle of the century a fourth office of Secretary of State was created to take over the War Department. The year 1854, therefore, marks the formal constitution of the Colonial Office as a separate and independent Department of State.

The years from 1854 to 1925 may be called the third phase. During this period the relationship of Britain with all the oversea possessions of the Crown (excepting India) was dealt with by the Secretary of State for the Colonies. In the course of these seventy years great changes took place in the scope and character of the work. The Colonial Office continued to be directly responsible for the administration of the smaller Colonies of Settlement, mainly in the West Indies, together with the considerable number of other islands and territories which had come into British hands as the result of the French wars. The administrative responsibilities of the Office also included trading stations on the African coast, and were immensely enlarged when the results of the 'scramble for Africa' brought large inland areas of the continent under British rule or protection. During the same period, however, the Office was increasingly occupied with the new complexities, of a diplomatic rather than of an administrative order, arising from the emergence of the larger of the old Colonies into fully self-governing national states. The war of 1914-18 intensified existing problems and created a host of fresh ones. The years which followed the Armistice saw the Office charged, in addition to all its former work, with the conduct of relations with the Irish Free State; with the task of setting up, under mandate from the League of Nations, new administrations in Iraq, Palestine, Trans-Jordan, and former German territories in Africa; and with the affairs of Southern and Northern Rhodesia, for which the British South Africa Company had formerly been responsible.

No single organisation could long cope efficiently with so vast, diverse and continually expanding a range of functions; and so in 1925, on the advice of the then Secretary of State, the Rt. Hon. L. S. Amery, a separate 'Dominions Office' was set up, to take over from the Colonial Office business relating to the self-governing Dominions (Canada, Australia, New Zealand, the Union of South Africa and Newfoundland), the Irish Free State and the Imperial Conference. For reasons of convenience the new Office also took over the work connected with the self-governing Colony of Southern Rhodesia and the South African High Commission Territories (Basutoland, Bechuanaland Protectorate and Swaziland).

Mr. Amery continued to hold the two offices of Secretary of State for Dominion Affairs and for the Colonies, but separate Parliamentary and Permanent Under-Secretaries were appointed forthwith. Mr. Amery was succeeded in 1929 by the Rt. Hon. Sidney Webb (Lord Passfield) who held the two offices for a short time only, remaining as Secretary of State for the Colonies when, in 1930, the Rt. Hon J. H. Thomas became Secretary of State for Dominion Affairs.

The fourth, and present, phase of the history of the Colonial Office dates, then, from 1925. This book is not primarily an historical study, and although on occasion it will be necessary to reach back beyond 1925 when considering some particular subject, it is in the main with the development and work of the Office during the last thirty years that we shall be concerned. In this period the geographical range of the Office's work has largely remained constant, though there have been one or two notable changes, marking both accessions to and deletions from the list of territories with which the Office deals. Ceylon ceased to be a Colony on becoming independent in 1948, and the Mandate for Palestine was terminated in the same year. The formerly mandated territories of Iraq and Trans-Jordan had ceased to be dealt with in the Colonial Office in 1932 and 1946 respectively. On the other hand, the Office, which had taken over the administration of Northern Rhodesia in 1924, assumed new and direct responsibilities for the Aden Colony and Protectorate in 1937 and for North Borneo and Sarawak in 1946.

TERRITORIAL RESPONSIBILITIES OF SECRETARY OF STATE

The responsibilities of the Secretary of State for the Colonies since 1925 may be defined in principle as follows. The Crown acts on the advice of Ministers—in the government of the United Kingdom on the advice of United Kingdom Ministers, and in the government of the other independent Members of the Commonwealth on the advice of the Ministers of the country concerned. The Commonwealth includes, as well as sovereign States, a number of territories which are separate administrative units but which are not completely self-governing in external or, in most cases, internal affairs. Most of these territories are dependencies of the United Kingdom. They include Colonies, Protectorates, Protected States and Trust Territories. The significance of these terms will appear later; the point to observe at present is that the Crown in the United Kingdom has some form of jurisdiction in these territories and, in exercising that jurisdiction, acts on the advice of United Kingdom, and not of local, Ministers. The Secretary of State for the Colonies is the United Kingdom Minister charged with the duty of advice to the Crown in this sphere.

No one acquainted with British constitutional arrangements will be surprised to learn that this general statement is subject to qualifications. Certain territories which fall inside the definition (notably the South African High Commission Territories) are not in practice dealt with in the Colonial Office. Relations with the self-governing Colony of Southern Rhodesia and with the Federation of Rhodesia and Nyasaland are handled by the Commonwealth Relations Office (previously Dominions Office), but the domestic affairs of the other two component parts of the Federation (Northern Rhodesia and Nyasaland) are still dealt with in the Colonial Office. So, up to the time of writing, are the affairs of Malta, which is self-governing within certain limits. The suggestion was made, however, in 1953, that the conduct of relations between Malta and the United Kingdom might be transferred to the Home Office.

To complete the negative side of the picture, it should be added that although the Colonial Office deals with the Anglo-French condominium of the New Hebrides, it never had any responsibility for the Anglo-Egyptian Sudan, or for the States of the Persian Gulf. The relationship of these States to the United Kingdom is not widely dissimilar, in principle, from that of some of the Protected States dealt with in the Colonial Office, but their affairs come within the province of the Foreign Office.

Having thus indicated briefly what the Colonial Office does not deal with, we may turn to consider what is in fact the range of its operations. It will be enough at this point to list the territories in the manner of a catalogue, leaving discussion of their individual characteristics and problems for a later part of the book. Statistics of area and population are given in Appendix I.

'And now, Mr. Merivale,' said a new Secretary of State a century ago, on being welcomed at the Office by his Permanent Under-Secretary, Herman Merivale, C.B., 'tell me, where *are* the Colonies?'

The map shows that they consist to-day in the main of a broad band of islands and continental areas unequally distributed round the world in the region of the equator. Apart from these, there are a few Colonies which fall outside the limits of the tropics: Gibraltar, Malta and Cyprus in the Mediterranean; Bermuda and Bahamas in the North Atlantic: Tristan da Cunha, the Falkland Islands and their Dependencies in the South Atlantic.

Within the tropical zone the territories of West, East and Central Africa claim first notice by virtue of size and population. On the West Coast are the Gambia, Sierra Leone, the Gold Coast and Nigeria. In Eastern Africa, the Somaliland Protectorate lies out to the north, and the islands of the Zanzibar Protectorate to the east. Kenya, Uganda and Tanganyika form a massive block extending from the ocean to the great lakes. South of these are Nyasaland and Northern Rhodesia.

Eastward from Africa, the Colony of Aden with the adjacent Protectorates guards the passage between the Red Sea and the Indian Ocean. In that ocean itself are the island Colonies of Mauritius and Seychelles.

The territories in South-East Asia with which the Colonial Office is concerned are the Federation of Malaya, Singapore, Hong Kong, North Borneo and Sarawak, with the Protected State of Brunei.

Scattered over the South Pacific Ocean is a vast assembly of islands, divided for administrative purposes into two groups. The Governor of the Colony of Fiji is responsible for relations with the Protected State of Tonga and for the administration of Pitcairn Island. Her Majesty's High Commissioner for the Western Pacific is responsible for the British Solomon Islands Protectorate, for the Gilbert and Ellice Islands Colony and for the British share in the administration of the Anglo-French condominium of the New Hebrides.

On the mainland of Central and South America are two Colonies: British Honduras and British Guiana. Of the island Colonies in the Caribbean Sea, Jamaica (to which the Cayman Islands and the Turks and Caicos Islands are attached for administrative purposes) is the largest. The isle of Barbados stands alone, a Colony in its own right, over which no flag but the British has ever flown; the other Colonies are formed of island groups: Trinidad and Tobago, the Leeward Islands, and the Windward Islands.

Finally, to complete the tropical circle, the ancient Colony of St. Helena stands far out in the waters of the Southern Atlantic.

This multitude of countries and islands, so various in size, wealth, climate and population, constitutes the bailiwick of the Secretary of State for the Colonies. He is the Minister of the Crown on whose advice the Crown acts in the exercise of its sovereignty and jurisdiction in these territories.

TYPES OF DEPENDENT TERRITORY

It was observed above, in passing, that the dependent territories fall into four categories: Colonies, Protectorates, Protected States and Trust Territories.

A Colony, in modern constitutional definition, is a territory which, by settlement, conquest, cession or annexation has become a part of Her Majesty's dominions and over which Her Majesty, as Queen of the United Kingdom, exercises absolute sovereignty. The Colonies, properly so-called, include the old settlements in the Atlantic islands (Bermuda, Bahamas, Barbados and the rest) and on the coasts of Central and South America, West Africa and the Malay Peninsula; together with a number of other islands and ports captured from other Powers or ceded to the Crown by the local inhabitants. Examples of Colonies acquired by capture are Mauritius, Trinidad, and Seychelles; of Colonies acquired by cession, Fiji and Hong Kong. The Colonies also include certain territories more recently 'annexed' by the Crown, such as Ashanti (part of the Gold Coast), Kenya Colony, North Borneo and Sarawak. The inhabitants of Colonies are British subjects and share with the inhabitants of Great Britain and Northern Ireland the legal status of 'citizens of the United Kingdom and the Colonies'.

Protectorates are territories which have not been annexed by the Crown but in which the Crown has acquired jurisdiction by agreement with the inhabitants, represented by their rulers or other authorised persons. Most of the Protectorates are in Africa, and owe their existence to Britain's part in the 'scramble for Africa' in the nineteenth century. Though constrained, for various reasons, to extend British spheres of influence in Africa, Queen Victoria's governments were not bent on annexation of territory. They preferred to offer the Great Queen's 'protection' to the indigenous chiefs and peoples, in return for the right to trade and evangelise and for the control of the external relations of the countries. Hence all the four West African territories—the Gambia, Sierra Leone, the Gold Coast and Nigeria—include to-day in a single administrative unit what is technically a Colony on the coast and what is technically a Protectorate inland. In Eastern and Central Africa, where no coastal Colonies were founded, there are only two areas with the technical status of Colony, and both are inland and of recent creation—Southern Rhodesia, formally annexed in 1923, and Kenya Colony, annexed in 1920. Before that date, Kenya was called the East Africa Protectorate, and (reversing the order of things in West Africa) its coastal belt is still a Protectorate, being technically part of the dominions of the Sultan of Zanzibar.

In practice, there is little if any difference in the actual working administration of Colonies and Protectorates. Though the constitutional relationship with the Crown rests on different legal foundations, it is exercised in the same way. The inhabitants of a Protectorate are not British subjects by birth but British Protected Persons; but this distinction, too, is little more than a technical one.

Protected States are of two kinds. One kind is exemplified in Nigeria and Uganda, where a number of local Kingdoms or Chiefdoms are included in a single administrative unit under a Governor representing the Crown. The rulers retain certain powers over their own subjects, but they are, in effect, local government authorities within a unitary State.

Examples of the other kind of Protected State are Tonga and Zanzibar. In these cases the traditional rulers (Her Majesty the Queen of Tonga and His Highness the Sultan of Zanzibar) retain their sovereignty. Their relationship with the United Kingdom rests upon treaties by virtue of which the United Kingdom is responsible for their external relations but does not intervene in internal affairs except in so far as this is provided for in the treaty. Relations between the United Kingdom and Tonga are conducted through the Governor of Fiji who is represented in Tonga by an Agent and Consul. Relations with Zanzibar are conducted through a British Resident who corresponds directly with the Secretary of State.

The Malay States are in a special position, partaking in some respects of both categories of Protected State. The nine States of the Malay Peninsula are all under their own rulers, whose relationship to the Crown is regulated by treaty and who exercise sovereignty within their own spheres. But these States, together with the 'settlements' of Penang and Malacca (which are Colonies) are combined in a federation which possesses a central legislature and many of the characteristics of a unitary state.

Lastly, there are the Trust Territories. These are areas of Africa which were German colonies or protectorates up to the 1914-18 war and thereafter were assigned to Great Britain for administration under mandate from the League of Nations. The administration begun under the mandate has been carried on under the Trusteeship Agreement approved by the General Assembly of the United Nations in 1946. These territories are three in number: Tanganyika, which is administered as a separate country in its own right; the British Cameroons, which are included in the Federation of Nigeria; and British Togoland, which is administered as part of the Gold Coast. The actual administration differs in no significant way from that of a

Colony or Protectorate, but Her Majesty's Government in the United Kingdom has to render accounts of its stewardship to the Trusteeship Council of the United Nations and to show that the conditions of the trust are being duly observed.

These, then, are the four principal classes of territory dealt with by the Colonial Office. But the tale is not quite complete. The New Hebrides, in the Western Pacific, are an Anglo-French condominium, the British and French governments being jointly and equally responsible for their administration, and being each represented locally by a Resident Commissioner. Also in the Western Pacific is Canton Island, an important international airport, which, with the neighbouring island of Enderbury, is under joint Anglo-American administration.

These last, however, are the exceptions which proverbially prove the rule, and the rule is that the territories dealt with by the Colonial Office, whatever their technical status in international law, are organised as separate and self-contained administrative units, each with its own apparatus of government, and each presided over (except for those Protected States which have their own Rulers) by a person (usually called the Governor, sometimes High Commissioner) who 'is the single and supreme authority responsible to, and representative of, Her Majesty'.[1]

GOVERNMENT OF OLDER COLONIES

We must now go back to our history. When Englishmen (Englishmen first, to be joined later by Scotsmen, Irishmen and Welshmen) began to found oversea settlements in Northern America and the islands of the Atlantic in the sixteenth and seventeenth centuries, they set a pattern for the future. These early colonists were, no doubt unconsciously, following a Greek rather than a Roman model, though it was the Roman word 'colony' which came to be associated with their enterprises. As in the first millennium B.C. the men of Athens, Corinth and other city-states of ancient Greece sailed out along the Mediterranean coasts, and where they found suitable sites established new city-states modelled upon, and linked by ties of blood and culture to, the metropolis; so the English seafarers did not attempt to extend the boundaries of England but set up new Englands wherever they settled.

As the Thirteen Colonies along the Atlantic seaboard of North America began to come into existence, the mother country granted to each as a matter of course a constitution, consisting of a Governor, a nominated Council and an elected House of Assembly, roughly comparable to King,

---

[1] Colonial Regulation 105.

Lords and Commons at home. It was intended that the assemblies should confine themselves to voting taxes to meet the costs of their own government and to making local by-laws, but that in all important matters they should obey and implement the laws of the Imperial Parliament in London.[1]

The same is true of the island settlements.

The present constitution of the Bahamas is similar to those of the North American Colonies prior to the War of Independence. The government is modelled upon that of England in the early days, the Governor representing the Sovereign, and the nominated Legislative Council and the elected House of Assembly representing respectively the Houses of Lords and Commons.[2]

Barbados and Bermuda, too, retain to the present day what is in essence the standard 17th century colonial constitution, though in the former there have been important recent developments.

Although friction between the United Kingdom Parliament and the local assemblies led eventually to the secession of the Colonies on the American mainland, the principle of setting up Colonies as separate States, each with the formal apparatus of self-government, had been firmly established and was followed as new settlements, in Professor Harlow's phrase, 'took root and grew' in Canada, Australia, New Zealand and South Africa. But the sharp lesson of the American War of Independence had been learned, and the problem of relationship between Colony and Mother Country was solved by the ingenuity of Lord Durham, who was sent to Canada as Governor-General in 1837 when Canada, in her turn, was finding her position as a dependent Colony intolerable. The Durham Report of 1839 pointed the way to the modern conception of the Commonwealth by establishing responsible Cabinet government in Canada. From then on, the history of the countries which came to be known as the Dominions is one of increasing independence· in external as well as in internal affairs, ultimately leading to their recognition, in the words of the Balfour Declaration of 1926, as 'autonomous communities, equal in status and freely associated under one Crown as members of the British Commonwealth of Nations'.

GOVERNMENT OF NEWER TERRITORIES

Meanwhile, the British Colonial Empire was receiving accessions of a very different kind from the early settlements. Trading and missionary enterprises had led to the establishment of posts or forts at many points on the coasts of Africa and Asia. European wars, in which British victories depended upon sea power, left as their legacy a series of islands and strategic points, occupied, or wrested

---

[1] V. T. Harlow, *Origins and Purpose.*
[2] *Colonial Office List,* 1954.

from other occupying Powers, primarily for war purposes but remaining to be administered in peace. British governments of the nineteenth century were not, in fact, consciously acquisitive of territory for its own sake. Some places were kept because of their strategic importance. In other cases it was rather a matter of the flag following trade. Expansion inland from the coastal settlements in Africa and Asia was due partly to the necessity of protecting them and their trade, partly to the impossibility of keeping out of the scramble for territory in which French, Germans and other European Powers were actively engaged, but largely also to a genuine desire to cut off the slave trade at its roots and to bring the message of Christianity to the heathen.

The motives and the circumstances were varied and complex; but the result was to bring under the British Crown an increasing number of territories, mainly in the tropics, which had existing populations of their own, and in which, for the most part, there was no question of colonisation, in the sense of establishing permanent British communities, as in the relatively empty and healthy spaces of the old Dominions of the temperate zones.

Some arrangements had, however, to be made for the administration of these territories, and, faced with the problem, the British did what was natural for them, that is to say, they set up in each place the apparatus of a separate state, reproducing, in simplified form, the traditional British pattern. Everywhere a Governor was appointed to represent the Sovereign, and was provided with an advisory Council representing, in theory at least, and increasingly in practice, the people of the country.

For example, in Ceylon, which was constituted a Colony in 1802, the Governor's Council consisted at first entirely of officials. In 1833, a Legislative Council, which was in effect a single House of Parliament, was established which included a number of 'unofficial' representatives of the local population in addition to the 'official', that is, civil service, members. A similar type of constitution was conferred at about this time on other Colonies, such as Mauritius, the Gambia, the Gold Coast and Trinidad.

This—the typical Crown Colony constitution—became standardised during the nineteenth and early twentieth centuries for all newly-established Colonies, and indeed in some of the older Colonies it replaced the original North American type which has already been described. The latter, as has been observed, was based upon the two-Chamber constitution of England under Tudor and Stuart, that is to say before the evolution of Cabinet government in the mother country. The new form of Crown Colony government provided the Governor, representing the Sovereign, with a body of advisers, called

B

the Executive Council, which in some sense acted as a Cabinet. The Legislative Council (which was the Upper House in the original American type) became a single Chamber corresponding in principle to the House of Commons, and capable, as later events have shown, of developing from a primitive stage, in which it consisted wholly or mainly of civil servants and unofficial members nominated by the Governor, into a fully elected representative Assembly.

This short and over-simplified account of Colonial constitutional history has been necessary in order to show first, that the territories are separate units and not extensions of the United Kingdom; secondly, that they are not independent sovereign States but dependent upon the United Kingdom; and thirdly, that the degree of dependence and the manner in which the control of the United Kingdom is exercised are extremely flexible. To maintain, so far as may be, the delicate balance between too much and too little control according to the infinitely variable circumstances of place and time, is the task of the Secretary of State for the Colonies.

TWO-FOLD RESPONSIBILITY OF UNITED KINGDOM

The responsibility of Her Majesty's Government in the United Kingdom, and of the Secretary of State as the Minister particularly concerned, will be seen to be two-fold. In both aspects these responsibilities derive from the fact that the Colonial territories are by definition not sovereign States, however great a degree of local self-government they may possess. So long as Her Majesty's Government in the United Kingdom retains any power whatsoever of tendering advice to the Crown in regard to the affairs of a territory, the supreme final authority for that territory must be the Parliament of the United Kingdom, to which Her Majesty's Government is responsible; and any powers conferred upon or exercised by local assemblies or officials must be in the nature of delegated powers which can, in the last resort, be abrogated or overridden by an Act of the Parliament of the United Kingdom.

Her Majesty's Government, therefore, is answerable to Parliament for the peace, order and good government of the territories. Her Majesty's Government is also responsible for the external relations of the territories since, not being internationally recognised sovereign States, they cannot negotiate or enter into treaty relations with foreign powers on their own account. It is upon Her Majesty's Government that the responsibility rests for the performance by the territories of their international obligations. Her Majesty's Government is accountable to the United Nations for the administration of Trust Territories (Tanganyika, British Cameroons and British Togoland) and has also undertaken to supply certain information to the United

Nations about the territories for which it has full responsibility.

As a corollary to all this, Her Majesty's Government is ultimately responsible for the external defence and internal security of the territories and for their financial integrity.

In summary, this first aspect of the work of the Colonial Office is directed from the Colonies towards Parliament, other British Government Departments, Commonwealth and foreign countries, international organisations and the general public, both in the United Kingdom and abroad, whose opinion is the ultimate sanction for the policies and actions of governments. On this side of its work, the task of the Colonial Office is to represent the interests of the territories, to see that they get a fair deal and to justify the way in which they are governed.

The other and complementary aspect of the work is directed from London towards the territories. The decisions of Her Majesty's Government on matters affecting them have to be conveyed and in their turn justified to the governments and peoples of the territories. The services which the territories may need for their peace and progress have to be organised and made available. Where the territories lack money, materials or staffs, these have to be supplied. In an era of rapid social and political advance, constitutions have to be adapted to changing circumstances. This means not only that the substance of new constitutional developments must be thoroughly and patiently negotiated, but that the instruments giving effect to the results of negotiations must be drafted by experts in this highly specialised kind of legal business and submitted in proper form for the approval of the Sovereign and where necessary of Parliament.

THE COLONIAL GOVERNOR

The Governor may justly be called the king-pin in the system of relationship between the United Kingdom and the dependent territories, and his position deserves close examination. It is at once simple and complex. The Governor personifies the Crown in its government of the territory. He is appointed by, and holds office at the pleasure of, the Sovereign. The executive powers of the Crown in the territory are vested in him. Except in certain specified matters such as the granting of honours and the power of assenting to legislation on matters reserved for the Sovereign's personal pleasure, he exercises all the constitutional functions of the Crown within the territory, including the Royal prerogative of mercy.

This seems clear enough. But, in British constitutional practice, the Crown acts on the advice of Ministers. In appointing Governors and in furnishing them with the Commission and Royal Instructions defining their authority, the Crown acts on the advice of Her Majesty's

Government in the United Kingdom. A Governor is also removable from his office on the same advice.

These facts may suggest that a Colonial Governor is, in effect, subject to the direction of the Secretary of State, as being the Minister who advises the Crown on matters affecting the Colonies. This is true, up to a point. But there are qualifying factors. The Secretary of State does not function in a vacuum. He must have information before him in order that he may decide upon any action. And he necessarily relies mainly upon the Governor to lay before him all the necessary information and considerations which affect, from the point of view of the territory concerned, the decision which has to be taken. Further, the Secretary of State is answerable to his Ministerial colleagues, and the Government as a whole is answerable to Parliament, for his actions. To overrule the considered and maintained advice of a Governor is a thing which no Secretary of State would do lightly or unless he was convinced that his action was right and could be publicly defended.

The Governor, then, is not a 'stooge' of Her Majesty's Government in the United Kingdom, though he could hardly hope or wish to retain his office if he were in fundamental disagreement with the policies or principles of Her Majesty's Ministers. Moreover, if to this extent he is subject to control from above, his technically supreme authority in the territory is itself tempered by local constitutional limitations. As has already been made clear, even the most rudimentary form of Colonial constitution makes some provision for the Governor to take counsel with other persons who directly or indirectly represent the interests of the local community. In practically every territory there is an Executive Council which the Governor is required to consult, and though he is not bound to follow its advice, he cannot unreasonably ignore it. In a very few territories the Executive Council consists entirely of officials, but in most territories now there are also unofficial members, and in the more advanced places the Executive Council has developed into what is actually or virtually a Cabinet of Ministers. In the most advanced constitutions of all, the spheres in which the Governor must act on the advice of his Ministers and those in which he may act in his own discretion are precisely set out. It is true that, so long as Her Majesty's Government retain any responsibility for a territory, reserved powers continue to be provided under which the Governor can act on his own account in case of emergency or a breakdown of the administration; but such powers are in practice very rarely invoked. The important point, for the present purpose, is that the Governor has to take account not only of the views of Her Majesty's Government in London but of the views of his advisers in the territory. Furthermore, he and his advisers have to take account of local public opinion. In practically all territories now there is some form of Legislative Council or Assembly which discusses legislation and finance. In more than half the territories this body contains a majority of unofficial members (nominated or elected) capable of outvoting the official members (civil servants). Even where the unofficial representatives are in a minority, their views, as expressive of public feeling, must carry great weight in assessing the possible, which is proverbially the art of government.

The Governor's position, then, is not precisely the same in every territory, but always he is the focus of authority and of communication. It is he who is responsible to the Secretary of State for seeing that the territory is properly governed, and it is he who receives from the Secretary of State the views and decisions of Her Majesty's Government and has the task of translating these into local terms and of securing their acceptance by explanation, persuasion and, if necessary, use of his constitutional powers. It is he, too, who has the duty of representing to Her Majesty's Government the views of his advisers and himself on all matters affecting the interests of the territory and its people. He is the territory's spokesman; but he is also the leader of the community, and the central figure of its public life.

The whole elaborate system of relationships, therefore, is concentrated upon two personages: the Secretary of State for the Colonies in London and the Governor in the territory. All official communications take place between these two. The Secretary of State, and no one else, speaks by telegram or despatch to the Governor on behalf of the Sovereign and Her Government in the United Kingdom. The Governor, and no one else, speaks to the Secretary of State on behalf of the territory under his charge.

The Colonial Office is nothing more or less than the Secretariat of the Secretary of State—the tool with which he does his work.

CHAPTER II

Britain and the Colonial Territories

BASIC POLICY

The central purpose of British colonial policy is simple. It is to guide the colonial territories to responsible self-government within the Commonwealth in conditions that ensure to the people concerned both a fair standard of living and freedom from oppression from any quarter.[1]

IN this short paragraph an official report of 1948 crystallised the purpose of the whole work of the present-day Colonial Office. Although the principles embodied in the statement were well established by the time that they were thus formulated, they are essentially a modern development, following logically upon the conception of trusteeship which in its turn succeeded to the conception of 'dominion over palm and pine'.

These general principles, assuming, as is indeed the fact, that they are being sincerely and effectively put into practice, should be a sufficient answer to those who carp and sneer at 'Imperialism' and 'Colonialism', for reasons often quite unconnected with the welfare or interests of the peoples of the territories concerned.

In carrying out its policy, the British Government is subject to numerous pressures—from the Colonial territories themselves; from Parliament, Press and public at home; from foreign and Commonwealth countries and the United Nations. To some extent these pressures may cancel out, but the balance, or at any rate the vocal balance, is apt to be on the side of more rather than less speed in the devolution of responsibility, and the Colonial Office, though at times attacked for going too fast, is even more loudly urged to go faster and is regarded in some quarters as reactionary if it maintains a prudent pace. So far, however, as political parties in the United Kingdom are concerned, all are in fact agreed upon the general lines of policy and even upon most questions of method and timing. There may be party differences regarding the right action in certain particular contingencies which arise in practice, but in such cases it is the application of principles to a given situation, not the principles themselves, about which controversy occurs.

For it is, of course, a fallacy to suppose that there is just one Colonial problem. There are at least as many problems as there are

[1] Cmd. 7433.

territories, and the problem of each territory is a complex and fluid product of many factors, economic, social and political.

CONDITIONS OF SELF-GOVERNMENT

From what has been said earlier it will be clear that, from the beginning of their colonial adventure, the British were committed to the principle of evolution towards self-government. They set up everywhere the embryonic structure of separate states, and the development of the self-governing Dominions was an inevitable consequence. Their history naturally gave rise to the assumption that other 'Colonies' would ultimately reach the same goal. The assumption was vindicated in 1948 by the achievement of independent sovereign status by Ceylon. This achievement—notable for the fact that it took place smoothly, without disturbance and in an atmosphere of universal goodwill—is a legitimate encouragement to other territories, but it is worth while to examine the factors which made it possible for Ceylon, since it does not necessarily follow that the same pattern of development will be precisely observed in places where the circumstances are not similar. The factors in any given place must obviously differ from those in any other: the question is whether at a given time they add up to a total which spells the possibility of independence.

The official statement quoted at the beginning of this chapter was, of course, carefully thought out. It indicates a goal but it also lays down conditions. The goal is 'self-government within the Commonwealth', but that is not an exact definition. 'Self-government' must, at the least, mean the right of a people to order its own domestic affairs, but there may yet be compelling circumstances which force the people to look outside for defence, for the management of their external relations, for financial and technical assistance. Moreover, the statement postulates 'freedom from oppression from any quarter', which implies not only defence against external aggression but the protection of the common folk against domestic tyranny. The kind of self-government envisaged by British policy does not include either the coercion of the people at large by an irresponsible minority, or the denial to racial or religious minorities of human and civic rights.

The ability of a territory to fulfil the conditions of independence is governed by some factors which are fixed and unalterable and by others which are transient and malleable. A small island lacking natural resources, strategic or commercial importance, poorly served by communications, cannot by taking thought add cubits to its stature. But a territory handicapped by backward social conditions or interracial strife can overcome these disabilities with time, effort and goodwill.

Ceylon is an island, but one of reasonable size (about equal to Holland and Belgium), reasonably healthy for the tropics, well placed in the line of world communications, and sufficiently equipped with natural resources. A century and a quarter of British colonial rule, followed by a long period of virtual self-government in internal affairs had brought the island by 1948 to a point at which its people were ready to take over full responsibility and its economy was sufficiently developed to ensure viability. Though the population was not entirely homogeneous the rights of minorities to the safeguarding of their liberties were fully recognised. In short, Ceylon possessed the basic desiderata for independence and had overcome its transient handicaps.

A similar process may be observed to-day at work in the Gold Coast, where, although the details are very different, the broad conditions are in many respects comparable with those in Ceylon. Other territories present more complex situations. In some cases, as in the West Indies, it is a question of federating small units which could not stand by themselves. In others, as in Kenya or Fiji, it is a question of creating a partnership between indigenous and immigrant peoples of different race and culture. Some places, such as the Falkland Islands or Seychelles, can only be dealt with individually, and it is a question of finding a form of constitutional development which will suit their individual circumstances and allow the fullest realisation of their aspirations which is practicable in those circumstances.

ASSISTANCE AND CONSULTATION

To follow out the implications and ramifications of this policy is the basic theme of all Colonial Office work; but the function of the Colonial Office, though essential, is not that of direct administration. Here the British system differs fundamentally from that of France. The French Parliament (which includes Deputies from oversea territories) legislates for the Colonies and the French equivalent of the Colonial Office maintains, through an official Inspectorate, a close control of the territorial administrations. The British way— the product, as has been shown, of empirical improvisation—places upon the territorial peoples the responsibility for working out their own salvation as separate communities; 'yet', as the report already quoted says, 'their governments are not established and then left without direction or advice'.[1] The Colonial Office supplies that direction and advice, and organises the help which the territories need. It does this by working through and in consultation with the Governors, who, as the Sovereign's representatives, are in close touch with the Secretary of State as well as with their local official and un-

[1] Cmd. 7433.

official advisers. When a territory reaches the stage of having a ministerial government, its Ministers may come to the Colonial Office for direct consultation with the Secretary of State and his staff, though the Governor remains the official channel of communication and is of course fully informed of what takes place at such consultations if he is not himself present.

As a corollary, it is a growing practice for the Secretary of State himself, or other Ministers, as well as officials of the Colonial Office, to visit the territories and discuss their problems on the spot with the Governors and all others concerned. Such visits may take place for the general and informal exchange of ideas, for the settlement of some particular difficulty or for the holding of a formal conference.

Ideas of setting up a Colonial Council or Conference with standing machinery have been canvassed from time to time, but have never commanded general acceptance. The variety of the territories, the individual character of their problems, the difference in their stages of political evolution—all these have been held to preclude the practical possibility of successfully maintaining such a form of organisation. A full-dress Conference of Colonial Governors and senior officials was indeed convened by the Secretary of State in London in 1927 and another in 1930, but the experiment has not been repeated since, though a conference of Governors of African territories was held in 1947. On the whole, successive British governments have preferred to proceed in the traditional British way, with arrangements that are flexible and adaptable to continually changing circumstances. Such tentative experiments as have been made in the direction of organised assemblies of Colonial representatives have indeed produced some valuable results, but the general conclusion drawn from them has been that the traditional way is probably right. In October, 1949, a conference of unofficial representatives from all African legislatures was organised in London by the Colonial Office. Many important problems were debated and explanations of policy were given by United Kingdom Ministers. Valuable work was done, but there was some feeling that, even though the conference was limited to Africa, the territories were too diverse in conditions to have a great deal of common ground for discussion.

In the summer of 1951, on the occasion of the Festival of Britain, unofficial representatives from all the territories were invited to London as guests of the British Government, and the opportunity was taken to hold a number of meetings in which the Prime Minister and other United Kingdom Ministers took part. This again was felt to be useful, but it did not result in a clear lead being given in favour of a regular repetition of the exercise. It would seem that, on the whole, the territories are more concerned about their individual

B*

relations with the United Kingdom than about establishing any collective relationship; and that the conference technique is most suited to dealing with the affairs of specific regions or with specific subjects.

In the latter field, this technique has in fact been highly developed, and many meetings for the exchange of ideas and settlement of policy have been held under the auspices of the Colonial Office during the last few years. These meetings have included conferences on African Education and Agriculture in Africa, as well as various discussions on local government and other aspects of administration arranged by the African Studies Branch of the Office; conferences of Commissioners of Police, Heads of Medical Departments, Labour Officers, Co-operative Officers, Finance Officers, Civil Aviation experts, Information Officers and Government Statisticians. In the field of regional policy, there have been important conferences on West Indian Federation, Central African Federation and the Constitution of Nigeria.

Another suggestion occasionally canvassed is that the peoples of the territories should elect Members to the United Kingdom Parliament. This idea, also, has never secured general acceptance, if only because it runs counter to the whole historical tradition of establishing the oversea territories as separate units and not as extensions of the United Kingdom. What is universally accepted, however, is the desirability of establishing close links between the British Parliament and the oversea legislatures and of encouraging the latter to profit by the experience of the former in maintaining democratic principles. In this sphere the work of the Commonwealth Parliamentary Association is invaluable. The constitution of the Association permits the legislatures of the dependent territories to form affiliated or subsidiary branches linked to the United Kingdom branch, and most have taken advantage of this. General meetings of the Association are held from time to time in oversea centres; one took place at Nairobi in 1954. Visits by Parliamentary delegations to oversea territories are organised by the United Kingdom Branch. And at all times the headquarters in Westminster Hall are open to visiting members from overseas who can be sure of a welcome and of any help which they may want in making contacts or enquiries. In addition to looking after visiting members of the legislatures, the United Kingdom branch, in co-operation with the General Council of the Association and with the Colonial Office, arranges organised courses at Westminster. The visitors or their governments are responsible for passage expenses, but during the course the visitors are guests of the Association. At Westminster they see the working of Parliament and meet members of both Houses. They hear talks on the traditions and procedure of Parliament and on the machinery of government, and take part in discussions. The course includes some study of British local government arrangements and a visit to the Parliament of Northern Ireland.

Taking it all round, we can safely say that consultation and personal contact between the responsible authorities in the United Kingdom and those in the oversea territories have never been so close, continuous and broadly based as they are to-day. And the focus of it all is, inevitably, the Colonial Office, for here all the threads are drawn together, here resides the ultimate authority, here is the essential link between the needs of the territories and the means of supplying those needs—needs of money, needs of material, needs of men.

FINANCIAL AID

This idea of supplying needs is a modern conception. Before the first world war the question hardly arose. After that war, the undeveloped state of the African territories and the backward social condition of their peoples began to impress the consciences of statesmen and officials. The chief need as seen at that time was for the application of modern scientific knowledge to the problems of what Professor W. M. Macmillan has called 'Africa Emergent'. Under the leadership, especially, of Mr. W. Ormsby-Gore (now Lord Harlech) who was Parliamentary Under-Secretary during a critical period, the Office began to be transformed into an organisation for mobilising the resources of science in the service of the dependent and especially of the African territories. In agriculture, medicine, animal health, forestry, education and other fields a campaign was on foot; but it was a campaign waged without the sinews of war. There was no money to back it up, except what the territories themselves could raise by taxation or loan on their own account. It is true that in 1929 a Colonial Development Fund of £1,000,000 a year was voted by Parliament, but this was partially for the purpose of relieving unemployment in the United Kingdom, and grants from the fund were limited to objects which involved the placing of orders here for manufactured goods.

As the years went on—years in which a wholly disproportionate amount of time and effort had to be devoted by Ministers and senior officials to the thankless task of administering Palestine—it became increasingly apparent to those concerned with the Colonies that it was both futile and dangerous to attempt to carry on a policy of development without financial support. Unfortunately, outside a limited circle, there was little public knowledge of or interest in the Colonies and their problems. The small attendance at Colonial debates in Parliament was notorious.

However, during the years which led up to the second world war, public opinion began to be stirred. In 1938, Parliamentary interest was strong enough to justify the preparation for the first time for ten years of a comprehensive report[1] by the Secretary of State (Mr. Ormsby-Gore) to accompany the Estimates for Colonial and Middle Eastern Services. (This experiment was repeated in the following year, and resumed, after a hiatus due to the war, in 1947, since when these surveys have appeared annually.)

This increased public concern had been stimulated largely by news of extensive labour troubles and civil disturbances in the West Indies, indicating serious deficiencies in the social and economic conditions of the colonies in that area. In 1938 a Royal Commission was appointed under the Chairmanship of the late Lord Moyne (who afterwards became Secretary of State) to enquire into these conditions. In its report[2] (which was submitted at the end of 1939 but not published until 1945) the Commission made drastic recommendations for more positive action to promote economic development and social services, including the provision of a West Indian Welfare Fund to be financed by an annual grant of £1,000,000 from the Exchequer for 20 years and to be administered by a special organisation under a Comptroller.

But the Secretary of State (by then Mr. Malcolm MacDonald) was concerned about other places as well as the West Indies, and by his direction the Office had been engaged, while the West India Royal Commission was at work, in formulating a comprehensive scheme applicable to the Colonies generally. In spite of the outbreak of war, it was decided to press on with this, and to include provision for assistance to the West Indies in the general programme. Accordingly, in February, 1940, proposals were published, following which the first Colonial Development and Welfare Act was passed, providing for expenditure up to £5,000,000 a year for ten years on development and an additional £500,000 a year on research. This provision was substantially augmented by a further Act in 1945. Two years later, the Colonial Development Corporation was set up, with borrowing powers up to £110,000,000 to assist in providing capital for desirable projects of development and enterprise.

The effect of these measures will appear in later chapters. The point to be observed here is that for the first time the British Government was committed to a definite policy of promoting economic development and social welfare in the Colonial territories and of supplementing local self-help by financial support from the Exchequer on a really large scale. Naturally, this revolution in thought and practice

[1] Cmd. 5760.
[2] Cmd. 6607.

hastened and enhanced the transformation of the Colonial Office from an institution confined to general supervision into the busy headquarters of an all-out drive against the disabilities which were holding back economic and social progress of the Colonial peoples.

TWO SETS OF PROBLEMS

If an attempt is made to classify the problems which the Colonial Office and the oversea governments and peoples are seeking in partnership to solve, it will be found that they are of two kinds: those which arise out of the dependence of the Colonial and other territories upon the United Kingdom and those which arise out of physical, economic or social conditions having nothing to do with political status. There is obviously no problem of Colonial agriculture, Colonial public health or Colonial education, as such: there are only problems of agriculture, health and education which arise in the Colonial territories but would equally arise if the territories were independent or were dependent upon some other Power than Britain. In dealing with such problems, the fact of dependence should, if the Colonial Office is doing its job, be for the advantage of the territories, by making available to them experience, knowledge and resources which they could not otherwise command. It would be difficult for any impartial observer with a knowledge of the facts to suggest to-day that the British either exploit the Colonial territories for their own benefit or use their controlling powers to damp down development which the territorial peoples could and would carry on faster if they were free to do so. The reverse is, of course, the truth, though it is fair to argue that a people conscious of dependent status may not always experience the same incentive to better itself as does a nation which feels responsible for its own destiny. The answer is to see that reasonable national aspirations are not frustrated and that constitutional advance is allowed to keep step with developing capacity for self-government.

It would be a misleading simplification to suggest that the two kinds of problem correspond exactly to the division of work in the Colonial Office between the 'geographical' and 'subject' departments, but there is some substance in the idea. The subject departments are on the whole concerned with matters which affect the Colonial territories generally. The Colonial Office has to deal with these matters because they arise in connection with territories for which the Secretary of State is responsible. But for the most part they are not, in themselves, 'Colonial' problems. They are universal problems considered in their specific relation to this particular group of territories.

The geographical departments, by contrast, are concerned

primarily with the individual relationship of each territory to Her Majesty's Government in the United Kingdom. They must take into account both the matters dealt with in subject departments as they affect the several territories, and also the purely local and special factors, complex, subtle and ever-changing, which determine the degrees of supervision and devolution in regard to each place.

It is difficult to describe in words the 'work' of the geographical departments. The best that can be done is to outline the background to that work by briefly examining the territories dealt with in the various sections. This survey will indicate the diversity of the field and suggest the nature of the problems that call both for individual and for comprehensive handling.

PART TWO

Background of
Colonial Office Work

CHAPTER III

The West Indies and their Neighbours

THE CARIBBEAN REGION

FIRST place in a geographical survey of the territories dealt with in the Colonial Office must in all justice be conceded to the West Indian or Caribbean area and the other Colonies whose affairs are handled in the same division of the Office. For here is the scene of Columbus's first landfall, and of some of the earliest ventures of British colonists. All territories in this area are Colonies in the true as well as the technical sense. All have been British for more than one century, some for more than three.

Through most of Office history, the affairs of these Colonies have been handled in one Department, under an Assistant Under-Secretary of State who had other responsibilities as well. But to-day the work is so intensive and extensive as to call for two Departments and for the whole attention of an Assistant Under-Secretary. The division of labour between the two Departments is a matter of current convenience, but roughly speaking one Department deals with the affairs of the Colonies which in the strict sense are West Indian (Jamaica, Trinidad, Barbados, Windward Islands and Leeward Islands); the other with the mainland Colonies (British Guiana and British Honduras) and the islands (Bahamas and Bermuda) which are not part of the West Indies properly so-called. General questions affecting the area as a whole are divided between the two Departments.

Before considering the individual characteristics and problems of the Colonies and their relations with the Colonial Office, it will be convenient to look at the Caribbean region generally.

The modern regional approach to West Indian affairs is based upon the Report of the West India Royal Commission[1] which, as already mentioned, was presented in 1939 and published in full in 1945. Before the appointment of this Royal Commission, ideas of federation and amalgamation were canvassed from time to time but never came to anything. That this should be so is not surprising when one looks at the facts. Even within this limited area of the Colonial Empire the territorial units exhibit great diversity in size, wealth, accessibility, racial composition, religions and historical background. Most of them are islands, and island peoples must be expected to

[1] Cmd. 6607.

be insular in temperament. British Guiana is not geographically an island, but its main contact with the world is on the seaward side, and the same can be said of British Honduras. Of the total regional population of about $3\frac{1}{4}$ million, nearly $1\frac{1}{2}$ million are in one island—Jamaica. Density of population varies from 1,300 per square mile in Barbados to 5 per square mile in British Guiana. Distances between the units are great (Jamaica to Trinidad, 1,000 miles; British Honduras to British Guiana, over 2,000), and shipping communication unsatisfactory. There is no metropolitan centre within the region forming a natural focus for trade or organisation.

And yet, since 1939, it has been recognised, both by British authorities and by the United States and other Powers with interests in this part of the world, that a regional approach is essential. If these places cannot exactly be said to share common problems, they do at any rate have to deal with parallel problems. The very diversity of conditions and the small resources of many of the individual units make it desirable that there should be central machinery which is at the disposal of all and which can ensure that each unit can command what service it needs in order to deal with its own local manifestations of the difficulties confronting all.

Very broadly stated, these difficulties are as follows. The West Indian Colonies as a whole depend primarily upon agriculture, and in some of them prosperity stands or falls upon a single crop. Nearly everywhere the main crop is sugar; and the Commonwealth Sugar Agreement of 1951, by giving security to the sugar industry, has had a most profound and beneficial effect upon the economy of the region.

Though at one time the agricultural industries brought great wealth to the proprietors, this has not been so for very many years. The economic history of the region for the past century is one of crisis after crisis. Meanwhile populations have increased and are still increasing. The bulk of the populations consists of the descendants of Africans brought to the West Indies as slaves, but in some Colonies—notably Trinidad and British Guiana—there are also substantial East Indian communities, descended from the indentured labourers recruited in India after the abolition of slavery. Though to some extent land is now increasingly in the hands of peasant proprietors, most of it is still held in the form of estates, and the great majority of the people depend on earning wages for a living. The result of these complex factors, as summarised by the Royal Commission in 1939, was that a demand for better living conditions was becoming increasingly insistent among an expanding population at a time when world economic trends seriously endangered even the maintenance of the deplorably low existing standards.

The first and chief manifestation of the new regional approach, following the Royal Commission's report, was the establishment in 1940 within the region of a Comptroller for Development and Welfare. This officer, assisted by a team of expert advisers, is appointed by the Secretary of State and is employed and paid by the United Kingdom Government. He is, naturally, in close and constant touch with the Colonial Office and in particular with the West Indian Departments. His headquarters are in Barbados.

The position of the Comptroller and his organisation is unique: there is nothing similar in any other colonial region. The Comptroller has no authority over the territorial governments and does not intervene in their relationship with the Secretary of State. The main duty of his organisation is to be at the service of all the governments in the region, to provide them as required with assistance and advice in planning and executing social and economic development, and to advise the Colonial Office on schemes put up by the territories for the expenditure of money allocated to the region under the Colonial Development and Welfare Acts—money which, in the period 1946-52, amounted to a total of £14½ million. Generally, the Comptroller and his organisation have an important part to play in promoting regional co-operation, especially in the economic field. Closely linked with the organisation is the Regional Economic Committee, on which all the Colonial governments in the region, including British Guiana and British Honduras, are represented.

This is a purely British organisation serving the British Colonies in the region. But there are other territories concerned. The United States, for example, have oversea dependencies of their own which present some of the same problems as our Colonies. In order to promote co-operation, an Anglo-American Caribbean Commission was set up in 1942, the British Comptroller being one of the Co-Chairmen. In 1946 the French and Dutch Governments joined in what was henceforward called the Caribbean Commission, and headquarters were set up in Trinidad. Two auxiliary bodies were added: the Caribbean Research Council and the West Indian Conference, the latter consisting of delegates from all the territories concerned, together with officials and advisers.

Returning to the British territories, we may now notice the progress of the federation idea. In 1947 a conference was held at Montego Bay, Jamaica, under the presidency of the Secretary of State (Mr. A. Creech Jones). As a result, a Standing Closer Association Committee was set up in 1948 and this Committee made specific recommendations for a federal scheme in 1950. These recommendations were remitted to the territorial governments for study, and matters were carried to a further stage in 1953, when another conference was convened by the Secretary of State (Mr. Oliver Lyttelton) in London. This conference (which included representatives of the islands, but not of the mainland Colonies which were not, at that time, disposed to commit themselves to taking part in the federal scheme) agreed on a detailed plan for federation which was in its turn sent back for discussion by the island legislatures. At the time of writing, all the islands have accepted the London Conference plan (with one amendment) and the next stages are being worked out.

THE WEST INDIES

Having indicated briefly the arrangements for dealing regionally with the affairs of the Caribbean area, we may now consider the several Colonies included in the work of the West Indian Departments. It will be convenient to take first the Colonies proposed to be covered by the federation plan, namely Jamaica with its dependencies, Trinidad and Tobago, Barbados, the Leeward Islands and the Windward Islands.

Jamaica

Largest of the West Indian Colonies in size and population, Jamaica lies well away from the rest. It is mountainous and well watered, and possesses, at Kingston, one of the finest natural harbours in the world. After its discovery by Columbus, it was at first occupied by Spain, but it has been British since 1655. Its political and economic history has been chequered, but social services and local government organs are well established, and there are many features in the Colony's public life of which its people are justly proud. Agriculture is the main source of wealth, but there are important bauxite mines and the tourist trade is second only to the sugar industry in its contribution to the prosperity of the country. A major and inescapable difficulty from which the island suffers is the occasional incidence of earthquakes and hurricanes. A particularly disastrous hurricane which occurred in August, 1951, practically wiped out for the time being the whole of the banana cultivations as well as causing much other damage: but the people reacted to the disaster with resource.

Jamaica to-day is virtually self-governing in its domestic affairs. It would be outside the scope of this book to give details of the constitutional arrangements in each Colony, and I propose to do no more than summarise their general effect so as to show the nature of the relationship between the Colonial and United Kingdom Governments. In Jamaica, the principal instrument of policy is the Executive Council, which is now in effect a Cabinet of Ministers, presided over by the Governor and including three officials and two nominated members.

The Legislature of Jamaica had originally and has now a two-Chamber form, consisting of a Legislative Council (Upper House) and a House of Representatives, the latter being wholly elected on the basis of adult suffrage and presided over by a Speaker elected by the House.

There are many notable things about Jamaica, but it must suffice here to mention that the island is the seat of the University College of the West Indies, founded in 1948 with substantial financial assistance fom the United Kingdom under the Colonial Development and Welfare Act.

Attached to Jamaica as dependencies, but with their own constitutions and financial arrangements, are the small groups known as the Cayman Islands and the Turks and Caicos Islands.

Trinidad and Tobago

These islands, lying a short distance off the Venezuelan coast, were finally ceded to Britain, after several vicissitudes, in 1802 and 1814 respectively. They have been administered as a single Colony since 1888. While, as in the other islands, agriculture is an essential industry (the Imperial College of Tropical Agriculture is located in Trinidad), the Colony is fortunate in possessing important sources of petroleum and asphalt. (It is also the world's only supplier of angostura bitters.) It is well served by sea and air communications and is sufficiently prosperous to be able to maintain social services at a comparatively high level.

The constitutional arrangements of the Colony differ in many respects from those of Jamaica, partly because of the difference in historical background. Trinidad never had, as Jamaica did, the old Stuart type of colonial constitution, but began with the nineteenth century Crown Colony model. It has, therefore, only a single Chamber, mainly elected, and presided over by a Speaker, but containing three official members. These are the same three who sit in the Executive Council which, as in Jamaica, is the principal instrument of policy, is presided over by the Governor, and contains elected Ministers who are in a majority. Broadly speaking, therefore, Trinidad, like Jamaica, is self-governing in domestic affairs.

Barbados

'Barbados', wrote Anthony Trollope, 'is a very respectable little island.' About the size of the Isle of Wight, and standing eastward of the other Caribbean islands, it was first claimed for King James in 1625 and has been British ever since. Its constitution, going back in essentials to 1652, is different from those of Jamaica and Trinidad, but is like those in providing for internal self-government.

A ministerial system of government has very recently been introduced, with the title of Premier for the leading Minister.

Barbados, first nicknamed 'Little England' by the Cavaliers, reproduces many traditional features of English life, such as the parochial system. The economy of the Colony is entirely dependent upon sugar, and it is one of the most intensively cultivated countries in the world. The pressure of increasing population is great and presents the government with its most serious problem, for the possibilities of further economic development are limited.

The Leeward Islands

This Colony consists of a group of numerous islands which have been British since the 17th century and have always been associated politically as well as geographically. The island of Dominica was for a time included in the group for administrative purposes, but since 1940 has been included in the Windward Islands.

The Colony at present[1] is a federation of four 'Presidencies': Antigua (with Barbuda); St. Kitts—Nevis—Anguilla; Montserrat; and the British Virgin Islands. Each Presidency has its own Executive and Legislative Councils, presided over by an official who is called Administrator in the first two mentioned, and Commissioner in the other two.

Though the oldest settlement (1623) was in St. Kitts (or St. Christopher) and the other islands were colonised from there, the seat of the federal government is in Antigua. There is a Federal Executive Council consisting of the Governor and seven official members (including the Administrators and Commissioners) and seven unofficial members; and a General Legislative Council in which the representative members from the Presidencies have a majority. Under the Leeward Islands Act, 1871, the General Legislative Council has concurrent powers of legislation with the local legislatures on certain specified subjects. This means that in these matters the General Legislative Council can overrule the enactments of the island legislatures if it thinks fit. The Federal Establishment includes the Colonial Secretary, Attorney-General, Principal Auditor, Commissioner of Police and an Economic and Financial Adviser. The costs of this establishment are apportioned among the Presidencies. The Judiciary is maintained jointly with the Windward Islands.

Antigua, the largest island of the group, was an important naval station in the Napoleonic wars, and possesses, in English Harbour,

[1] At the request of the local governments, the federation is shortly to be dissolved, the Presidencies becoming separate Colonies like the Windward Islands.

the relics of Nelson's dockyard, which efforts are now being made to preserve. (Nevis, too, has associations with Nelson, for it was in the church here that he was married.) To-day, Antigua depends mainly upon sugar and cotton. St. Kitts is a 'sugar' island. Montserrat's principal exports are cotton and lime products. The Virgin Islands (there are 36 of them, of which 11 are inhabited) specialise in livestock.

The Windward Islands

Unlike the Leeward Islands, this group is not a federation, but consists of four separate Colonies—Grenada, St. Vincent, St. Lucia and Dominica—each with a resident Administrator who works under the general supervision of the Governor of the whole group. They have no common legislature, common laws or revenues, nor any joint establishment, apart from the Governor, Chief Secretary and a few other officials and advisers. The Governor normally resides in Grenada, visiting the other islands as circumstances require.

The historical background of the Windward Islands differs from that of the Leewards. The possession of all four islands was long disputed between British and French, and the British claims were not finally established until the era of the Napoleonic wars. The bulk of the populations are of African descent; a few of the aboriginal Caribs still remain in St. Vincent and Dominica. Each Colony has an Executive Council containing both elected and nominated members, and a Legislative Council with an unofficial majority. It is expected that a form of Ministerial government will be introduced in some at least of the islands during 1955.

The economy of the islands is diversified. St. Lucia depends largely upon its sugar production, but cocoa, cotton, bananas and copra are included in the exports of the group as a whole. Grenada is famous for nutmegs, St. Vincent for arrowroot and Dominica for limes.

ATLANTIC ISLANDS

The other Colonies dealt with in the West Indian Division of the Office comprise the mainland territories of British Guiana and British Honduras and the islands of the Bermudas and Bahamas.

The Bahamas

The Bahamas consist of an archipelago of some 700 islands of which only 20 are inhabited. One of the islands was the first land discovered by Columbus after his crossing of the Atlantic in 1492. The islands were, however, first settled by British colonists, and had some form of constitutional government before 1670. It was not, however, until 1729 that the islands were finally constituted as a

British Crown Colony. Since then there has been little change in the pattern of government, which vests executive power in the Governor and Executive Council, while the legislature consists of a Legislative Council (upper House) and an elected House of Assembly.

Owing to their pleasant sub-tropical climate and their accessibility from the mainland of the United States, the islands are much favoured as a holiday resort, and the tourist traffic is the main source of the Colony's prosperity. It also has the effect of making the cost of living for the ordinary inhabitant extremely high in the popular centres.

Bermuda

Bermuda, too, depends mainly upon its tourist industry, especially since the closing of the Naval dockyard in 1951, and has benefited greatly from the development of air communications during the last few years. The airfield, which was built by the United States under a war-time lease, is now a very important airline junction, and most of the 100,000 or so visitors which the Colony attracts year after year travel by air.

The Colony consists of a chain of coral islands on the summit of a submarine volcano. Bridges and causeways connect the main islands so as to form a continuous territory. Though discovered by a Spaniard named Bermudez in 1515, the islands were first settled by shipwrecked mariners in 1609 and were at one time called the Somers Islands after the admiral of that name who commanded the party. They have had representative government continuously since 1620, and the Bermuda Legislature is the oldest Parliamentary body in the Commonwealth apart from Westminster. The form of the constitution has changed little since 1684, and is generally similar to that of the Bahamas as already described.

THE AMERICAN MAINLAND
British Guiana

British Guiana, the legendary land of Eldorado, presents a very different picture. On the map, it is a territory nearly as large as Great Britain, but over nine-tenths of it is forest or savannah. The bulk of the population of about 450,000 is concentrated in a fairly narrow coastal belt, and is mostly employed in various capacities connected with the sugar and—to a less extent—the rice production industries. The economy of the country depends mainly upon sugar growing, rice production, bauxite mining and timber extraction. Owing to geographical conditions, difficulties of communication and poverty of resources, the interior of the Colony is largely undeveloped and indeed it is not clearly known what, if any, potentiality of development it may possess. The coastal region itself, upon which so much depends, is flat and below sea level, and therefore needs continuous defence against inundation.

Historically, British Guiana was colonised at various times by British and Dutch, and, after some fluctuations of ownership, became finally British in 1814. As in other parts of the Caribbean area, the early prosperity of the colonists depended upon the employment of imported African slave labour. After the emancipation of the slaves, indentured labourers were recruited from India. As a result, the population to-day includes about 200,000 East Indians and about the same number of African or mixed descent.

This very brief sketch gives the background to the events of 1953-54 which brought the Colony prominently before the notice of the British public. The constitutional history of the Colony is peculiar, and it is only necessary to say here that from 1928 onwards the arrangements were of the standard Crown Colony type, with Executive and Legislative Councils presided over by the Governor. In 1943 the composition of the Legislative Council was adjusted so as to give a clear majority to members elected on a franchise based on a literacy test and a property qualification. Demands for further reforms led to the appointment in 1950 of a Constitutional Commission, whose report resulted in the inauguration, in 1952, of a new constitution providing for universal suffrage, a bicameral legislature with a lower House consisting almost entirely of elected members, and the transformation of the Executive Council into a ministerial body.

In subsequent elections, a majority of seats was won by the People's Progressive Party. All efforts to make the constitution work with Ministers drawn from the Communist leaders of this party failed, and the economic as well as the political stability of the Colony began to be seriously threatened. Eventually, in 1953, it became necessary to suspend the constitution, strengthen the security forces, provide for an interim government, and appoint a new Commission to make recommendations for the future. At the same time, the Governor was encouraged to make and to put into effect extensive plans for pressing on with urgently needed economic and social developments which the People's Progressive Party Ministers had neglected; and substantial financial assistance was promised by Her Majesty's Government under the Colonial Development and Welfare Acts.

Such events well illustrate the part played by the Colonial Office in the affairs of the territories. It is the Secretary of State who has to consider, in consultation with his Cabinet colleagues and with the Governor concerned, whether conditions in a Colony call for investigation, and what form such investigation should take. If there is to be a Commission, its terms of reference must be fixed, its members selected after the necessary negotiation, and practical arrangements made for it to do its work. Its report has to be considered, in consultation with the Governor, decisions taken on its recommendations, and action put in hand to carry those decisions into effect. Almost certainly the report will be published and will be the subject of Parliamentary debate. Again, so extreme a decision as the suspension of a constitution can only be taken by Her Majesty's Government; it must inevitably be preceded by much consultation and discussion between the Colonial Office and the Governor; and it must thereafter be explained and justified to Parliament and to public opinion at home and overseas. While, fortunately, many Colonies go quietly on their way for long periods at a time without calling for any major operations on the part of the Colonial Office, deep currents of political and social change are running, and are liable at any moment to disturb the surface here or there. The Colonial Office, and especially the geographical departments, must be in close and continuous touch with developments so that the Secretary of State is kept informed and is enabled as far as possible to deal with impending difficulties before they reach a critical stage, and so that action, when it has to be taken, is prompt, decisive and effective.

British Honduras

This is a much smaller territory, the size, in fact, of Wales, with a population of some 70,000 of very varied racial origin. It is a country of strange and obscure history. In the Middle Ages it was the seat of a Mayan empire whose ruined monuments are numerous and impressive. The survivors of the Maya Indians to-day do not, however, possess any sense of historical continuity with their ancestral past. British and Spanish settlers disputed the control of the country for many years up to 1798, since when the British have remained in possession, though not in undisputed possession, for the neighbouring State of Guatemala has laid claim (as heir to Spanish rights) to the territory. She has not, however, accepted the British offer to submit the case to the International Court of Justice.

The Colony, at one time a dependency of Jamaica, has stood on its own since 1884. The chief industry has always been forestry and the territory has never been very prosperous. A disastrous hurricane in 1931 set it back a long way and for the next twenty years it had to be helped with grants in aid from the United Kingdom Exchequer.

British Honduras has its own particular variation on the constitutional theme. The Legislative Council (or Assembly) is constituted by local law, the Executive Council by Royal Instructions and Letters Patent. After a good deal of local deliberation, the Legislative Council recommended in 1952 that a new constitution should be introduced, under which the Legislative Assembly would have a majority of members elected by universal suffrage, and the Executive Council would have a majority of members elected by the Assembly. These proposals were accepted by Her Majesty's Government, and arrangements were made for bringing the new constitution into force in 1954. The arrangements were carried on despite the fact that the best organised political party, the People's United Party, was avowedly opposed to the continuation of the colonial régime. The Party was successful in gaining a majority of seats at the election held in April, 1954; its leaders then undertook to co-operate loyally with the Governor and administration in promoting the best interests of the country. This promise was kept, and in the autumn of 1954 representatives of the new government, together with the Governor, visited London at the invitation of the United Kingdom Government for what turned out to be a very friendly and fruitful discussion of the Colony's problems and prospects.

This short examination of the situation and problems of the Colonies whose affairs are dealt with in one division of the Colonial Office shows how wide are the differences between even territories contained in what on the map looks a comparatively small and homogeneous region. Variations of detail might be expected; but no two Colonies are alike even in general background. Yet these variations are not fortuitous. They spring from real differences in historical, geographical, economic and social conditions. They make the work of the Colonial Office vastly more complicated than it would be if there were a neat and uniform system of administration. Whether such a system, if it had been introduced in the past, would have produced any better results is a hypothetical question, but at least in the case of the West Indies it is most unlikely. However that may be, it would be impossible now to reverse the whole trend of British policy and to quench the rich and vital individualism which our precept, example—and even, on occasion, our neglect—have encouraged throughout the centuries.

CHAPTER IV

West Africa

THE GENERAL BACKGROUND

CROSSING the Atlantic from the Caribbean to Africa, we are transported to quite a different world. The four West African territories—the Gambia, Sierra Leone, the Gold Coast and Nigeria—have, as will be seen, their own immense diversities, but as a group they possess certain common characteristics which distinguish them from the territories in other areas for which the Colonial Office is responsible. To begin with, they are all inhabited by African populations which—whatever unwritten history of migration and conquest may lie behind them—can fairly be called indigenous. The geographical situation of these countries has lent itself to the establishment of long and continuous contact between European maritime powers and the coastal areas, but it has also discouraged any move for permanent settlement by Europeans. All the territories, therefore, present a contrast between coast and interior, the latter having been for a much shorter time—generally not more than sixty years—in direct touch with Western influence.

The four territories stand in the list above in the order of geographical location and also in an ascending scale of size, population and complexity of political and administrative institutions. The arrangements for dealing with their affairs in the Colonial Office have varied from time to time. At one period there was a Nigeria Department and a separate Gold Coast Department, which also dealt with Sierra Leone, the Gambia and the Mediterranean Colonies. Then the departments were amalgamated and responsibility for the Mediterranean transferred to another part of the Office. In 1953 the work had grown so much that the departments were split once more, one now dealing with Nigeria and one with the other three territories; regional matters being handled by a small staff shared by the two departments.

For West Africa is a 'region', though a political federation of the four territories is not a prospective reality. Some African statesmen indeed have a vision of a future 'United States of West Africa', embracing not only the British territories but those now under the tutelage of other Powers, as well as independent Liberia, but at present the several countries are busy finding themselves and building up integrated communities. It is indeed a remarkable fact that the effect of living together even for a comparatively short time in an administrative unit under the *Pax Britannica* has been to inspire a sense of nationhood strong enough to transcend great diversities of culture, language and tradition.

Yet, though federation may not be in the present picture, there are many things in which the British West African territories find it advisable and necessary to work together. In 1939 a Governors' Conference was established as a standing body, and during the succeeding war this was expanded into a West African War Council with a British Resident Minister as Chairman and a permanent secretariat. After the war the Council was continued for a time with the Secretary of State himself as titular Chairman, but in 1951 it was abolished and replaced by a West African Inter-Territorial Conference consisting of two members of the Cabinet, Executive Council, or Council of Ministers from each territory. The main work of the Conference is to foster international and inter-territorial collaboration on various technical subjects (for example communications and public health services), to supervise joint research organisations and to help in co-ordinating defence arrangements. It has a Chief Secretary seconded from the Colonial Office, and the headquarters are in the Gold Coast. The Chairman of the Conference is chosen by the Conference when it meets.

THE GAMBIA

All these West African territories are in some sense artificial creations, resulting from the fixing of international boundaries by the great Powers, but the Gambia is certainly the most deserving of this description. The Colony consists of an island and a small area of mainland at the mouth of the great River Gambia, and of another island some 150 miles upstream. The Protectorate is a strip of territory about ten miles wide on each side of the river for nearly 300 miles of its course, forming an enclave in the French territory of Senegal. British trading posts were established at the river mouth not long after the beginning of the 17th century, and the early history of the Colony was eventful and romantic. Settled occupation dates from 1816 when the present capital was founded and named Bathurst, after the Secretary of State at the time. At first the territory was annexed to the Colony of Sierra Leone, but it became a Colony in its own right in 1843.

Though the territory has paid its way, it has never been particularly prosperous. It may have seemed probable at one time that the site of Bathurst at the river mouth would be a key point for trade from and to the interior, but in fact Bathurst as a port has been eclipsed in importance by Dakar in French territory. During the second world war the Colony was a busy centre for international air communications, but post-war aviation developments left it on one side. An attempt made in 1948 by the Colonial Development Corporation to establish an extensive poultry industry proved to be ill-fated. Fortunately, the Gambia has a permanent and reasonably profitable industry in the shape of ground-nut production. This is carried on by the efforts not only of the inhabitants but of so-called 'strange farmers' who flock into the riverside lands from French and Portuguese territory during the farming season.

Politically, the Gambia may be considered as falling into two parts: the Colony proper, which in effect means the relatively sophisticated and cosmopolitan town of Bathurst and its immediate surroundings; and the Protectorate with its indigenous peasant tribes under their traditional chieftains. The aim and effect of modern developments is to promote the integration of the country. Bathurst itself has an elected Town Council, and the Protectorate districts have their own local government authorities. At the centre, there is a Legislative Council with an unofficial majority, partly elected and partly nominated, representing both Colony and Protectorate. In the Executive Council, as constituted in 1951, there were (in addition to the Governor) six officials and four African unofficial members, one of whom comes from the Protectorate. In 1953 proposals for constitutional reform were made by a Consultative Committee appointed by the Governor. These included a Legislative Council of five official and sixteen unofficial members and an Executive Council of four official members, an 'appointed' Gambian public officer and six unofficial members of whom not less than two nor more than three would be appointed Ministers. These changes were brought into effect in 1954.

SIERRA LEONE

The mountain peninsula of some 250 square miles, sheltering a fine natural harbour, which forms the Colony of Sierra Leone is one of the few places on the West African coast which can lay claim to scenic beauty. Though given its romantic name by Portuguese explorers in the 15th century, and visited from time to time by Hawkins, Drake and other adventurers—respectable and otherwise—no settlement was established until 1787, when land was acquired by a British philanthropic society in order to provide a home for slaves who had been freed and brought to England where they were destitute. During the succeeding years the Colony was extended, the population was increased by the settlement of liberated slaves, the capital town of Freetown was founded and the responsibility for government was taken over by the Crown. In the 19th century British influence expanded into the interior, and eventually in 1896 a formal Protectorate, more than a hundred times the size of the Colony, was established within boundaries fixed by agreement with the French and Liberian governments. Although, therefore, the history and background of the two territories are very different, Sierra Leone, like the Gambia, presents a strong contrast between Colony and Protectorate and is facing the problem of welding the two into an integrated State. It is not an easy problem, because the Colony population, while African by race, is mainly composed of the so-called Creoles whose ancestors came back to Africa after enforced sojourn overseas, having largely lost their African tradition and acquired a share in Western tradition; whereas the Protectorate population is native to the soil and looks back through generations of historical continuity. The Colony lives by the services it renders as the main channel for imports and exports. But the natural resources of the country are in the Protectorate, from which palm kernels and other agricultural products, iron ore, diamonds and other minerals come down to the coast for shipment to the world's markets.

The progressive integration of Colony and Protectorate is reflected in the constitutional development of the territory. Until 1924 the writ of the Colony's Legislative Council did not run in the Protectorate, which was directly administered by officials responsible to the Governor. Then the functions of the Council were extended over the whole country, and three Protectorate chiefs were included in the membership. There was still an official majority. Since 1951, however, the Council has had a majority of unofficial members, and these have included fourteen elected representatives of the Protectorate, the remaining elements being seven elected representatives of the Colony and two nominated members. In the Executive Council there are, in addition to the Governor, four *ex officio* members and not less than four (actually there are six) persons appointed by the Governor from amongst the elected members of the Legislative Council. In 1953 these were formally designated as Ministers and assumed responsibility for departments of government.

The relationship, therefore, of Sierra Leone (and indeed of the Gambia) to the United Kingdom is coming near to that of the West Indian Colonies described in the previous chapter. Her Majesty's Government in the United Kingdom retain the ultimate responsibility and the power to take action if need be: but the day-to-day administration, and the formation and execution of policy with regard to the internal affairs of the country, are now, by virtue of these modern developments, conducted by persons representing and responsible to the local community, assisted and advised by the

Governor and civil servants. In the Gold Coast, to which we now come, the process has developed further to the verge of independence.

THE GOLD COAST

Here is a territory, or rather group of territories, the size of Great Britain, with a population of 4½ million consisting almost entirely of indigenous Africans. It is divided, politically, into four parts: the Gold Coast Colony, which extends along the whole of the coastline to a depth of 50 to 100 miles inland; the ancient Kingdom of Ashanti, annexed to the Crown and declared a Colony in 1901; the Northern Territories, which are a Protectorate; and that part of Togoland which is under British Trusteeship, a narrow strip of country running alongside the other three sections from north to south.

As a source of gold, and later of slave labour, this part of West Africa attracted the interest of European nations as early as the 15th century, and the castles built by Portuguese, Dutch, English, Danes and others remain to-day as impressive monuments of bygone history. Gold is still an important export and the country's mineral resources include substantial quantities of manganese, bauxite and diamonds. But by far the most important product to-day is cocoa, of which more than £60 million worth was exported in 1951, as compared with £4½ million worth in 1938. Even more spectacular is the expansion in timber exports, from £77,000 worth in 1938 to nearly £5 million worth in 1951. Thanks to the success of its valuable industries, the financial condition of the territory is healthy and has enabled great and rapid progress to be made in social and economic development.

This in its turn has made possible and indeed inevitable corresponding developments in the political field, marking the emergence of the Gold Coast as a national State capable of standing upon its own feet in the modern world. After going through the usual pattern of political evolution under the Crown Colony system, the Gold Coast was in 1950 granted a constitution which provided, in effect, for the government of the country by a Cabinet of Ministers responsible to an elected Legislative Assembly. This system was, however, subject to certain provisions differentiating it from full Parliamentary government. The Governor, not the Prime Minister, presided over the Cabinet; and this body included three *ex officio* Ministers holding the portfolios of Defence and External Affairs; Finance; and Justice. These officials were also members of the Legislative Assembly, which included as well a small number of 'special members' representing commercial and mining interests.

In 1954 a further development has taken place, under which the *ex officio* Ministers disappear, as do the 'special members', leaving a wholly elected Assembly and an all-African Cabinet. The Governor retains certain powers which are essential so long as Her Majesty's Government in the United Kingdom has any responsibility whatsoever for the territory, but otherwise acts on Ministerial advice. The Gold Coast, in fact, has reached the last stage of political evolution short of independence.

As was suggested in Chapter II, this achievement has depended upon the fortunate combination of a number of favourable factors, amongst which are the compact nature of the territory and the relative homogeneity of its population. The Gold Coast's problem, though fraught with its own difficulties, is at least simple by comparison with the problem of Nigeria.

NIGERIA

No one could describe Nigeria as 'compact'. In mere size it is as large as the United Kingdom, France and Belgium put together. It contains about 30 million out of the 77 million people who inhabit the territories for which the Colonial Office is responsible. Practically the whole of this population is African, but this general term covers a wide variety of ancestry, language, religion and culture.

It is, very roughly, a square territory, with a coastline of 700 miles and an inland depth of about 650, reaching to the arid waste of the Sahara. Much of the produce upon which the country depends—cocoa, palm products, groundnuts, cotton, tin, rubber, hides and skins and the rest—comes from far inland and has to be brought to the coast for export. This is a strong unifying factor which weighs against other factors tending to separate Nigeria into component parts. Amongst these other factors one of the most important is the cultural and social difference between the peoples of the northern part of the country and those of the south. The former are predominantly Mohammedan and Hausa-speaking; and the area is divided into a number of Emirates under rulers who inherit in common an ancient tradition drawn from the Arab world. The southern peoples are much less homogeneous in language, history and social organisation, and owe much of their cultural tradition to their far longer contact with Europe.

In the 16th and 17th centuries the coast, with its numerous river mouths, was a hunting ground of slave traders from many nations, but no permanent colony was established until, in 1861, the British government somewhat reluctantly decided to occupy the port of Lagos as the only means of checking the slave trade and protecting legitimate commerce. Meanwhile, the explorations of the hinterland by Mungo Park and others had aroused interest in the possibilities

c

of trade and development. The British claim to a sphere of influence in Nigeria was internationally recognised in 1885, but it was not until the early years of the 20th century that the whole area was brought under formal British protection and administration. Until 1914 the northern and southern parts of the country were administered as separate units. In that year the units were amalgamated to form the Colony and Protectorate of Nigeria, and part of the former German Cameroons was later added as a mandated (now a trusteeship) territory. By general consent the title of maker of the modern Nigeria belongs to the late Lord Lugard.

In a new constitution introduced in 1947 the southern part of the country was divided into an Eastern and a Western Region (the North remaining as a third Region) and the beginnings of a federal system were set on foot. The Legislative Council (which had formerly legislated only for the Southern Provinces) was given functions relating to the whole country (and an unofficial majority); and Regional Houses of Assembly were also established with limited powers. In 1951 there was a further development. A Central Legislature consisting almost entirely of African elected members was set up, with corresponding Regional Houses; and central government was entrusted to a Council consisting of Ministers drawn from each Region together with a few *ex officio* members. This arrangement failed to work satisfactorily, and in 1953 a conference of the majority and principal minority parties in Nigeria was convened in London under the Chairmanship of the Secretary of State, Mr. Oliver Lyttelton. It was agreed to work out a new federal scheme, under which the functions of the central or federal government would be clearly defined and the regional governments would become autonomous in most matters not specifically reserved to the centre. Undertakings were also given concerning the grant of self-government at a future date to any Region which might desire it, subject to certain safeguards for the continuance of the Federation. The only issue upon which there was serious divergence of view was the status of the town of Lagos, the question being whether as Federal capital it should be a separate Federal territory or remain incorporated in the Western Region with which it had been merged since 1951. The Secretary of State, having been asked by the conference to resolve the difficulty by giving a decision, pronounced in favour of the former alternative.

The conference was resumed at Lagos in January, 1954, the Secretary of State flying there from Northern Rhodesia in order to preside; and agreement was then reached on the detailed provisions of the new constitution, which accordingly came into force on 1st October, 1954.

ROLE OF THE COLONIAL OFFICE

These brief notes are not, of course, intended to serve even as a summary of the history and present conditions of the four West African territories, but only as a background to the work of the Colonial Office departments concerned with their affairs. Enough has perhaps been said to indicate broadly the nature of the relationship between the territorial governments and the Office, and to suggest some observations of a general kind for which recent West African history provides a convenient text. It is easy to write that at a certain stage of a territory's political development certain constitutional changes took place. But of course these things do not just happen. The Nigerian conferences of 1953 and 1954 were an illustration, on a large scale, of what in one form or another must go on all the time; and they themselves did not take place in a vacuum but were the product of long and patient spadework on the part of statesmen and officials at both ends. In the Gold Coast, the outward pattern of events was different. There, in 1949, an all-African Committee was appointed locally to make recommendations for a constitution, and later developments have been initiated by the Gold Coast Cabinet itself. But before recommended changes could be put into force there had to be an intensive process of consultation and negotiation. So, too, in Sierra Leone and the Gambia.

This is part, and an important part, of the Office's dealings with the territories, and inevitably it receives much attention and much publicity. It is only a part, however. The machinery of government has to be continuously provided for. Staff must be attracted, recruited, trained and looked after. This brings in the Oversea Service Division. Expert advice has to be made available on every sort of subject. This brings in the social service and other subject departments of the Office and the Secretary of State's Advisers and Advisory Committees. Development plans have to be worked out. Generally this is done first of all in the territory, but if—as is almost always the case—the plans involve raising outside money either by grant under the Colonial Development and Welfare Acts or by loan on the London market, much discussion and negotiation must be gone through before final decisions can be reached, and in this the Finance Department of the Office, and the Treasury, too, have an indispensable part to play.

The territories depend for their livelihood on the export of their products and on the import of the supplies which they need. In these days most of the big trading questions are the subject of international agreements and of arrangements between governments. These are dealt with comprehensively for the Colonial territories by the Economic Division in close communication with the Board of Trade,

Ministry of Supply and other government offices. So, too, defence questions and international affairs, civil aviation and other forms of communication have their appropriate sections of the Office, linked to the appropriate other Departments of State.

The geographical department must, however, be a party to all these activities, even though some specialised section of the Office may be doing most of the actual work. This is necessary, not only because the geographical department alone is able to place each subject in its proper perspective in relation to the economic, social and political conditions of the territory in question but because, as must by now have become apparent to the reader, the Office's approach to the conduct of business with each territory has to be carefully adjusted to the territory's particular and individual relationship to the United Kingdom. In this and the previous chapters we have been considering territories all of which possess a considerable amount of local self-government. Even so, they present wide differences of relationship. In later chapters we shall find wider differences still. The Colonial Office, to put it bluntly, can say things to the Governor of A which it could not say, without provoking a crisis, to the Governor of B. It is all a question of tact; and the job of the geographical department is to see not only that the right things are done but that they are done in the right way.

CHAPTER V

East and Central Africa

THE EAST AFRICAN GROUP

IN almost everything, except for the facts that they are in the Tropics and are predominantly populated by peoples of African race, the territories now to be considered present a sharp contrast to those of West Africa. In the Colonial Office the work relating to these territories is divided between two departments. One department deals with the affairs of Kenya, Uganda, Tanganyika and Zanzibar, together with those of the East African High Commission, an organisation in which the first three territories mentioned are associated for certain purposes. The other department deals with the affairs of Northern Rhodesia and Nyasaland and collaborates with the Commonwealth Relations Office in matters concerning the Central African Federation. It also deals with the Somaliland Protectorate and with the Aden Colony and Protectorate which, though not, of course, in Africa, are more conveniently attached to this than to any other department of the Office.

In considering the individual territories it will be simplest to follow this departmental arrangement and to take first the three territories of Kenya, Uganda and Tanganyika.

The history of British connection with these territories is very different from that in West Africa. From the late fifteenth to the early eighteenth centuries the Portuguese had been established as traders on the east African coast, but they were driven out and replaced by the Arabs, who were interested in the interior of the country only as a source of slaves and ivory for export. In the nineteenth century British explorers, intent upon unveiling the mysteries of the Dark Continent and discovering the source of the Nile, found their way to Uganda and the great lakes. Some of them were Christian missionaries and others came in their tracks; and then, once again, trade followed the Cross, and a British sphere of influence was established.

In 1888 British interests in the region which is now Kenya and Uganda were entrusted by Royal Charter to the Imperial British East Africa Company, but during the next five years formal protectorates were established and eventually the area was divided into two administrative units, the Uganda Protectorate and the East Africa Protectorate.

It was the former of these which attracted particular interest, and the Uganda Railway was built for the purpose of providing a communication between Uganda and the coast. The building—officially described as 'an epic enterprise'—lasted from 1895 to 1901. This had the incidental effect of opening up the highlands through which the line passed, and of attracting British and South African farmers to settle there. The building of the railway had called for the introduction of Indian labour in many thousands, and so laid the foundations of a large Indian resident population.

All these developments took place under the supervision of the Foreign Office. The Protectorates were brought under the Colonial Office in 1905, and soon after this were provided with the usual government apparatus of Governor, Executive Council and Legislative Council. After the first world war large numbers of new settlers arrived in the East Africa Protectorate which, in 1920, was renamed Kenya after the great mountain, when the territory (with the exception of the coastal strip which is part of the dominions of Zanzibar and remains a protectorate) was annexed to the Crown as a Colony.

That war also left Britain charged with the administration of the greater part of the territory which had been German East Africa. The country had been occupied by British and Belgian forces in 1916 and 1917, and a provisional civil government established. At the end of the war, Britain received a mandate to administer the territory in British occupation, and a formal government of what was named Tanganyika Territory was set up in 1920. Administration was carried out under the mandate until the establishment of the Trusteeship system under the Charter of the United Nations.

EAST AFRICA HIGH COMMISSION

It has already been noticed in West Africa that administrative boundaries, determined originally by international more than by local considerations, tend to create national communities, though there may, indeed, be room for minor adjustments where, for example, a boundary is found to cut right through the lands of a close-knit tribal community. While these three territories—Kenya, Uganda and Tanganyika—are contiguous and clearly share many interests in common, each has developed its own special and individual characteristics, and these tend, perhaps, to become more rather than less pronounced as time goes on. Ideas, therefore, of amalgamation or even of political federation of the territories have never received general support. It has long been accepted, however, that the close association of the territories for certain practical purposes is desirable and indeed necessary. Customs and postal communications have for many years been run as joint services. So have railways, harbours and lake transport, though it is only recently that Tanganyika has come into this arrangement.

The first practical step towards closer association was the foundation of a Governors' Conference in 1926. The range of jointly operated services was greatly increased during the second world war, and in 1947 an East Africa High Commission was established. This is not a federal government but has certain executive and legislative powers in respect of defined interterritorial services, including transport, postal and telegraph communications, income tax, civil aviation, research and scientific organisations. The High Commission consists of the three Governors, assisted by executive officials, and there is a Legislative Assembly representing all three territories, with an unofficial majority.

KENYA COLONY AND PROTECTORATE

The special characteristics of the Colony and Protectorate of Kenya stem from its history which has already been very briefly outlined. Four main communal or racial elements go to make up the population of the country. There are, first, the Africans themselves, of many tribes and customs. Under the British flag they have increased and multiplied. Twenty years ago their numbers were estimated at 3 million: to-day they are getting on for double that figure. Next in order of numbers are the Asians (Hindus, Pakistanis and Goans), over 100,000 in all. The European population is somewhere about 35,000 and the coastal Arab community about 25,000.

The basic problem of Kenya is to weld these communal elements, so diverse in so many respects, into an integrated State. It is a difficult enough problem, to be solved only by the patient co-operation of men of goodwill over very many years. The notorious Mau Mau disturbances, which caused a state of emergency to be proclaimed in October, 1952, strikingly illustrated the gravity of the problem, while at the same time frustrating much of the work which had been done by men of many races to promote peaceful progress. In such an emergency the first purpose of government must be to restore law and order; but it is recognised as no less important to get to the root of the trouble and create conditions in which a fresh start can be made.

When a crisis of this order develops in a Colonial territory, the normal processes of consultation between the home government and the government of the territory are greatly intensified. Very soon after the declaration of the emergency, the Secretary of State (Mr. Oliver Lyttelton), accompanied by officials, flew to Kenya to examine the situation on the spot. Two months later the Governor (Sir Evelyn

Baring) flew home for further discussions with the Secretary of State and the Colonial Office. After further exchanges of visits at various levels, the Secretary of State went out once more in March, 1954, to preside at decisive meetings in Nairobi about the future government of the country. As a result of these meetings a new form of constitution has been introduced under which, while the Executive Council remains in being for certain limited purposes, the main business of government is entrusted to a Council of Ministers, including representatives of all the principal racial groups.

UGANDA PROTECTORATE

Meanwhile, events in Uganda were bringing that formerly unobtrusive country into the headlines. Unlike other parts of Eastern Africa, the Uganda Protectorate includes a number of African Kingdoms which were in existence before the coming of the British and with the rulers of which agreements were concluded at the time of the establishment of the Protectorate. The largest of these Kingdoms is Buganda, which has a hereditary Ruler (His Highness the Kabaka), a ministerial system, a form of parliament (the Lukiko), and a hierarchy of chiefs who are the executive officers of government.

The broad aim of British administration of the Protectorate has been to build the whole country into an integrated state capable of standing on its own feet, while preserving the traditional organs of local government. Hopes of attaining this objective are encouraged by the absence of serious racial rivalries and by the economic prosperity of the territory. The latter is due largely to the success of the cotton-growing industry, but production of coffee and other crops is important and a number of secondary industries have been established. The Owen Falls Dam, inaugurated by H.M. The Queen in April, 1954, must clearly have a profound influence on the economic and industrial development of Uganda and the neighbouring countries.

Constitutionally, the Uganda Protectorate has been organised from early days as a unitary state with a legislative and financial system covering the whole country. The usual pattern of a colonial government has been followed and has developed along what have become normal lines. The Executive Council consisted wholly of officials until 1946. Then two unofficial members were added, and this was later increased to six—two Africans, two Asians and two Europeans. The Legislative Council was also progressively broadened. Whereas in 1932 there were only three unofficial members, and no African representatives, the unofficial element has been increased by stages, until by 1950 the Council contained 16 unofficial members, including 8 Africans. At the beginning of 1954 further important developments took place, as a result of which the Legislative Council came to consist of nine *ex officio* members, 19 nominated and 28 representative members.

The difficulties which led to the British Government's withdrawal of recognition from the Kabaka Mutesa II of Buganda in November, 1953, were due to certain unacceptable demands put forward by His Highness for the separation of Buganda from the rest of the Protectorate. His declared intentions, persisted in against the Governor's advice, were held to be incompatible with the due performance of his obligation under the Buganda Agreement. During the summer of 1954 Professor Sir Keith Hancock carried out long and patient consultations with representatives of the Buganda people and a scheme for future constitutional arrangements was drawn up. As a result of subsequent negotiations, a settlement which provided, amongst other things, for the Kabaka's return was reached in the summer of 1955.

TANGANYIKA

Tanganyika, the largest (excepting Nigeria) of the territories dealt with in the Colonial Office, consists, as already stated, of the greater part of what was, until the 1914-18 war, German East Africa. Since 1917 it has been administered by Great Britain. The mandate laid upon the British Government by the League of Nations prescribed certain basic principles of administration and required an annual report to be made to the Council of the League. In 1946 the territory was placed under the international trusteeship system established by the United Nations Charter, and the British Government is now accountable for its administration to the Trusteeship Council and the General Assembly of the United Nations. This means that an annual report has to be rendered complying with certain specified requirements. Representatives of the administration may be called upon to appear before the Trusteeship Council and answer questions. Conclusions and recommendations of the Council and Assembly have to be given attention. From time to time a Visiting Mission from the Council may be sent to study conditions on the spot.

The population of the territory is estimated to be about eight million, or about a quarter of the population inhabiting the very little larger area of Nigeria. All but about 100,000 are indigenous Africans, the vast majority of whom depend on agriculture for their livelihood. Most of the agriculture is carried out by individuals working on their own account, and marketing their produce through co-operative societies, the most valuable export crops handled in this way being coffee and cotton. The largest agricultural product for export is, however, sisal, which is mainly grown on estates. The sisal industry—officially described as the most important single

C*

economic factor in Tanganyika—is highly organised and works under Government regulations.

As is well known, Tanganyika was the scene of the ill-fated ground-nut scheme, launched in 1947 on lines which proved in the event to have been too ambitious and to have made too little allowance for the factors militating against success. It is only fair to say that the failure cannot be laid at the door of the Tanganyika authorities, who were not directly concerned with the planning or operation of the scheme.

In addition to its agricultural industries, Tanganyika possesses an important mining industry, the most valuable mineral export being diamonds.

In its constitutional development, Tanganyika provides its own variation upon the now familiar theme. In the Executive Council the official members hold portfolios, each being in charge of a group of government departments; there are also unofficial members, European, Asian and African, who are as yet without portfolio. The Legislative Council has a Speaker, 15 official and 14 unofficial members. It has, however, been announced that the Council is to be considerably enlarged: there will be 30 unofficial members, ten from each of the three racial groups, and 28 government members— partly officials and partly unofficials who accept nomination on the understanding that they will not vote against the government.

Tanganyika so far has an enviable record of peaceful progress under British administration. From the comparatively primitive conditions which existed when the British took over the country, it has made notable advances in economic prosperity, the provision of social services and the organisation of local government; and it has been remarkably free from manifestations of interracial conflict or industrial dispute.

ZANZIBAR PROTECTORATE

The Zanzibar Protectorate consists of two islands—Zanzibar and Pemba—off the coast of Tanganyika. At the end of the 17th century the Arabs of Oman established an empire on the East African coast, and early in the 19th century the Sultan transferred his capital from Muscat in Arabia to Zanzibar. In 1861 the Sultanates of Oman and Zanzibar were separated, and in 1889 the then Sultan of Zanzibar placed his dominions under British protection. These dominions included a ten-mile strip of coast on the mainland. The German government purchased from the Sultan that part of this strip which lay in German East Africa, but the British recognised what is now the Kenya Protectorate (which includes the great port of Mombasa) as remaining under the Zanzibar flag, and the Kenya Government pays a rent of £10,000 a year to Zanzibar for the use of this territory.

British relations with Zanzibar are regulated by treaty. The government of the Protectorate is exercised by His Highness the Sultan with the advice and assistance of a British Resident. The usual pattern of colonial administration has been adapted to fit the special circumstances of the country. The Executive Council is presided over by the Sultan, with the British Resident as Vice-President, and includes the Heir Apparent to the Throne as well as official members. The Legislative Council is presided over by the British Resident and has nine official and eight unofficial members. The latter are appointed by the Sultan on the advice of the British Resident and include representatives of the Arab, African, Indian and European communities. The laws of Zanzibar are Decrees made by the Sultan, countersigned by the British Resident.

British relations with Zanzibar were conducted by the Foreign Office until 1914, when the Colonial Office took them over. At first the British Resident was placed under the control of the Governor of the East Africa Protectorate (now Kenya) who was also High Commissioner for Zanzibar. This arrangement came to an end in 1925, since when the British Resident has been directly responsible to the Secretary of State. It was shortly after this that the Executive and Legislative Councils were first constituted.

Zanzibar has progressed and prospered under the long and enlightened rule of the reigning Sultan, His Highness Seyyid Sir Khalifa bin Harub, G.C.M.G., G.B.E., who succeeded to the throne in 1911. The basis of the Protectorate's economy in the old days was its entrepôt trade. Although it is still the scene of a busy coastal traffic, this is only a survival of the time when Zanzibar was 'the emporium of East Africa', and as an international shipping centre Zanzibar has been eclipsed by Mombasa, Dar-es-Salaam and other mainland ports. Fortunately, Zanzibar has found an alternative source of wealth in the clove tree. The clove-growing industry was introduced into the islands by the same Seyyid Said bin Sultan who transferred the capital of his empire to Zanzibar in 1832. The islands proved to be peculiarly favourable to the cultivation of clove trees, and the Protectorate has become the world's principal supplier of this commodity. Although the trees are subject to certain diseases, and the harvest from year to year is very variable, the industry has held its own and the value of the annual export of cloves and clove oil now averages from £3 to £4 million.

NYASALAND PROTECTORATE

We now move southward to the region which is known as Central Africa. The territories here with which the Colonial Office is concerned are the Nyasaland Protectorate and Northern Rhodesia. Though adjacent to each other and both now included in the Central African Federation, their history and background are very dissimilar.

'Nyasaland is Livingstone's country', and its recorded history begins with the great explorer's discovery of Lake Nyasa in 1859. This was followed by considerable missionary activity in which the Church of Scotland played a leading part and—as in Uganda—commerce grew up alongside evangelistic endeavour.

Nyasaland is situated far inland, and its communication with the outside world was along the river line of the Zambesi to the Indian Ocean. Portugal and Britain were rivals for the privilege of opening up this part of Africa, but between 1889 and 1891 a settlement of boundaries was reached, and a British administration established, with 'the consent and desire of the Chiefs and People', over an area first called the Nyasaland Protectorate, then—from 1893 to 1907—the British Central Africa Protectorate. In 1907 (the affairs of the territory having been taken over from the Foreign Office by the Colonial Office) the old name was revived and Executive and Legislative Councils constituted. Since then, political development has followed the familiar pattern, with progressive increase of unofficial—and especially, in recent years, of African—representation.

The economic position of Nyasaland has always been difficult. The country is fertile and produces valuable export crops of tobacco, tea and other agricultural commodities; but in the past lack of capital resources and poverty of external communications have hampered development. The desirability, in these circumstances, of closer association of the Protectorate with the neighbouring territory of Northern Rhodesia became apparent as the latter developed, and a Royal Commission made recommendations to this end just before the second world war.

NORTHERN RHODESIA AND THE FEDERATION

Although Northern Rhodesia, also, first became known to the world through Livingstone's discoveries, the territory, as its name indicates, owes its modern state to the colonising enterprise initiated from South Africa by Cecil Rhodes. A British protectorate over Barotseland was established, at the request of the Paramount Chief, in 1891, but the administration of the whole area was entrusted, until 1924, to the British South Africa Chartered Company. In 1924 the Crown assumed direct control, a Governor was appointed and the affairs of the territory were thereafter dealt with by the Colonial Office in the normal way.

At that time it might have been supposed that the future course of Northern Rhodesia would be one of humdrum agricultural development, and the early attempts at prospecting and mining gave little hint of the spectacular expansion of the copper industry which during the last 25 years has transformed the whole economic outlook of the territory. 'A country whose progress rested on an annual revenue of about half a million pounds in a few years was netting ten million and more annually, and building up reserve funds of several million pounds. It is largely upon copper that the new schools, hospitals, roads and other recent witnesses to prosperity are founded.'[1] By 1953 the ten millions had in fact been more than tripled.

This great economic development has of course had its social and political effects. The mining and agricultural industries have brought people of European race in considerable numbers to the territory. These have naturally claimed a share in the government, and an advanced type of constitution is now in force. The Executive Council includes a number of unofficial members with departmental responsibilities, while the Legislative Council has an unofficial majority including elected European members and a number of African members.

The strong arguments in favour of closer association not only between Nyasaland and Northern Rhodesia but between these Protectorates and the self-governing Colony of Southern Rhodesia have long been appreciated. Southern Rhodesia does not come within the scope of this book, but it is necessary to explain that in 1923 this territory was formally established as a Colony and provided with a constitution which made it, subject to certain reservations, self-governing. When the Dominions Office was separated from the Colonial Office, the former naturally took over the conduct of relations with Southern Rhodesia, while Northern Rhodesia, as already stated, remained with the Colonial Office, and was dealt with as part of the Eastern and Central African group of territories.

In 1938 a Royal Commission under Lord Bledisloe's Chairmanship considered the question of closer association between the Central African territories. Its conclusions were against early amalgamation or federation, but in favour of setting up interterritorial machinery for co-operation. As a result, a Central African Council was established in 1945, but this was a purely consultative and advisory body, and as such was found in practice to have only limited usefulness. Between 1950 and 1953 a series of conferences and negotiations took place, and it was eventually decided to set up a Federation of Rhodesia and Nyasaland with its capital for the time being at Salisbury.

Under the federal constitution, which came into force in the autumn of 1953, the Federal Government consists of a Governor-

[1] *Annual Report*, 1953.

General who acts on the advice of a Cabinet of Ministers responsible to a Legislative Assembly elected from the three territories. There is an 'exclusive list' of subjects (such as external affairs and defence) which are reserved entirely to the competence of the Federal Legislature, and a 'concurrent list' of subjects (such as industrial development, public health and broadcasting) with which both the Federal and the territorial legislatures may deal, though, in case of conflict, federal law prevails. In all other matters, the territorial legislatures retain full responsibility. Special provision is made for safeguarding the interests of the African populations.

The Secretary of State for Commonwealth Relations acts as the channel of communication between the United Kingdom Government and the Federal Government (as well as the territorial Government of Southern Rhodesia). The Secretary of State for the Colonies remains responsible for the territorial affairs of Northern Rhodesia and Nyasaland. In practice there is close daily collaboration between the Central African Department of the Colonial Office and the corresponding department of the Commonwealth Relations Office.

ADEN COLONY AND PROTECTORATE

Aden Colony consists of the port on the Arabian coast at the southern end of the Red Sea, together with neighbouring islands. From 1839 the port, important as a coaling station for steamships, was administered by the Government of India. In 1937 it was constituted a separate Colony and its affairs were taken over by the Colonial Office.

Aden depends for its prosperity on its function as a free port and trading centre, the only local product being salt. A very important recent development is the establishment by the Anglo-Iranian Oil Company of a refinery at Little Aden.

The Executive Council of the Colony is entirely official in composition, but the Legislative Council contains an equal number (eight each) of official and unofficial members. The latter have hitherto been nominated, but the introduction of an elective element has been agreed to in principle.

The Governor of Aden Colony is also Governor of the Aden Protectorate, which consists of a number of Arab Sultanates and Sheikhdoms whose rulers, at various times since 1839, have entered into treaty relations with the British Government. The Protectorate includes the island of Socotra. The main part of it, however, consists of a belt of land stretching along the southern coast of Arabia, which falls, administratively and geographically, into two divisions, the Western Protectorate and the Eastern Protectorate. The former consists of eighteen states each of which is ruled over by its own Chief.

The British Government does not administer the country directly, but supplies a small staff of political officers who advise and assist the Arab rulers. The Eastern Protectorate consists of five States ruled over by Sultans, together with the island of Socotra. The mainland is chiefly desert and mountain country intersected by wadis, in which the principal towns and settlements are situated. Some of the towns are quite large, especially the capitals of the two important states of the Hadhramaut, which is the most highly organised part of the Eastern Protectorate. A British Agent and Resident Adviser, assisted by political officers, is stationed at Mukalla, the main seaport of the area.

SOMALILAND PROTECTORATE

On the southern side of the Gulf of Aden lies the Somaliland Protectorate. This was first established in 1884 and for some years was administered from Aden as a dependency of the Government of India. In 1898 it was transferred to the Foreign Office, and in 1905 to the Colonial Office. From 1901 to 1920 the Government was in sporadic conflict with the so-called 'Mad Mullah', but the country had twenty years of peace after his power was broken. In 1940 it was overrun by the Italians but they were driven out in the following year and after a period of military administration civil government was reconstituted in 1948.

Somaliland has no important natural resources. Though it produces frankincense and myrrh, it lacks the first and most profitable of the Magian gifts. The population is traditionally nomadic, depending for its livelihood on livestock. As an official report says, 'when rainfall is uncertain and pastures overstocked, the herds of camels and the flocks of sheep and goats can only offer their owners a life of precarious security.'[1] To maintain administration and to promote economic development and social services, financial aid from the United Kingdom has so far been continuously required. To make the country self-supporting is a long-term task to which the administration has applied itself energetically with the help of Colonial Development and Welfare funds. The main objects of the development plan are to expand educational and health services, to improve communications, and to encourage profitable industries, above all the cultivation of the land.

The conditions of Somaliland up to now have not been favourable to constitutional advance. The Governor has been the supreme authority, and there has been no Executive or Legislative Council. The Governor does, however, in practice consult with a Council consisting of his principal officials, and there is a Protectorate

[1] Report for 1950/51.

Advisory Council whose membership, partly elected, includes representatives of all sections of the community. The prospective creation of a Legislative Council was announced early in 1955.

AFRICAN STUDIES

Before leaving the African continent, we may mention here an organisation which is unique in the Colonial Office and serves the African Division as a whole. This is the African Studies Branch, which was founded in 1947 to meet a felt need for a small, specialist section, closely associated with but not part of the African geographical departments, for collecting and disseminating information on administrative and social questions arising in connection with the African territories.

The Branch is staffed by officers with field experience in Africa, assisted by panels of experts, and its work covers local government organisation, land tenure, African customary law, and sociological research in relation to administrative problems.

In addition to dealing (either by correspondence or by personal visits to the territories) with matters referred to it for study or advice, the Branch produces a quarterly *Journal of African Administration*, containing technical articles and reviews, for the assistance of administrative officers in the field and other interested persons. The Branch also organises periodical Summer Conferences on African Administration. These take place at a British University and are attended by administrative and specialist officers on leave who are nominated by their governments, together with representatives of the Colonial Office, academic institutions, missionary societies and foreign colonial powers. Each conference has a theme, such as Local Government, Agricultural Development, or the Encouragement of Initiative in African Society. Papers for discussion are circulated in advance, and the proceedings of the conferences are printed for restricted circulation.

Amongst the many distinguished experts who are good enough to give the Office and the oversea governments the benefit of their knowledge and counsel, special reference may be made here to Lord Hailey, whose contribution to the study of administrative problems, particularly in Africa, during the last twenty years has been outstanding.

CHAPTER VI

South-East Asia

MALAYA

THE fourth main region with which the Colonial Office is concerned includes the Malay Peninsula with the adjacent island of Singapore; the Borneo territories (North Borneo, Sarawak and Brunei); and Hong Kong.

Once again, in moving from one region to another, we find ourselves confronted with a wholly fresh set of conditions. These are not territories in which British colonists have made their homes and set up their own institutions. Their history is part of the complex story of the great Oriental civilisations and is bound up with the rise and fall of Empires. For about the first 1,500 years of the Christian era, India was the dominating influence in this part of the world. That influence was weakened and then destroyed by two factors: the conversion of the peoples of the Malay Archipelago to Islam, and the arrival of Portuguese, Dutch and British traders. The opening up of the region to international trade attracted immigrants of many races, especially Chinese, during the 19th century.

Although the ports of Malacca and Penang had an earlier British connection, the great landmark in the history of British Malaya is the foundation of Singapore, which, after lengthy negotiations between Sir Stamford Raffles and the rulers of Johore, was finally ceded in perpetuity to the Crown in 1824. The island, which lies less than a mile from the tip of the Malay Peninsula, had been an important commercial centre in the Middle Ages but had been neglected for some four centuries. Once established as a free port under British auspices, its prosperity grew rapidly. In 1826 Singapore was incorporated with Malacca and Penang under the name of the Straits Settlements, and the seat of government was moved from Penang to Singapore in 1832. At this time, and for the next 35 years, the Settlements were run as a dependency of India. The arrangement proved increasingly unsatisfactory, and in 1867 the Straits Settlements were constituted a Colony, and their affairs were brought under the Colonial Office.

With the change came a growing London interest in the Malay Peninsula, a territory about the size of England divided into a number of separate States under Malay rulers. Some of the rulers had already made approaches for British protection, but under the régime of the East India Company no sort of 'forward policy' was adopted. In the 1870s, however, the mineral resources of the peninsula began to attract attention, and in that age of colonial expansion it was certain that if Britain did not take a hand other powers would.

Accordingly, from 1873 onwards, treaties began to be negotiated with the various States under which the rulers agreed to accept British protection, to conduct foreign relations through Britain, and to accept the advice of a British officer on administrative matters not affecting Malay religion or custom. These officers were placed under the direction of the Governor of the Straits Settlements, as High Commissioner for the Malay States. In 1895 four of the nine States were constituted into a Federation (generally known as the F.M.S.) with a centralised government. The other States remained 'unfederated'. In 1932 the government of the Federation was to some extent decentralised and the powers of the Rulers and State Governments reinforced, thus placing the federated and unfederated States in a more equal position in relation to the High Commissioner.

Meanwhile the economic development of the peninsula had gone rapidly ahead, thanks to three factors. The first was the great importance of Singapore as a major international port and trading centre and (after 1921) as a naval base. The second was the growth of the tin-mining industry, and the third the extraordinary prosperity of the rubber-growing industry which was introduced first at the end of the nineteenth century. The combination of these factors, in the words of an official report, 'in a few decades converted an unhealthy, sparsely-populated and anarchic country into the most prosperous and best developed of all Britain's tropical dependencies'.

SINGAPORE AND THE FEDERATION OF MALAYA

In the short campaign from December, 1941, to February, 1942, the prosperity of this group of territories was laid in ruins by the Japanese, and for three and a half years they were in enemy occupation. On their recovery in 1945 a vast work of reconstruction had to be done. The British Government decided to separate Singapore from the peninsula as a Colony in its own right. The two Settlements on the mainland, with the nine Malay States, were, by agreement with the State Rulers, incorporated into a Malayan Union under a Governor. This arrangement turned out to be politically unworkable, and in 1948 the Malayan Union was transformed into a Federation of Malaya, and the title of High Commissioner for the Sovereign's representative was restored.

Before summarising the present constitutional positions of Singapore and the Federation, we must turn to consider what has been known since 1948 as the 'emergency', and its effects on the economic, social and political life of these territories. In order to understand it, some basic facts must be kept in mind. First, four-fifths of the Malay Peninsula consists of almost impenetrable jungle and mountains. The population and industries are mainly concentrated in a relatively narrow belt along the western coast. Secondly, the effect of pre-war immigration over many years was to bring the Chinese population (taking the Malay States and Straits Settlements together) up to approximate equality with the Malay population, and even to put Chinese in a majority not only in Singapore and Penang but in some of the more important Malay States. Substantial communities of Indians were also established in several places.

In the peaceful and generally prosperous conditions that obtained up to 1941, the immigrant communities took little part or interest in local politics, though it became increasingly clear that a potential political problem existed. The unsettlement caused by the war and the Japanese occupation, and the general upsurge of nationalist aspirations in the Eastern world created a situation urgently demanding a new political framework in which citizens of all races could be brought to work together for the common good. By 1948 much progress had been made though much more remained to be done. At this point there began what has been officially described as 'the all-out Communist effort to sabotage recovery in Malaya'. Unable to achieve their ends by infiltration and agitation, the Communists—a small but well-organised party mainly Chinese in membership—turned to violence. The activities of the so-called bandits, taking advantage of the geographical features of the country and the inability of scattered rural populations to resist terrorism effectively, have not prevented economic and political development. But they have cost Malaya— and Britain—many valuable lives and have greatly injured the country by making it necessary for large sums of money and immense administrative, police and military effort to be diverted from constructive work to the restoration of law and order and the protection of peaceful citizens.

It would not be fitting, in the context of this book, to attempt to describe the events of the Malayan emergency or the measures adopted to deal with it by the successive High Commissioners (Sir Edward Gent, who lost his life in an air accident while travelling on duty in 1948; Sir Henry Gurney, who was assassinated by terrorists in October, 1951; Sir Gerald Templer, who served from 1952 to 1954; and Sir Donald MacGillivray). While the chief burden of direction necessarily rested upon these men and their staffs, the Colonial Office was of course constantly involved in questions of policy, finance and manpower as well as in keeping Parliament and public in touch with what was going on. The Secretary of State (Mr. James Griffiths) visited Malaya in 1950 to discuss matters on the spot, and his successor (Mr. Oliver Lyttelton) went out after assuming office in the following year. In the other direction, the High Commissioners and senior officials had to pay frequent visits to London for consultation with the Secretary of State and his colleagues and advisers.

The long-term answer to the Communist threat is the setting up of stable democratic institutions, broadly based upon a common citizenship, and leading in course of time to the establishment of self-government. Since the recovery of Malaya after the war, unremitting efforts have been made to solve the complex problems involved, and by 1954 notable progress had been made, in spite of the emergency. In Singapore, following on the report of a Constitutional Commission, a form of Ministerial government, with a mainly elected Legislative Assembly based upon an electorate comprising all British subjects and protected persons resident in the Colony, was introduced early in 1955. In the Federation, political arrangements have to be considered against a far more complicated background. Agreement has however been reached, after examination of the problems by a local committee and after consultation with their Highnesses the Rulers, that the elective principle should be introduced for more than half the seats in the Federal Legislative Council, which hitherto has consisted wholly of official and nominated members. In the Executive Council, the 'membership system', by which certain Councillors were 'Members' for different branches of government work, without, however, exercising full Ministerial authority, had been in force since 1951. Under the 1955 constitution they have become Ministers. In the States themselves, executive authority is vested in the Ruler, who is assisted by a State Executive Council and a Council of State. The Councils of State, which are also to include an elected element, are empowered to legislate on all matters not reserved to the Federal Legislature.

REGIONAL ORGANISATION

Before the other territories in the region are considered, mention should be made of the special arrangements which exist for the co-ordination of policy in regional affairs. When civil government was resumed after the war, the plans included the appointment of a Governor-General whose functions extended over the Malay Peninsula, Singapore and the Borneo territories. A former Secretary of State for the Colonies, the Rt. Hon. Malcolm MacDonald, was appointed to this post. At about the same time a Special Commissioner responsible to the Foreign Office, with headquarters in Singapore, was appointed to advise the British government on general problems affecting the conduct of foreign affairs in an area which included Burma, Siam, Indo-China and Indonesia.

In 1948 the two posts were combined under the title of Commissioner-General for the United Kingdom in South-East Asia. As Commissioner-General Mr. MacDonald continued to exercise the same co-ordinating functions as before on behalf of the Colonial Office. The organisation includes a Colonial and a Foreign side, each of which has its own staff. The Commissioner-General has no executive responsibility for the government of the territories.

THE BORNEO TERRITORIES

Except for the island of Labuan (which was formerly part of the Straits Settlements Colony) and the protected State of Brunei, the Colonial Office was not directly concerned with the Borneo territories until after the second world war.

Historically, the whole island of Borneo was at one time under the Sultanate of Brunei, and indeed the two words 'Brunei' and 'Borneo' are really the same; but the Brunei Empire declined after the sixteenth century, and eventually the southern and larger part of the island became included in the Dutch sphere of influence. In 1841 James Brooke, an Englishman, who had succeeded in pacifying a province which had got out of the Sultan's control, was rewarded by being made ruler of a territory which, with later additions, became the State of Sarawak. The Sultan of Brunei ceded the island of Labuan to the British in 1846 and entered into treaty relations with them in 1847. In 1872 a large area of the Sultan's mainland possessions was ceded to a private syndicate which eventually developed into the British North Borneo Company.

To-day Brunei is a small State, but a prosperous one owing to the fact that it contains an important oilfield which has been greatly developed since the end of the war. In fact the State was at the end of 1952 the second largest producer of oil in the Commonwealth. The oil is not refined locally, but is pumped to a refining station in Sarawak territory. Thanks to this source of wealth, Brunei has been able to repair the very serious damage which was done to the country during the Japanese occupation and to embark on an extensive programme of social and economic development.

The State is governed by His Highness the Sultan with the assistance of a Council. There is a British Resident whose advice the Sultan is required by a treaty of 1906 to seek and act upon in matters other than those affecting the Mohammedan religion. The Resident is responsible to the High Commissioner for Brunei who was formerly the Governor of the Straits Settlements and is now the Governor of Sarawak.

Sarawak itself was benevolently ruled by the Brooke dynasty from 1841 until the second world war. It became formally a British protectorate in 1888, but the British government did not intervene in the local administration. After a century of Brooke rule, the State was in a sound position and could look forward with confidence to the future. In 1941 the Rajah, Sir Charles Vyner Brooke, marked the centenary by granting a constitution which put his people on the road to democratic self-government.

All this was smashed by the Japanese, and when Rajah Brooke returned in 1946 it was to a ruined country. He decided that the time had come to ask the Crown to take over the administration, so that Sarawak could benefit by the resources and experience of the Colonial Office organisation. And so Sarawak became a Colony, with a constitution based on that which had been inaugurated by the Rajah. It provides for a Supreme Council, which is the counterpart of a Colonial Executive Council, and for a legislative body known as the Council Negri.

Sarawak is a difficult country to administer and develop. It consists of a long strip of coastland, broken by numerous mountains and river gorges; three-quarters of the land is thick forest. Away from the main centres the indigenous population is still living in simple conditions. There is an important and long-established Chinese community.

Under colonial administration much progress has already been made in the development of central and local government organisation, in the expansion of social services and in economic development. Apart from isolated incidents, Sarawak has been free from disturbance during the post-war period. The assassination of the Governor, Mr. Duncan Stewart, in December, 1949, was the work of a small fanatical group and was not symptomatic of any general dissatisfaction with the régime.

As already stated, the adjacent territory of North Borneo was administered by a Chartered Company until the second world war. The Charter placed certain limitations upon the Company, such as a requirement that the appointment of their principal representative (in effect Governor of the territory) should be approved by the Secretary of State, but the Colonial Office was not concerned with the details of administration. As an important rubber-producing area, the State progressed peaceably until 1942.

North Borneo suffered at least as badly as any other territory from its forcible inclusion in the Japanese Co-prosperity Sphere. On its liberation in 1945 it was found in a condition of 'appalling devastation'. Negotiations had already been on foot between the British Government and the Company with a view to the Crown taking over the administration after the war, and the new Colony (which includes the island of Labuan) was formally brought into being in 1946. An interim constitution was granted, which was superseded in 1950 by a constitution providing for Executive and Legislative Councils of the usual colonial type.

Inevitably the task of the administration since 1945 has been one of reconstruction and rehabilitation, and local efforts have had to be supported by large financial assistance from the United Kingdom. In spite of all difficulties, great progress has been made in rebuilding the towns, improving communications and promoting social and economic development. The difficulties are indeed great. The Colony is about the size of Ireland and is (very roughly) square shaped, three sides of the square consisting of heavily indented coastline. The interior is largely mountain and jungle, and there is no land communication between the Colony's two chief towns, Jesselton (the capital) and Sandakan.

Co-ordination of policy in the Borneo territories is helped by periodical conferences held under the chairmanship of the Commissioner-General.

HONG KONG

If every Colony is unique, it might be said that Hong Kong is more unique than any other. 'Hong Kong,' says an official report, 'is a product of history, the history of relations between East and West.' Until the 1830s this small, barren, rocky island off the China coast was unimportant and almost uninhabited. In 1841 it was occupied as a British trading centre, owing to the disadvantages under which foreign traders laboured in Canton. In 1843 the island was formally ceded to Great Britain and the Colonial Office took over. After many early difficulties, the growing prosperity and settled conditions of the Colony attracted large numbers of Chinese to make their homes there. In 1860 the ceded territory was enlarged by the inclusion of the Kowloon peninsula on the mainland. The mile-wide strait between Victoria, the capital of the Colony, and Kowloon is the entrance to seventeen square miles of landlocked harbour, geographically placed so as to form the trading gateway to the whole of South China.

In order to secure settled administration and to give elbow-room to the urban areas which were already becoming overcrowded, a further tract of mainland with adjacent islands, known as the New Territories, was leased for 99 years from the Chinese Government in 1898. Much of the land is mountainous and infertile, but it provides some rice, fruit, vegetables and dairy produce for the towns. Nearly half the Colony's water supply comes from reservoirs in the New Territories.

Like the other territories dealt with in this chapter, Hong Kong was occupied by the Japanese during the second world war and suffered very severely. In 1941 the population was estimated at rather over 1½ million, as compared with rather under 1 million at the 1931 census. During Japanese occupation the number sank to half a million, but by the end of 1946 it had returned to the pre-war level. The civil war in China then drove large numbers of people to seek the shelter of the Colony, and since 1950 the population—a large part of which is even in normal times of a 'floating' character—has been anything from 2¼ to 2½ million.

The provision of accommodation and social services for this great influx of people called for immense efforts on the part of government. Large numbers of the recent immigrants had to settle themselves as best they could in temporary 'squatter areas', in conditions involving serious risks of fire and disease. The clearing of these areas and the resettlement of the inhabitants in proper houses and flats is one of the major activities of the authorities.

'Activities' is the right word, for every visitor to Hong Kong is struck by the immense vitality of the Colony. Since 1945 it has not only shown extraordinary recuperative power, but has made exciting progress with all kinds of new developments. For instance, government expenditure in 1952-53 on education and on health services was about ten times as great as in 1938. Even allowing for the change in the purchasing power of money, that represents a spectacular advance.

The huge population, the bulk of which is concentrated in the twin cities of Victoria and Kowloon, is supported by the proceeds of commerce and industry. Even during a period of restricted trade with China, the port handles on an average more than £20 millions worth of goods each month. Light manufacturing industries are strongly established, making textile goods, electric appliances, kitchen ware and rubber footwear for export to neighbouring countries and even to Africa and the United Kingdom itself.

Because of the peculiar local conditions, political institutions have not developed in Hong Kong in the same way as in other Colonies. During and since the end of the civil war in China the Colony has had to be kept in a state of defence, and from this point of view alone firm and stable government is essential. In any event, ordinary electoral machinery would be difficult to introduce, since much of the population is not permanently resident in the Colony, and considerable numbers of residents are not British subjects. There is a measure of election for the Urban Council, but for appointments to the Legislative Council of the Colony itself no satisfactory alternative has yet been devised to nomination by the Governor (who naturally takes counsel with those best able to advise before making his nominations). The Legislative Council consists of nine official and eight unofficial members; the Executive Council of six of each.

CHAPTER VII

The Rest of the World

THE SOUTH-WEST PACIFIC

THE last four chapters have been about territories which fall into natural geographical or regional groups. Most of the remaining territories—representing broadly the work of two geographical departments of the Colonial Office, though the departmental allocation of territories may vary from time to time—cannot be so conveniently classified and have to be considered individually. The islands of the south-west Pacific, however, though mostly small in themselves, scattered unevenly over a vast area of ocean and not linked by any system of internal communications, have many problems in common with one another and indeed with other islands in the area which are administered by other Powers. They are, therefore, properly to be considered as a regional group.

The group is subdivided into a number of administrative units. The principal unit is the Colony of Fiji, which until 1952 was the centre of all British administration in the area. The other main units are the British Solomon Islands Protectorate, the Gilbert and Ellice Islands Colony and the Anglo-French Condominium of the New Hebrides. The Kingdom of Tonga is an independent State under British protection. The tiny Colony of Pitcairn lies out in mid-ocean, about half-way between Panama and New Zealand.

Until 1952 the Governor of Fiji was also High Commissioner for the Western Pacific and as such was generally responsible for the administration of all the territories. Owing to the growth in the volume and complexity of the administrative work in modern conditions, it was decided then to separate the two offices. The Governor of Fiji assumed responsibility for the conduct of relations with Tonga and for the government of Pitcairn. The High Commissioner took over the rest and established his headquarters in 1953 at Honiara, the capital of the Solomon Islands.

Along with this decentralisation of administration has gone a development of machinery for co-operative action on general problems affecting the region. In 1946 the Government of Fiji, the Western Pacific High Commission and the Government of New Zealand (on behalf of New Zealand's island dependencies) agreed to set up a South Pacific Health Service under a Board of Health. The

Director of Medical Services, Fiji, was appointed Inspector-General of the Service. Tonga joined in the arrangement in 1947. In 1948, a South Pacific Commission was set up by the Governments of Australia, France, the Netherlands, New Zealand, the United Kingdom and the United States. The Commission, whose headquarters are at Noumea in French territory, meets once a year. It advises with regard to matters affecting the economic and social development and welfare of the islands in the region. Under its auspices a South Pacific Conference, including representatives of the island peoples, was held in 1950, and again in 1953. There is also a South Pacific Air Transport Council.

FIJI, PITCAIRN AND TONGA

The Fiji Islands were voluntarily ceded to the British Crown (after more than one offer of cession had been turned down by the British Government) in 1874. Since then the Islands have been a British Colony. The island of Rotuma was added to the Colony in 1881.

Soon after the Colony was taken over, a local government system called the Fijian Administration, based on local custom, was set up and is still in operation. It is controlled by a Fijian Affairs Board, chairman of which is the Secretary for Fijian Affairs. Until recently the post was held by one of Fiji's most distinguished sons, Ratu Sir Lala Sukuna, K.C.M.G., K.B.E. By this arrangement the Fijians—who enjoy special rights under the Deed of Cession—are organised and governed as a self-contained community within the framework of the general government of the Colony.

Although the Fijians are the indigenous people of the land, they are not now the largest racial community, being exceeded in numbers by the Indian population. The Indians are mainly descendants of immigrants attracted to the islands from the 1880s onwards to work on the sugar plantations. Sugar is the Colony's principal export crop, and its cultivation is almost all carried on by Indians. Fijians produce most of the copra and bananas for export, and work in the gold mines which provide the only important industry other than agriculture.

The third chief element in the population consists of Europeans and persons of European descent.

As in other territories with 'plural societies', the long-term objective must be to establish a common Fijian citizenship: but this must be the fruit of long and patient co-operation, and for the present the fact of separate communities living side by side is inescapable. It is reflected in the central government arrangements, which provide for an official majority in the Legislative Council and for separate unofficial representation—partly elected and partly nominated—of the three communities. One unofficial member of each community serves in the Executive Council.

As already stated, the Governor of Fiji is also Governor of Pitcairn, a remote island group colonised by the mutineers of the *Bounty*. It is administered by the leading inhabitant, who is styled Chief Magistrate and is assisted by an Island Council.

The Governor is also H.B.M. Consul-General for the Kingdom of Tonga, where he is represented by an official called British Agent and Consul. Tonga has become better known to the world public since the visit of H.M. Queen Salote Tupou, G.C.V.O., G.B.E., to Britain for the Coronation in 1953 made so happy an impression. Under the Treaty of Friendship and Protection of 1900, Tonga is self-governing in its internal affairs.

WESTERN PACIFIC HIGH COMMISSION

The islands of the Western Pacific High Commission are organised in three main groups, with Resident Commissioners in the Gilbert and Ellice Islands and in the New Hebrides, under the general supervision of the High Commissioner, whose headquarters are in the largest group, the British Solomon Islands Protectorate. This group has been under British administration since 1893. Some of the islands were occupied in 1942 by the Japanese, who were driven out only after fierce and bloody battles, in which victory was greatly assisted by the loyalty of the population. These events set back the peaceful progress of the Protectorate, but economic and social development has been resumed since the war and the Protectorate Advisory Council, first established in 1921, has become a more effective body for associating the people with the policy and activities of government.

The Gilbert and Ellice Islands Colony consists of 37 islands scattered over two million square miles of ocean. One island—Ocean Island—is an important source of phosphate, but the rest depend on copra production for their external trade. Local government institutions, with popular representation, have been set up in the main populated islands and operate under the supervision of District Officers. There is an important international airport at Canton Island, which is jointly run by Britain and the United States.

The New Hebrides were recognised as an Anglo-French joint interest in 1887 and administrative arrangements were agreed upon in 1906. Each government appoints a Resident Commissioner and provides certain national officers. There are also certain joint services carried on by the condominium as such. So far lack of money has prevented any extensive development of the islands from being undertaken. Until 1955 the New Hebrides did not qualify for British financial assistance from Colonial Development and Welfare funds.

MAURITIUS AND SEYCHELLES

Before turning to the nearer waters of the Mediterranean, we may conveniently consider the remaining oceanic Colonies. There are two in the Indian Ocean: Mauritius and Seychelles.

Mauritius, with its neighbouring dependent islands, is an important, interesting and beautiful Colony having many affinities with the West Indies although so far away from them in space. The first settlers there were the Dutch, who named it in honour of Prince Maurice of Nassau. The settlement was abandoned after a century, and in 1715 the French took possession and named the island Ile de France. It was captured by the British in 1810 and formally ceded in 1814.

The near-century of French colonisation has left its mark on the institutions, laws and language of the Colony. To-day, however, well over half the population consists of Indian immigrants and their descendants. There are also substantial communities of the descendants of Africans brought to the island by the early settlers and of Chinese. The population is increasing rapidly and is already high in relation to the area, considering that the Colony depends entirely upon agriculture and indeed upon one form of agriculture, the cultivation of sugar.

With its long history of settlement, Mauritius is in many ways a highly organised Colony with advanced educational and other social services. Elected members have served on the Legislative Council since 1886, and since 1948 the Council has had an elected majority based on a wide franchise; all adult residents are entitled to be registered as voters on passing a simple literacy test. The Executive Council also has an unofficial majority, some of the members being elected by the Legislative Council.

In 1951 a step was taken which was designed to give members of the Executive Council experience of government work with a view to the introduction of a ministerial system in the future. Under this arrangement, certain members of Council are appointed as 'Liaison Officers' for specified departments. As such, they are expected to familiarise themselves with the work of their departments, represent their interests in the Executive Council, and take part in formulating the financial needs of the departments when the annual estimates are being prepared. They also take charge in the Legislative Council of measures relating to the work of their departments.

Seychelles, like Mauritius, began as a French Colony, though rather later in time, and became British in 1810. For nearly a century after that Mauritius and Seychelles were run together, though the administrative machinery was gradually separated. In 1903 Seychelles was constituted a Colony in its own right.

The Colony, which consists of 92 islands, differs from Mauritius in having no sugar industry, and in consequence there has been no substantial Indian immigration. The main export product is copra, derived from the coconut which here is largely grown as a plantation crop. Cinnamon and other spices are also produced. There is a small tourist industry which could certainly be developed if communications between these attractive islands and the outside world were better.

Within the limitations set by geography and finance, Seychelles has made notable progress in social development during the post-war period. Water supplies, roads, hospitals, preventive medicine, schools, housing and other public services and cultural activities have been improved or introduced for the first time. A more democratic system of central and local government has also been set up. The Executive Council includes four unofficial members in addition to the Governor and three official members. The Legislative Council has six official members, four elected unofficials and two nominated unofficials.

THE FALKLAND ISLANDS AND THEIR DEPENDENCIES

From the Indian Ocean we pass to the South Atlantic.

The Falkland Islands, first sighted by an English navigator in 1592, are as far south of the equator as Britain is north, and the climate is officially described as 'dour', being rather cold and characterised by persistent strong winds. After various vicissitudes, in which the islands were successively occupied or claimed by French, British, Spanish and Argentine representatives, the British finally established a settlement there in 1833 and set up a formal government in 1841. The population—mainly of British descent—now numbers about 2,250 and lives directly or indirectly by sheep farming. About half the people live in Stanley, the capital town, and the rest are dispersed over the islands. This makes the provision of education and social services difficult. Even so, quite a lot is done, and the modern conveniences of broadcasting and air services have done much to break down the isolation of the small and scattered settlements. In the educational field, the Colony has an arrangement with the Dorset County Council by which the latter lends teachers to the island schools and accepts selected island children for secondary education.

The Colony is financially self-supporting. It has a constitution of the usual kind, but on a small scale commensurate with the population. There is an Executive Council with three unofficial members, and a Legislative Council with an unofficial majority consisting partly of elected and partly of nominated members.

The Falkland Island Dependencies fall into two groups: the island of South Georgia, with the South Sandwich and South Orkney Islands; and the peninsula of Graham Land which juts out of the

Antarctic continent, with the South Shetland Islands lying off-shore. South Georgia was first visited and claimed for the Crown by Captain Cook in 1775; his reports led to the development of an important whaling and sealing industry and to the discovery of other islands and of the continent itself.

The only settlements in the Dependencies are whaling and scientific stations. A small administrative staff is kept on at South Georgia where the main headquarters of the whaling industry is located.

In 1925 the Colonial Office set up a Committee called the 'Discovery' Committee to carry out a programme of biological and oceanographical research with special reference to the whaling industry. At first the expeditions organised by this Committee, and financed by revenue derived from the industry, were carried out in Captain Scott's famous ship *Discovery*. Later, more modern research vessels were brought into service. After the second world war these activities were taken over by the Falkland Islands Dependencies Survey, and in 1948 the direction and administration of the Survey was transferred from London to the Governor in the Falkland Islands. The work of the survey includes the investigation and charting of the area, the study of the land and marine fauna, meteorological observations and, generally, the collection of information of scientific and economic interest about this remote and little-known region.

The British possession of the Dependencies is disputed by the Argentine and Chilean governments, and indeed the former do not admit the British right to sovereignty over the Falkland Islands themselves. In 1955 the case was submitted by the United Kingdom to the International Court.

ST. HELENA, ASCENSION AND TRISTAN

Farther north, in mid-Atlantic, between the tropic of Capricorn and the equator, lies the ancient and renowned Colony of St. Helena. In the 17th century it was an important port of call for ships travelling between Europe and the East Indies. Its possession was claimed at different times by British and Dutch, but the latter were finally driven out by the Royal Navy in 1673 and the East India Company received a charter from Charles II to occupy and govern the island. It remained under the Company until 1834 and found its place in history as the seat of Napoleon's exile from 1815 to 1821. Since 1834 it has been administered by the Crown as a Colony. Its importance as a port of call ceased with the coming of steam and the opening of the Suez Canal. To-day it is isolated from the world except for the regular calling, about once a month each way, of the Union Castle steamers plying between Britain and South Africa, and the occasional visits of other ships. There is no air service. The population of rather under

5,000 depends on agriculture, the only important industry being the cultivation and processing of flax.

The Colony has a constitution suitable to the simplicity of its social organisation. Laws are enacted by the Governor (who also acts as Chief Justice). There is an Executive Council, consisting of officials, and an Advisory Council consisting of unofficial members.

The Colony of St. Helena has two Dependencies. Ascension Island, a naval station until 1922, is an important cable junction. There are no inhabitants apart from the staff maintained there by Cable and Wireless Ltd., their families and domestic servants, and two policemen. The Company's manager is Resident Magistrate. The island was used as an air force base during the second world war.

The other Dependency is Tristan da Cunha, which was formally claimed as British in 1816 and attracted a small number of settlers during the following sixty or seventy years, after which, with the decline of the sailing ship, contact with the outer world almost ceased.

From the early days the island community was served more or less continuously by chaplains of the Society for the Propagation of the Gospel, though there was a long break between 1909 and 1922. In 1932 the Chaplain was officially recognised as Honorary Commissioner and Magistrate and an Island Council was appointed. In 1938 the island and its neighbours were constituted a dependency of St. Helena.

During the second world war a naval meteorological and wireless station was set up at Tristan and the period of isolation ended. Thanks to the enterprise of a naval Chaplain, arrangements were made with a commercial company to start a crawfish industry, the revenue from which is placed in a fund to provide for the administration of the island and social welfare of the people. An official Administrator was appointed in 1950 and the Island Council was given legal status. With the funds thus made available, the islanders have been provided with medical and educational services and with agricultural advice.

Although for convenience Tristan is legally a dependency of St. Helena, it is 1,500 miles away without any regular means of communication. In practice, therefore, the Administrator works directly under the Colonial Office.

A Tristan incident illustrates the kind of queer thing that is always liable to crop up in Colonial Office work. Early in the second world war, Tristan was in the charge of a naval surgeon whose wife was with him. A baby was born, and the question arose, how should his birth be registered? The island arrangements did not run to producing birth certificates. Asked for advice, the head of the Colonial Office department remembered that in the first war Ascension had been treated as a naval establishment. An enquiry of Somerset House supplied the information that deaths on Ascension had been duly entered in the Marine Register. And so all was simple. *H.M.S. Atlantic Isle* was commissioned, and the baby's birth was properly registered at Somerset House in accordance with Article 869 of *King's Regulations and Admiralty Instructions*.

GIBRALTAR

The remaining territories to be considered are all in the Mediterranean. In size, Gibraltar is the smallest of all British Colonies, being a rocky peninsula of 2¼ square miles connected with the Spanish mainland by a sandy isthmus. From A.D. 711 to 1462 it was held by the Moors. Then the Spaniards took it and held it until 1704, when it was captured by the British. After a number of unsuccessful sieges, the Rock has remained unmolested in British hands since 1783. Its importance to the free world as a fortress and naval base was proved in both world wars. During the second war the civil population were evacuated to the United Kingdom. They were repatriated between 1940 and 1944 and much was done to improve their housing and social conditions on their return.

Gibraltar being primarily a fortress, its Governor is by usage a senior officer of the fighting services who is also actual as well as titular Commander-in-Chief. In his administration of the Colony the Governor is assisted by an Executive Council composed of the Deputy Fortress Commander, three civil officials and three unofficial members. Since 1950 there has been a Legislative Council consisting of the three senior civil officials, five elected unofficial members and two nominated members of whom at least one must be an unofficial. Municipal affairs are dealt with by a City Council containing a majority of elected members.

Most of the people depend directly or indirectly for their living on the dockyard and other Service and government activities. The resident population is reinforced by large numbers of Spaniards who live in the neighbourhood and come into the Colony for their daily work.

MALTA

Malta, the G.C. Island, stands in a very special position. A fortress and naval base of great strategic importance, it is also a country small indeed but with a long and distinguished history and a highly developed national tradition. Its association with Britain dates from 1800. Two years before that the French had driven out the Knights of St. John of Jerusalem, who had held the island since 1530.

Malta is poor in natural resources and most of the needs of the

D

population have to be supplied by imports. There are some light manufacturing industries and a certain amount of tourist trade. In the main, however, the people depend for their livelihood directly or indirectly on expenditure by the Services, and especially on the work provided by the Admiralty dockyard. Over-population is a serious problem and the government does much to promote emigration, especially to Australia.

The government of Malta is a form of diarchy. In internal matters the country is self-governing. With certain reservations the Governor acts on the advice of a Cabinet of Maltese Ministers presided over by a Prime Minister and responsible to a wholly elected Legislative Assembly. This is known as the Maltese Government. Matters concerning or incidental to defence and external relations are dealt with by the Maltese Imperial Government, and in these matters the Governor acts on his own authority, with the advice of a Nominated Council of officials and representatives of the fighting services. Joint consideration of matters affecting both sides of the diarchy is provided for by the existence of a Privy Council, which consists of the Cabinet and the Nominated Council sitting together under the presidency of the Governor.

The relationship of Malta to the United Kingdom is therefore a special one, differing in many respects from that of a Colony or Protectorate. Maltese affairs have, however, always been dealt with in the Colonial Office as a matter of practical convenience. In 1953, with a view to meeting some objections raised on the Maltese side to the continuance of this traditional arrangement, the British Government offered to transfer Maltese affairs to the Home Secretary, who is the Secretary of State immediately concerned as the Queen's Minister in relation to the United Kingdom and neighbouring islands. Subsequent discussions between British and Maltese political leaders had not been concluded at the time of writing.

CYPRUS

Cyprus is another Mediterranean island with a long and eventful history. The first connection with Britain came about by its conquest by Richard I in 1191, but he did not permanently retain the island. The dynasty founded by the crusader Lusignan ruled it until 1489, after which it was held by the Venetian Republic until 1571. It was then conquered by the Turks, under whom it remained for over 300 years. In 1878 the British took over the administration of the island by agreement with Turkey, and it was formally annexed to the Crown on the outbreak of war with that country in 1914. In 1925 it was constituted a Colony.

Until 1914 Cyprus remained technically a part of the Ottoman

Empire, but it was governed from 1882 onwards on the usual British Colonial pattern, with an Executive Council and a Legislative Council with an elected majority representing both the Turkish and the non-Turkish inhabitants. The latter are in fact the great majority, over 80 per cent of the population being Greek. The modern political history of Cyprus is largely bound up with the movement amongst the Greek community for Union (*Enosis*) with Greece. This movement, in which the Orthodox Church has taken a prominent part, is strongly opposed by the Turkish community. In 1931 the movement led to serious disturbances, in consequence of which the constitution was suspended and the Legislative Council abolished. The offer of a new constitution, which would have given the people of the island a considerable measure of autonomy, was made in 1948. This offer was not accepted by the leaders of the Greek community, and Her Majesty's Government announced, in 1954, their intention to introduce instead a modified form of constitution. In the meantime the Governor continues to govern with the aid of the Executive Council, which includes unofficial Greek and Turkish representatives.

Despite this hold-up in central political progress, the development of local government institutions based on popular representation has gone ahead satisfactorily, and the island is covered by a network of Municipal and District Councils, Village Commissions and elected Boards.

There has also been very considerable development of economic resources, public utilities, social services, and cultural activities of all kinds. A notable modern achievement of the public health service has been the total eradication of malaria. Cyprus has now one of the lowest death rates in the world. The scenic beauty, attractive climate and archaeological interest of the island attract an increasing number of visitors and residents.

The strategic importance of Cyprus in modern world conditions has resulted in the increasing use of the island as a naval, military and air force base, with consequent beneficial effects on employment and trade. It was announced in 1954 that British Military Headquarters in the Middle East would be moved there from the Suez Canal Zone.

VARIETY AND COMMUNITY

This concludes a necessarily brief and greatly over-simplified survey of the territories whose affairs are dealt with in the Colonial Office. The account, with all its inadequacies, does at least demonstrate the immense variety of these countries and islands and the strength of their individuality. Yet it may also suggest that, underlying this variety, there is some broad community of needs and interests. If all general statements must be subject to some reservation and qualification, there are some general statements that can be made which cover most (but not in each case with the same lot of exceptions) of the territories.

In the economic field, for instance, most of the territories depend principally upon agriculture, and many depend upon a single crop. Most must export primary products and import manufactured goods in order to maintain and improve the standard of living of the people. Most must rely upon seaborne trade to take their goods to the markets and to bring in their imports. Most are deeply concerned in the trend of world prices obtainable for such staple agricultural products as vegetable oils, cotton, fruit, cocoa, coffee, sugar and rubber. Equally, most are acutely interested in the application of scientific research to the problems connected with the improvement of production and the fight against diseases and pests, with special reference to conditions in the tropics, where most of the territories are situated. Most of the territories, again, cannot within any reasonable time develop their potential resources without financial assistance from outside, whether in the form of capital or of 'pump-priming'.

In the field of social organisation, the peoples of most territories have great problems and handicaps to overcome. Few of them could now, if they wished, continue in a life of primitive simplicity, isolated from the world. They have been caught up into the turmoil of a world-wide social revolution and must take their part in it. Huge efforts are required to combat ignorance, disease, poverty and the disadvantages of their physical environment. The efforts, indeed, must be their own, but they need inspiration, help and guidance from those more favourably placed. They need, too, peace—'freedom from oppression from any quarter'—and cannot rely upon their own unaided resources to secure it.

In political organisation, the territories differ in detail, but all have set before them the goal of self-government. The form which self-government may take may not, indeed cannot, be the same for all. But there is a clear pattern of progress, from authoritarian government to representative government, from representative government to responsible government. As the survey has shown, most of the territories have now reached the representative stage, and some have reached or are closely approaching the responsible stage. How to secure this progress by orderly evolution, how and when to introduce constitutional changes so that the political organisation meets the true interests as well as the legitimate aspirations of each community —these are questions which continually have to be answered. The precise answers depend upon the circumstances of time and place, but to find the right answers demands experience of the practical working of political institutions under a great variety of conditions.

And, finally, all these problems require the services of competent people who can deal with them. Some territories are better placed than others to find the necessary supply of qualified men and women from their own populations. But all the territories in some degree, and some in a very high degree, need the help of men and women who have absorbed and can apply and transmit the accumulated knowledge and experience of the Western civilisation, with all its complex inheritance drawn from Jerusalem, Athens and Rome.

Her Majesty's Government in the United Kingdom have the responsibility—and the privilege—of seeing not only to the good government of the territories but to the social and political progress of their peoples and the development of their resources. This great field of activity and enterprise needs a focal point, and that focal point, naturally and necessarily, is the Colonial Office in London. The remainder of this book, therefore, will be concerned with a closer examination of the organisation of the Colonial Office and of the work which is being done at the centre to deal with the general problems of Colonial administration in modern conditions.

PART THREE

Colonial Office Organisation

CHAPTER VIII

The Making of the Modern Colonial Office

COLONIAL ADMINISTRATION BEFORE 1925

WHEN, in 1925, the Colonial Office ceased to be concerned with the affairs of the self-governing Dominions and began to deal exclusively with dependent territories, its organisation was comparatively simple, and indeed had undergone no significant change since 1907, when a Dominions Division had been created which would in time develop into the Dominions Office. The Colonial Office itself, in 1925, was divided into eight 'geographical' departments, each responsible for the business connected with a particular region or group of territories. There was also a 'general' department which dealt with Office establishment matters, promotions and transfers within the Colonial Service (recruitment for the Service being conducted by the Private Secretaries to the Secretary of State),[1] and a miscellaneous assortment of subjects affecting the Colonies generally, such as pensions and ceremonial. There was also a Legal Adviser, shared with the Dominions Office.

Between the departments and the Permanent Under-Secretary of State and Ministers, there were three Assistant Under-Secretaries of State. One of these dealt with Tropical Africa; one with the Middle East (that is to say, the mandated territories of Iraq, Trans-Jordan and Palestine, which had been assigned to the Colonial Office in 1921); and the third with the other non-African territories and the General Department.

This uncomplicated pattern was traditional, and its inadequacy for modern requirements was only beginning to become apparent to far-seeing observers, in which class, fortunately, were included the Secretary of State and Parliamentary Under-Secretary of State at the time, namely the Rt. Hon. L. S. Amery and the Hon. W. Ormsby-Gore (afterwards Lord Harlech) respectively.

If British Colonial policy up to the first world war had to be summed up in two words, those words would be 'sound administration'. It is broadly true to say that, apart from a general feeling of satisfaction at the large number of spots of red on a world map, there was no significant public or Parliamentary interest in the affairs of

---

[1] Except for the Eastern Cadetships, which were filled by the Civil Service Commission through the same examination as the Home and Indian Civil Services.

the dependent territories. This had perhaps some advantages. It enabled a great deal of patient, unspectacular work to be done without interference or interruption. It enabled questions to be decided on their merits without regard to political expediency. Since the persons responsible for the administration, both at home and in the territories, were of a high standard both of quality and of integrity, this was all to the good. Governors were, it is true, tied down by regulations requiring them to obtain Colonial Office approval for all kinds of administrative and financial details; but they had a very free hand in matters of local policy, in which the Colonial Office was not competent or desirous to intervene. Civil servants are popularly supposed to lack initiative; but in some ways the peculiar circumstances of the Colonial Office encouraged it, and it was due to civil servants of the Office as much as to anyone that, for example, during the first decades of the twentieth century effective measures were begun for the prevention and treatment of tropical diseases, the chief obstacle to the progress and welfare of the peoples of the territories.

Finance, however, was a problem. The Colonies were expected to pay their way, and to cut their coat according to their cloth. If they were prosperous, they were free to go ahead with whatever economic and social developments the local authorities wished. Most of them, however, were far from prosperous, and could afford little from their own resources beyond the bare minimum needed to preserve law and order and to provide for the administration of justice and the collection of revenue. (And indeed the functions of government were not generally considered in those days as going much outside these limits.) Some could not even afford this minimum; and in these cases the United Kingdom Exchequer was prepared to make grants in aid, though this was always considered as a temporary expedient, and the finances of any territory 'on the dole' were subject to strict control by the Treasury.

CONTROL BY SECRETARY OF STATE

Traditionally, the main ostensible function of the Colonial Office was to administer the Colonial Regulations—'Col. Regs.' colloquially, 'Regulations for His (or Her) Majesty's Colonial Service' in full. Nothing is more significant of the great change that has taken place than the fact that this code—once the Bible and *vade-mecum* of the Office—is now seldom referred to except to settle some point of dispute. It is not now even printed in the annual *Colonial Office List.* The Colonial Regulations date back to 1837, and are 'directions to Governors for general guidance given by the Crown through the Secretary of State for the Colonies'. In their original form the regulations were extremely detailed, the Governors and their officials being treated as agents, and not very free agents, of the Government in the United Kingdom in financial and administrative matters. As time went on, control was necessarily relaxed in regard to 'Colonies possessing Representative Assemblies', but the regulations continued to be strict and detailed for the rest. In the regulations the powers and responsibilities of the Secretary of State in relation to the territorial governments were defined, and the bulk of the Office work was concerned with the exercise of these powers and responsibilities.

Under Colonial Regulations, the right of appointment to all vacant offices in the public service was reserved to the Secretary of State, and except in the purely subordinate posts a Governor could make no appointment or promotion without the approval of the Secretary of State. Governors were required to furnish quarterly returns of all changes in offices above the lowest grades. The disciplinary control of officers was similarly subject to the overriding authority of the Secretary of State. Although the officers of the Colonial Service were employed and paid by the territorial governments and not by the Colonial Office, it was the Office, by virtue of the supervisory powers vested in the Secretary of State, which was the effective headquarters of the Service. Thus, in addition to corresponding with the Governors about personnel matters, the Office would deal at first hand on its own responsibility with questions requiring action in this country, such as the grant of extensions of leave, the arrangement of medical examinations and the instructions to be given to the Crown Agents for the Colonies about payment of salaries and allowances or the booking of passages.

A second important field of work arose from the regulations governing public finance. The annual estimates of each territory required the prior approval of the Secretary of State, and had to be submitted well before the beginning of the financial year with detailed explanations. Rigid rules were laid down for the actual expenditure of the approved appropriation, for any variation from the estimates as sanctioned, for the submission and auditing of the accounts. The Governor had no power to add to the fixed establishment of the territory or to alter any salary without the approval of the Secretary of State. The Office took its financial responsibilities seriously and the estimates and accounts even of territories not subject to Treasury control were examined with great care. The Secretary of State's right to veto expenditure with which he (or his staff) did not agree was freely exercised. Doubtless this often caused some exasperation at the Colonial end, but it has to be remembered that in those days all but the older Colonies were run by civil servants, and the Colonial Office, acting for the Secretary of State, had a duty to see that the territories did not run into debt and become a charge on the British Treasury.

Another not negligible body of work was derived from the Colonial Regulation which laid down (and still does) that every person in a Colonial territory whether a member of the public service or a private individual, has the right to petition the Secretary of State, provided that he does so through the Governor. It was a traditional rule that all petitions—and there have always been plenty of them—should go up to the Secretary of State or at least the Parliamentary Under-Secretary, who of course required a full report and advice from the department.

Finally, the Regulations required all legislative Acts to be forwarded to the Secretary of State with certificates and explanations. This was to enable the Secretary of State to fulfil the duty, laid upon him not by the Regulations but by the constitutional instruments, to decide whether or not to advise the Sovereign to exercise the power of disallowance. Apart from this general provision, the Governor would be required by the instruments to submit certain kinds of legislation to the Secretary of State in draft, or in other cases to reserve his assent until the Sovereign's pleasure were made known.

CHANGING DEMANDS ON COLONIAL OFFICE

Since practically all government activities require legislative sanction and involve employment of staff and expenditure of public money, it is clear that the functions of the Secretary of State implied a close and detailed supervision of the administration of the Colonial territories. But in form, at any rate, it was on the whole a negative supervision, an elaborate system of check against abuse. The specific job of the Colonial Office was to see that the regulations were duly observed and to advise whether the approval of the Secretary of State could properly be accorded to the actions or proposals of the Governors. In practice, of course, there was frequent consultation between the Office and the Governors about questions of policy, but the extent of this depended upon personalities and circumstances: it was not inherent in the system.

In such conditions, the convenience of a geographical subdivision of the Office is readily understandable. Each department of the Office had its own files of correspondence with the territories which it covered, and was in a position to deal with all the matters which might be referred to the Secretary of State by the Governors. Experience, precedent and common sense determined the action to be taken. Reference could be made to the other geographical departments, to the general department, to other government offices, or to outside sources such as Kew Gardens (the Director of which was Botanical Adviser to the Secretary of State), for guidance when necessary. Co-ordination in important matters was secured by the submission of papers through the Assistant Under-Secretaries of State to the Permanent Under-Secretary and Ministers. Some of the civil servants in the Office had visited Colonial territories as Secretaries of Commissions and the like, but the majority had no personal knowledge of the places with which they dealt. This was not considered in those days a serious disadvantage. The Office did not seek to govern the territories: that was the business of the Governors. The job of the Office was to see that the London end was properly looked after. Knowledge of the rules and the practice and of the views and policy of the Secretary of State; ability to take decisions in the Secretary of State's name and to express them in proper form and suitable language; skill in negotiation with the Treasury and other government offices: these were the important qualifications in a civil servant of the Colonial Office.

But while, in 1925, the organisation and system of the Office were very much what they had always been, they were already overdue for review in the light of new developments. The Colonial situation in the years following 1918 was very different from that which had prevailed before 1914. Many factors had contributed to the change. The war had stirred things up generally throughout the Empire. The Tropical African Dependencies in particular, the remoter parts of which before the war had barely been brought under administration, were beginning to throw up political and economic problems of a novel kind. The war left Britain with the responsibility for reconstruction and administration in Iraq, Palestine, Trans-Jordan, Tanganyika and some of the former German territories in West Africa. Moreover, these places were to be administered under mandate, and Britain was accountable to the League of Nations for her administration. This fitted in with and reinforced the idea, which had already begun to pervade the climate of opinion, that Britain's role in the territories with backward populations (as distinct from the old Colonies of settlement) was that of a trustee. A notable contribution to and exposition of this new conception was Lord Lugard's book *The Dual Mandate in British Tropical Africa*, published in 1922. Lord Lugard's thesis was that in Africa Britain was called to discharge a double trust: to develop the African lands for the benefit of their inhabitants and also for the benefit of the world at large, which needed their products.

The desirability of 'developing the great estate', and of realising the potential economic resources of the territories for the general good of mankind was not of course new, but what had previously been a vision seemed now to be capable of translation into achievement, thanks to improvements in communications and advances in scientific research. The time was ripe for a forward policy; but it was not to be a policy of exploitation. The inhabitants of the territories were to share in the achievement and in the resulting benefits. Education, health and other social services had, therefore, to be provided, both for their own sake and to enable the people to play their part in the new era. The resources of modern science had to be mobilised in order to intensify the war upon the diseases of men, animals and plants which were hindering progress, to improve the quality and quantity of Colonial products, and to promote their use in manufacture and industry.

CHANGES IN ORGANISATION SINCE 1925

These needs were apparent by 1925 to Ministers and officials in the Colonial Office and to Governors and officers of the Colonial Service overseas. But it was not until the Office was freed from the preoccupations of business connected with the Dominions that the necessary reorganisation could be effected.

One of the first needs was to establish a closer and more intimate relationship between the Office and the Governors and staffs in the territories. To this end, a Colonial Governor with wide experience both in Whitehall and overseas, Brigadier-General Sir Samuel Wilson, was appointed as the first Permanent Under-Secretary of State for the separate Colonial Office. His period of administration (1925-33) was marked by the opening phase of an extensive development of the 'subject' side of the Office, that is to say of the machinery for dealing comprehensively with matters affecting the territories as a whole; by a similar development of the expert advisory services maintained by the Office for the general benefit of the Colonial Empire; by the adoption of a policy of unification for the Colonial Service; and by the establishment of the conception of partnership between the Office staff and the Colonial Service as component members of a single team, diverse in function but united in purpose.

In pursuance of this programme, the staff and functions of the General Department were enlarged, and split off into new departments when the appropriate stage had been reached. In 1930, a new Personnel Division (afterwards called Colonial Service Division and now Oversea Service Division) was set up under an additional Assistant Under-Secretary of State, and a distinguished retired officer of the Colonial Service, Mr. (afterwards Sir George) Tomlinson, was brought in to take charge of it. This Division incorporated the recruiting staff which, as explained in Chapter XI, had been in the position of Private Secretaries to the Secretary of State. Enlarged staffs were provided for dealing with promotions, transfers, pensions and conditions of employment in the Colonial Service. Office establishment matters were also taken over from the General Department by the new Personnel Division.

The idea of an actual amalgamation of the Colonial Office staff and the Colonial Service was indeed considered. It was, however, decisively rejected by a Committee on the system of appointment to the Colonial Office and the Colonial Service which sat in 1929–30 under the Chairmanship of Sir Warren Fisher, then Permanent Secretary to the Treasury.[1] The arguments against amalgamation were based upon the great disparity in size between the home and oversea establishments, and upon the essential differences between their work. While the Colonial Office was a Ministerial secretariat in London, most of the administrative officers overseas were directly engaged in the actual practice of governing peoples placed under their authority. Moreover the Colonial Service must include a wide variety of professional and technical branches which would have no counterpart in the home organisation.

The Warren Fisher Committee concluded that the interests of the Colonial Service would best be served by a loose form of unification of that Service, leaving the Colonial Office to be staffed, as in the past, by home civil servants. They advised, however, that various steps should be taken to promote interchange and better understanding between Downing Street and the staffs overseas. In consequence, it was arranged that a number of administrative posts in the Colonial Office should regularly be filled by officers of the Colonial Service seconded for a period (usually two years), and that administrative civil servants joining the Colonial Office staff should be under a liability to serve abroad as required and, in particular, should as far as possible be attached for a time to one of the oversea governments during their early years of service. Apart from these formal arrangements, it was part of the job of the new Personnel Division to establish closer personal relations between the Office and the officers of the Colonial Service. With this object, men on leave were systematically invited to call at the Colonial Office and social as well as official contacts at all levels were encouraged.

The scope of the General Department itself was gradually broadened to deal with economic and social service questions. In 1934 it became a General Division, comprising two departments— one general and one economic. In 1938 a separate Social Services Department was hived off to make a third section of the General Division. A year later the scope of this department was enlarged to cover Colonial Development, in view of the new policy then projected, reference to which will be made in its place. At the same time, with war-clouds gathering, a separate Defence Department within

[1] Its report was published in 1930 as Cmd. 3554.

the General Division was created. Finally, the Economic Department was expanded and sub-divided to meet war-time needs and the demands of post-war development, and became a Division in its own right, first under an Assistant and then, since 1947, under a Deputy Under-Secretary of State.

The organisation will continue to be adjusted to meet changing circumstances. Some fixed date must be taken for purposes of description, and it is proposed, in describing the present state of the Office, to consider this as it stood on 1st January, 1955. A comparison of the position then and at the separation of the Colonial and Dominion Offices in 1925 well illustrates the transformation which has taken place in 30 years:

1925 NINE DEPARTMENTS, comprising:

8 *Geographical Departments:*
East and Central Africa (2)
West Africa (2)
West Indies
Middle East
Far East
Mediterranean

1 *General Department* (including Establishment affairs of both the Colonial and the Dominions Offices)

1955 THIRTY DEPARTMENTS, comprising:

9 *Geographical Departments:*
East and Central Africa (2)
West Africa (2)
West Indies (2)
S.E. Asia
Pacific
Mediterranean

Oversea Service Division:
(4 departments)

Economic Division:
(7 departments)

Legal Division:
(2 departments)

8 *other departments,* viz:
Communications
Defence and General

Establishment and Organisation
Information
International Relations
Social Services (2)
Students

THE OFFICE BUILDINGS

An 'Office' is both a human organisation and a material edifice. Until 1875 the Colonial Office was housed in the buildings which stood at what is now the open end of Downing Street, looking on to the Horse Guards Parade, that is, beyond No. 11, the present official residence of the Chancellor of the Exchequer. The only surviving part of these houses is the low building now used as the Whips' Office. The records show that towards the end of their life, these houses fell into a lamentable state of disrepair, and the conditions in which the staff worked were far from comfortable. Even so, the Colonial Office had its reputed attractions, one of which was that a gentleman employed therein could at least count on a good rubber of whist after luncheon, and another was the availability of certain empty rooms for use as fives courts.

When the new Government buildings (designed by Sir Gilbert Scott—'shuddering with horror', as Lytton Strachey wrote—on Lord Palmerston's instructions, in the Renaissance and not in the currently fashionable Gothic style) were put up on the south side of Downing Street, the north-east corner of the block was assigned to the Colonial Office; the Foreign Office being on the north-west corner, the India Office on the south-west and the Home Office on the south-east. The corner into which the Colonial Office moved in 1875 was the last to be completed, and (no doubt because the funds provided for the building were running out) was finished off more plainly than the rest of the block. It contained, however, a very fine room for the Secretary of State and a few other good rooms for Under-Secretaries. It was also provided with a very large Library, which was intended to serve all the government Offices. This intention was not realised, and this was fortunate for, large as it was, the accommodation proved in time to be quite insufficient for the Colonial Office collections.

Some of the fireplaces in the old Colonial Office were salvaged from the demolition and incorporated in the new structure. That which stands in the room provided for the Secretary of State for the Colonies and now occupied by the Secretary of State for Commonwealth Relations came from the waiting-room of the old building in which Nelson and Wellington met for the first and only time shortly before Trafalgar, both having chanced to call upon the Secretary of

State at the same hour. The event is commemorated in a well-known painting by John Knight, in which the detail of the fireplace is clearly seen.

The new building occupied by the Colonial Office in 1875 was to be its home for more than seventy years. As the work expanded and the staff increased, basement and attic rooms intended for storage and menial purposes were brought into use for administrative and clerical staff, and the capacity of the building was sufficient for its purpose until the end of the first world war. Then it began to be overstrained, and after 1925, when the accommodation was shared by two Offices, each with its own official hierarchy, the position grew daily more difficult. To meet a succession of accommodation crises, various expedients were devised. Rooms were borrowed from the Home Office. Small self-contained sections of the Office were found places in Richmond Terrace and other neighbouring buildings. Great ingenuity was shown by the Office of Works in constructing new rooms on the roof amongst the chimney-stacks, and otherwise making use of waste space.

But all was of no avail. During the second world war, the pressure became so intolerable that there was no choice but to 'out-house' a large part of the Office. At various times during the war the Office found itself divided between Downing Street, Queen Anne's Gate, Palace Chambers, No. 2 Park Street (a mile and a half from the main building) and 15 Victoria Street.

It was obvious that only a major surgical operation could meet the case. Neither the Colonial Office nor the Commonwealth Relations Office (as the Dominions Office came to be called in 1947) was anxious to leave the historic ground of Downing Street; but while, if the Colonial Office went out, the accommodation there could suffice for the Commonwealth Relations Office, it could not have housed anything like the whole of the Colonial Office if the Commonwealth Relations Office had moved elsewhere. It was therefore decided by the Government that a new Colonial Office should be built on the site of the old Westminster Hospital, and that, while the building was in progress, the headquarters of the Office should be moved from Downing Street to that part of the Church House in Great Smith Street which was held by the Government under lease from the Church of England. The staff which could not be accommodated there would be concentrated as quickly as possible in Sanctuary Buildings on the opposite side of Great Smith Street. While this arrangement was far from ideal, it would provide a reasonably compact unit and enable the Office to be run as a coherent organisation.

The exodus into Great Smith Street took place in 1947, and the concentration of the whole staff in the two buildings in that street was completed in 1954. Hopes of early transfer to the new building were, however, dashed owing to the state of national finances, which caused the work of construction to be held up. It will clearly be some considerable time—though, one may hope, not forty years in the wilderness—before the Office can move into the promised land.

CHAPTER IX

Ministers and Civil Servants

THE OFFICE AND THE SECRETARY OF STATE

GEOGRAPHY, as Mr. E. C. Bentley's immortal lines remind us, is about maps; biography is about chaps. The Colonial Office is very much concerned with maps, but the problems with which it has to deal are, essentially, human problems. The Colonial territories are important not as places on a map but as places in which men, women and children live; and the work of the Colonial Office has to do with the lives of people and with the effects of the interactions of people upon each other, both within a territory and between a territory and the world outside. And this work is done by people: the staff of the Colonial Office is a corporate body of men and women with a continuous organic life. Men and women come into the Office, absorb the tradition; are transformed, perhaps, by it; help, perhaps, to transform it and to adapt it to new conditions.

Before considering in detail the work of the various departments of the Office, we may profitably examine its general lay-out and organisation, and see what manner of people are comprised in its staff.

It has already been made clear that the Colonial Office has no existence except as the secretariat of the Secretary of State for the Colonies. Officially, every act of the Office is done by him, as the person to whom the Sovereign has entrusted for the time being the seals of the Colonial Department. When a novice joins the staff of the Office, the first thing he learns is that if he is drafting a despatch to a Governor he begins 'I have, etc.'—which when typed out in full becomes 'I have the honour to . . .'—and continues in the first person, since the Secretary of State's signature will appear at the end of the finished article. If a letter to any person or body other than a Governor is being drafted, it must begin 'I am, etc.'—which is automatically translated by the typist as 'I am directed by Mr. Secretary ———— to'; and throughout the letter all opinions and emotions must be ascribed to the Secretary of State and not to the writer or signatory—'Mr. ———— regrets to observe,' or 'has noted with satisfaction'; 'The S. of S. has decided'; and so on: this is the invariable form of communication, whether or not the Secretary of State has personally seen or heard of the correspondence in question.

For although no one man could handle personally the vast mass of documents which pass into and out of the Office of to-day, it is all one man's responsibility. He is answerable for what is done in his name. Many things indeed do require and receive his personal consideration. Which things these are is a matter for him and is not the business of anyone outside. All communications from the Office are of equal validity. A disgruntled correspondent once wrote: 'You say that you are directed by Mr. Secretary ———, but well I know it is a man called Read!' He was alluding to the late Sir Herbert Read, who had signed the letter complained of. But it happened to be a bad shot, for that particular letter had been personally authorised by the Secretary of State.

The duties of the Office staff, then, are: to supply the Secretary of State with the information and advice which he may need for reaching decisions; to carry out his general or specific directions for action; to correspond, negotiate or decide on his behalf along lines which it can be assumed would be approved by him if he were able to deal personally with the subject in question. If it is to perform these duties satisfactorily the Office staff must clearly possess, both collectively and individually, a large fund of knowledge, experience and discretion. Successive Secretaries of State have testified in generous terms to the fact that the staff does possess these qualities. This is due to the merits of individuals, but most of all to that living tradition built up by generations of civil servants to which I referred in the Introduction.

THE PARLIAMENTARY UNDER-SECRETARY OF STATE AND MINISTER OF STATE

The office of Parliamentary Under-Secretary of State for the Colonies goes back to 1830. If the Secretary of State is a member of the House of Lords, the Parliamentary Under-Secretary will almost certainly be a member of the House of Commons. If the Secretary of State is a commoner, the Under-Secretary may or may not be a peer. Should he not be, some other member of the Government would have to answer for the Colonial Office in the House of Lords.

The function of the Parliamentary Under-Secretary of State is to act as a deputy and counsellor of the Secretary of State; to help him in his Parliamentary work; and within the Office to exercise such authority as the Secretary of State may delegate to him.

Although, when the Dominions Office was separated from the Colonial Office in 1925, the two portfolios of Secretary of State continued for a time to be held by one Minister (Mr. L. S. Amery), a new and separate post of Parliamentary Under-Secretary of State for Dominion Affairs was created. In 1930, owing to the growing pressure of work upon Ministers, the Secretary of State for the Colonies was relieved of Dominion Affairs, and successive holders of the office were able to carry on with the help of a Parliamentary Under-Secretary for several years. During and after the second world war, however, their ability to do so was affected not only by the general growth in the volume of business but by the increasing need for personal travelling by Ministers to various parts of the Colonial Empire. To assist in meeting these new demands, a new post of Minister of State for Colonial Affairs was created in 1948. The Minister of State ranks intermediately between the Secretary of State and the Parliamentary Under-Secretary. He is not a Cabinet Minister, and does not exercise authority independently of the Secretary of State, since it is in the latter that all constitutional authority remains vested.

The division of labour within the Office between the three Parliamentary chiefs is a matter of personal arrangement, as settled by the Secretary of State for the time being, and depends upon the individual qualifications and interests of those concerned. One Secretary of State, for example, might wish to keep economic affairs, or business connected with, say, Africa, in his own hands. Another might prefer to let these be the primary concern of the Minister of State or Parliamentary Under-Secretary and to concentrate his own attention on some other subjects. But, however things are arranged for domestic convenience, the final decision and responsibility in all important matters rests with the Secretary of State himself. It is he who represents his Office in the Cabinet; it is he who advises the Sovereign; it is he who is the ultimate spokesman and target in Parliament.

THE PERMANENT, DEPUTY AND ASSISTANT UNDER-SECRETARIES OF STATE

At the head of the Office staff is the Permanent Under-Secretary of State, who is both the Secretary of State's chief official adviser and the superior officer of all civil servants in the Office. He is also Accounting Officer for all Parliamentary Votes administered by the Office. When this post is vacant, selection is made from a wide field, not confined to the Office itself or even to the Civil Service. Of the five men who have held it since 1925, two—including the present incumbent—have been promoted from within the Office. None of the other three was or had been a home civil servant.

The Permanent Under-Secretary is now assisted by two Deputy Under-Secretaries. Until 1916 there were normally two Assistant Under-Secretaries of State. A third (for Dominions business) was added in 1916, and a fourth (for Middle Eastern business) in 1921. As already stated, an additional post was created for the Personnel Division in 1930. One post was upgraded to Deputy Under-Secretary in 1931, and a second Deputyship was added in 1947, one of the two Deputies being specifically charged with the economic, financial and development side of the Office work.

In former days, everything that went to the Secretary of State passed through the Permanent Under-Secretary. Nowadays such a rule would create an intolerable bottleneck, and, while the Permanent Under-Secretary is kept in touch with all important developments, he and the two Deputies divide the work between them and deal directly with Ministers on matters within their respective spheres. One Deputy Under-Secretary continues to look after the Economic Division, including the Finance Department, and also supervises the Social Service Departments. The Permanent Under-Secretary deals with Office establishment, defence, international relations, African, South-East Asian and Mediterranean affairs; the other Deputy with the work of the Oversea Service Division, the Information, West Indian, Pacific, and Students Departments. The arrangement is elastic and can be adjusted to suit changes of circumstances.

The Legal Division of the Office is outside this scheme, and consists of two departments, staffed by qualified legal officers, under the Legal Adviser, who is equivalent to a Deputy Under-Secretary of State, and who also serves the Commonwealth Relations Office.

The Permanent and Deputy Under-Secretaries of State are supported by eight Assistant Under-Secretaries. Of these, two are concerned with economic affairs, one with the work of the African Division, one with that of the Oversea Service Division and Students Department, and one with that of the West Indian Departments. The others divide the remaining work.

ADVISERS

Modern developments in the administrative machinery have been matched by the creation of an expanding system of advisory services. To a limited extent the Colonial Office had always called upon the services of outside experts for particular purposes in case of need. In 1909 a standing Advisory Medical and Sanitary Committee for Tropical Africa had been set up, and the scope of this Committee was extended to cover all the dependent territories in 1922. In 1923 an Advisory Committee on Native Education in Tropical Africa was appointed; its functions, too, were extended to all the territories in 1928.

These Committees were at first provided with whole-time professional secretaries, paid from funds contributed by the Colonial governments, and these officers acted to some extent as expert advisers to the administrative departments. In 1926, however, a Chief Medical Adviser was appointed to the Office staff. Three years later, an Agricultural Adviser was appointed, and at the same time an Advisory Council of Agriculture and Animal Health was constituted. A Labour Adviser was appointed in 1938, Advisers on Education and Animal Health in 1940. Since then, Advisers on Co-operation, Fisheries, Forestry, Social Welfare, Surveys and Geological Surveys have been appointed; also a Police Adviser whose title has been changed to Inspector-General of Colonial Police. Some other advisory posts have been created to meet temporary needs but have not survived as part of the permanent establishment. Amongst these were an Adviser on Inland Transport, a Financial Adviser, a Business Adviser, an Adviser on Development Planning, an Adviser on Demography, and an Adviser on Oversea Information Services. The work of the Advisers and their staffs, and of the numerous advisory bodies and research organisations attached to the Office today, will be noticed later.

PRIVATE SECRETARIES

Much of the smooth and efficient working of the Office depends upon the Private Secretaries. Nowadays all senior officers have their Personal Assistants (P.As.), though it took a second world war to get this revolutionary idea established. But Private Secretaries properly so called are attached only to the Secretary of State, the Minister of State and the Permanent and Parliamentary Under-Secretaries. The Secretary of State's 'Private Office' is an important part of the departmental machinery, and the Principal Private Secretary is a key man not only from the point of view of his master but from the point of view of the Office generally, though he has no co-ordinating or executive authority comparable with that of the *chef de cabinet* in the French system. In the past, Secretaries of State have sometimes brought in their own Private Secretaries, and they have the right to do so. But usually today the appointment goes to a specially selected Principal with experience of the Office. He gets an allowance in addition to his pay, and earns it, for he has to work all hours, accompany his chief on journeys abroad, and be continuously tactful and cheerful, interpreting the Office to the Secretary of State and *vice versa*.

There are two Assistant Private Secretaries to the Secretary of State—one an Assistant Principal assigned to the post for a year or two, and the other a Senior Executive Officer who works more or less permanently in the Private Office and deals with Parliamentary business and with ceremonial matters. Both these subjects call for experience and continuity. The ceremonial work, which includes making up the lists of Colonial guests for Palace functions and other social events, and the arrangement, in conjunction with Government Hospitality, of reception and entertainment for distinguished colonial visitors, was done by a Ceremonial and Reception Secretary shared with the Commonwealth Relations Office until the last holder of the post (Rear-Admiral Sir Arthur Bromley) retired after the Coronation.

The Minister of State has a Principal as his Private Secretary; the Permanent and Parliamentary Under-Secretaries of State have Assistant Principals. All these posts are much valued by those eligible for them, not merely because they carry allowances, but because they give their holders a most useful conspectus of the whole Office work and its relation to Cabinet and parliamentary policy.

CHAPTER X

General Organisation and Office Services

ADMINISTRATIVE ORGANISATION

THE Office to-day is the product of historical development, and its various departments, branches and sections have come into being to meet developing needs. In Colonial Office terms, a 'department' normally means an organisation under an Administrative Officer of the rank of Assistant Secretary, supported by two or more Principals, under whom are Assistant Principals and such officers of the Executive and Clerical Classes as the particular work of the department may require. All these are general service officers, not specialists, and are interchangeable. To this rule there are some exceptions. The principal posts in the Legal Division and in the Statistics Department are staffed by specialists. The head of the Information Department is a Chief Information Officer, and the department includes a number of officers of the Government Information Service. The Librarian, again, is a specialist, and is assisted by members of the Librarian class, though the rest of his staff is drawn from the executive and clerical staffs of the Office at large.

The head of a department is charged with the conduct of all the work within the departmental sphere. The members of the department take their instructions from him, and he assigns to them their duties and responsibilities. He has to see that higher authority is kept informed of all developments or prospective developments of importance, and to seek directions, when necessary, about action to be taken. An important part of his job is to make sure that other departments of the Office are consulted as may be necessary. If his department is geographical, much of its work will be of concern to one or other of the subject departments. If his is a subject department, he has always to bear in mind that his work is of concern to one or more of the geographical departments. There must, therefore, be constant interdepartmental consultation.

ADVISORY STAFFS AND SERVICES

Alongside the administrative departmental organisation which has been described are the Advisory Staffs. Their position, again, is the product of historical development. It would no doubt have been possible to proceed by way of establishing a Medical Department, a Labour Department and so on, but in fact this was not done. As has been seen, what happened was that at various times from 1926 onwards, experts in different fields were appointed as Advisers to the Secretary of State. As time went on, the range of advisory services was expanded, and some of the principal Advisers were provided with one or more specialist assistants. But the constitutional position under which these persons are advisory to the Secretary of State and do not take executive action in his name has been preserved and this system seems to command general satisfaction.[1] Under this arrangement, the Advisers neither are directed by, nor do they give directions to, the administrative departments of the Office. The Secretary of State, whether personally or in the persons of his officials, consults them, receives their advice, and takes his decisions. The responsibility for executive action is his, not theirs. Similarly, in dealing with the territorial governments when on tour, the Advisers give their opinions as experts in their own right and not as emissaries of the Colonial Office. In fact, visits to the territories are an important and essential part of the functions of the advisory staff. Although no Adviser has as yet managed to visit every territory, several Advisers have during their term of office visited practically all territories.

The Advisers are at the service of, and accessible to, all departments of the Office. But, although they have not departments of their own, they have special links with certain departments. There is no Medical, Education, Labour or Social Welfare Department; but there are two Social Service Departments in which these subjects and others are dealt with, and with which the Advisers concerned are in intimate and continuous touch. Similarly, the Advisers on Agriculture, Animal Health, Fisheries and Forestry have special affinities with the Production Departments of the Economic Division; the Inspector-General of Colonial Police with the Defence Department. This arrangement preserves the Advisers' independence of the official hierarchy, while providing machinery for bringing them into all administrative and executive action affecting their subjects.

Advisory Committees are now a prominent and indispensable feature of the Colonial Office organisation. There are in all twenty-six of these bodies, and through them the Office is able to command the willing and indeed enthusiastic help of a great company of the highest authorities in a wide range of scientific and social studies. Some of the Committees are essentially technical in character, others are called to assist in the formation of policy. The latter are usually presided over by the Minister of State or Parliamentary Under-Secretary of State, with a senior administrative officer as deputy

[1] The position of the Legal Adviser is exceptional. See Ch. XIV.

chairman. The Adviser concerned (if there is one) and the head of the Office department concerned sit as members. The staff of the department carry out the secretarial work, and arrange both for the reference of matters to the Committee and for the recording and consideration of the Committee's advice. While the function of the Committees is to advise on matters referred to them by the Secretary of State and not to take executive decisions, they have in practice ample scope for initiative, and their views and opinions necessarily carry great weight, both in the Office and with the oversea governments.

ASSIGNMENT OF RESPONSIBILITY

As, no doubt, in other government departments, the general theory on which Colonial Office business is conducted is that communications coming into the Office are opened, sorted out, assigned to the appropriate department, placed on the proper file with the relevant previous papers, considered and minuted up from junior to senior until somebody decides what should be done. By time-honoured Colonial Office custom he signifies his decision by adding the words 'at once' to his initials. Usually what has to be done consists of composing a letter, despatch or telegram; back goes the file to the junior, who prepares a draft, which in its turn goes up until someone passes it by inscribing the magic letters 'f.s.', meaning 'for signature'. Of course there are many variations on this pattern and many ways in which the process can be short-circuited; but this is the general idea. In many government offices the nature of the work is such that it is possible to lay down rules as to who decides what; for instance it can be laid down that officers of a certain rank have authority to deal with claims not exceeding a stated figure. Practically none of the Colonial Office work is of this kind. Every officer has to exercise judgment in dealing with any question, whether to settle it or 'send it on'. This is where tradition, training and experience count.

Because of this, there is no clear-cut distinction between the duties of the various grades and classes. The work of the Office is essentially of an 'administrative' character, and is done by civil servants of the administrative class, with assistance from the executive, clerical and other classes. Until after the second world war, indeed, the executive class was not represented in the Office. There were however certain posts of 'Staff Officer' which were filled by officers of what used to be the Second Division of the Civil Service or by promotion from the Clerical Class. Nowadays there is a fairly large executive staff which carries out both higher clerical duties and the kind of work which used to be done by the Staff Officers, work often very little different in character from some of that performed by administrative officers.

This absence of a clear-cut official hierarchy has helped to encourage a steady flow of promotions to administrative rank from the executive and clerical classes, who have benefited by this in addition to the opportunities of advancement within their own classes. Out of 30 Assistant Secretaries in post in 1953, no fewer than six were men who had started their careers in the Office as clerical or second division officers.

But, although in the middle part of the Office it is not possible to distinguish very clearly the functions of the various grades, the differences being of degree rather than of kind, the position above and below this middle part is more easily defined.

HOW THE OFFICE IS STAFFED

Except in so far as it is reinforced by the temporary attachment of officers from the Oversea Service, or by the employment, also in a temporary capacity, of retired members of that Service, the staff of the Colonial Office consists of home civil servants recruited through the ordinary machinery of the Civil Service Commission or Ministry of Labour. For the administrative, executive and clerical classes, the Civil Service Commission assigns candidates to the Office from the normal examinations. Because of the special interest and variety of the work, assignment to the Colonial Office is eagerly sought by successful candidates.

When permanent specialist and advisory staffs are recruited from outside, the same principle of appointment through the Civil Service Commission machinery is followed. Many of the advisory staff, however, are retired officers of the Oversea Service who give the Office the benefit of their special combination of professional knowledge and practical experience in the oversea territories. For similar reasons a few administrative posts have been filled in the same way, and in times of shortage of regular staff it has been of great advantage to the Office to be able to tap this valuable source of supply.

The secondment of serving officers of the Oversea Service to the Office, on the other hand, is not arranged to relieve shortages but mainly in order to give useful experience to the officers concerned. The seconded officers usually serve for two years and generally occupy posts in the grade of Principal. From time to time, however, Assistant Secretaryships are held by such officers. Between 1937 and 1942 one of the posts of Assistant Under-Secretary of State was occupied in succession by three Colonial Governors; but this has not happened lately.

The Colonial Office staff, being part of the home civil service, is interchangeable with that of other home government departments and not with the Oversea Service, which is a separate service, or rather series of services, employed and paid by the territorial governments. Occasionally, however, permanent transfers are made from the Oversea Service to the Office and *vice versa*. A few Governorships and other senior posts abroad have from time to time been filled by members of the Office staff, the most recent example being the appointment of Sir Andrew Cohen, an Assistant Under-Secretary of State, to be Governor of Uganda in 1952. The temporary secondment of administrative (and sometimes other) officers to the territories is a regular part of the Office system, and, like the secondment here of officers from the territories, is mainly arranged for the purpose of enlarging the experience of those concerned.

Transfers from and to other government departments are fairly common. A substantial proportion of the present staff originally came into the Office on transfer, and quite a number of those who have left the Office on transfer have risen to the highest posts in other departments.

ESTABLISHMENT AND ORGANISATION

Under the Permanent Under-Secretary of State, the Establishment and Organisation Officer is responsible for the general staffing and working arrangements of the Office. As is the rule in the civil service, the selection of the person to hold this key post is subject to the approval of the Prime Minister. The post ranks as an Assistant Secretaryship, and the practice during the last ten years or so has been to appoint one of the younger officers of the grade for a limited period, after which he goes on to take charge of a more normal department. But there is no fixed rule about it.

When the Personnel Division was set up in 1930, one Assistant Secretary combined the headship of the Colonial Service Department with the post of Establishment Officer. By 1939 it had become clear that the latter should be a whole-time post, and it has so remained. With the great expansion of staff during and after the war, what was until then a very small department has grown into quite a substantial organisation, including a Deputy Establishment Officer, who ranks as a Principal, and a fairly large staff of Executive and Clerical Officers.

Like other government departments, the Colonial Office has a Departmental Whitley Council which is under the Chairmanship of the Permanent Under-Secretary. The Council meets ceremoniously on occasion, but in practice it is seldom called together except for the necessary annual meeting. Day-to-day relations between the 'authorities' and the staff are almost entirely conducted by means of constant and informal contact between the Establishment Officer and his assistants on the one hand and the Chairman of the Staff Side and other accredited representatives of the various grades on the other. This arrangement gives general satisfaction.

In his general responsibility for staffing arrangements, the Establishment Officer presides over the promotions boards which are held for all non-administrative grades.

The Establishment and Organisation Department includes a Security Section and an Office Services Section. The latter deals with accommodation and equipment, the reception of visitors, the supervision of the registry, copying, paper-keeping and messenger services, the printing and stationery section and the travelling arrangements for members of the staff—quite a considerable matter in these days.

Attached to the Department are a Staff Welfare Officer and a Training Officer. Civil defence and fire services are also provided for. Payment of the staff is not dealt with in the Establishment Department but is handled by the Accounts Branch of the Finance Department. It is the Establishment Officer, however, who negotiates with the Treasury about the number and grading of staff and the fixing of salaries for posts which do not fall into the normal civil service classes.

CORRESPONDENCE

The work of the Colonial Office does not involve much direct contact with the general public, though requests for information about the Colonies from members of the public are much more common now than they used to be. The great bulk of the Office's correspondence is conducted with Colonial governors, other home government departments, public bodies and business organisations. The only individuals with whom the Office has to deal on any large scale are officers of the Oversea Service on leave or retirement in the United Kingdom; candidates for appointment to the Oversea Service and their referees; and people from the territories who are here as students.

The Office therefore, and its correspondents, are largely free from the infliction of form-filling, though in some things, such as applications for appointments, a certain amount of this is unavoidable. Most of the Office correspondence with individuals is about their personal affairs and problems, and it is the tradition and rule to adopt, as far as possible, a human and sympathetic tone in drafting letters, and to consider what a letter will look like to the recipient. Special care is taken over the letters of condolence which unfortunately have to be sent to the relations of officers of the Oversea Service who die abroad. These letters are specially typed, worded in a less formal way than the usual official communication, and signed by a senior officer.

In its official correspondence, the Office is heir to a tradition dating back to the days when it was laid down that 'despatches must be written in a large and distinct hand, with dark ink', and when there was plenty of time between mails to indulge in elegant orotundity. The advent of the electric telegraph (so referred to in minutes of the days when this method of communication was a novelty),[1] the typewriter and the dictaphone (to say nothing of the long-distance telephone) have had their effect.

But the office style is still on the whole of the kind described by Sir Ernest Gowers in his *ABC of Plain Words*: 'The style is perhaps pompous, but it has the charm of ancient custom, and it is quite easy to learn. It is easy to overdo also, and a warning not to overdo it is the only advice that need be given about it. Do not be too free with its well-starched frills. . . . Even in the traditional field there is a salutary movement towards simplicity.'

Jargon is horrible; but official English at its best is an admirably precise instrument for conveying exact shades of meaning with a general air of grave old-fashioned courtesy. The Colonial Office 'grand manner' is perhaps best seen in the circular despatches which an irreverent colleague in a Colonial Secretariat once described as 'Sermons on the Mount'. Printed traditionally in italic type on beautiful blue paper, these communications form a record of the views of the Secretary of State and his advisers on an immense variety of topics, from routine administrative matters to the most serious questions of policy. If at times they seem to invest the trivial with unduly portentous significance, they provide as a whole a good example of traditional style in which the well-turned phrase and even the occasional epigram are not eschewed. But this is to speak of the past rather than of the present, for as the relationship between the Office and the Colonial governments changes, the need for general pronouncements becomes less, and the use of circular despatches tends to be confined to practical and utilitarian matters. The advent of the 'savingram', too, has had its effect on the Office's literary style. This revolting but convenient word denotes a message written in the form of a telegram, but carried by air mail and not by the 'electric telegraph'. Such messages have very largely superseded the cocked-hat despatch, and I suppose that if the saving effected in woman-hours by not having to type 'I have the honour to be, Sir, your most obedient, humble, servant', were computed over a year, it would be found to be not inconsiderable.

No doubt the Colonial Office, like any other human institution, sometimes lapses from its own high standards. One matter which has always been regarded inside the Office as well as outside as being open

[1] In 1864 the only existing cable was to North America; telegraphic communication with the West Indies and the Far Eastern Colonies was established a few year later.

to legitimate criticism is delay in answering letters from the public. Delay may often be unavoidable because the questions raised involve complicated issues and may need reference to a Colonial government. Shortage of typing staff, which the Office could not help, made it very difficult indeed during and immediately after the last war to deal promptly with any but the most urgent correspondence. For a long time the copying pools were as much as two or three weeks in arrear, despite all efforts to catch up. The position in this respect has, however, greatly improved, and most letters that cannot be answered immediately are acknowledged by postcard, which does something to remove grounds of complaint. Government departments can never, in fact, deal with everything by return of post. It is partly due to the system, but the system itself is dictated by necessity. Whatever the Office says is, as has been pointed out, said by the Secretary of State. Any inaccuracy or ineptitude in an Office communication has to be answered for by him; the Office must therefore always be most careful not to let him down. Not only decisions, but the arguments upon which decisions are taken must be recorded, not only for immediate purposes but because the decisions may have to be justified at some future time, especially if they are unpalatable to the correspondent or involve expenditure of public money. The mills of a government office are forced to grind exceeding small, and they must inevitably grind somewhat slowly. But at any rate it can be said that the Office is aware of the temptation to prolixity and over-meticulousness which besets the civil servant; and that it does its best to resist.

REGISTRIES, COPYING AND COMMUNICATIONS

The general arrangements for the handling of correspondence comprise the Registries, the Copying Service and the Oversea Communications Service. Registration methods are one of those matters about which no finality seems possible. At one time the registries were broken up and attached to the several divisions of the Office. Then there was a move to concentrate them in one or at most two central registries. Latterly the tendency has been towards decentralisation, some degree of which became inevitable when the Office was split up amongst several buildings. But the separate registries are all under the supervision of a Chief Registrar and all work on the same system.

The Copying Service, under a Chief Superintendent, is organised in 'pools' dispersed about the Office. An important section is the telegram copying and distribution organisation, which ties up with the Oversea Communications Service. This latter Service, under its own Controller, handles both telegrams and mails.

Because the Office is so large and continuous a customer, Messrs.

E

Cable and Wireless Ltd. have a room in the building itself, where telegrams are handed in and from which they are passed, by tele-printer or courier, to the Company's office in Whitehall.

Some idea of the volume of the Office's correspondence is given by the following figures for the years 1953 and 1954:

	Inward		Outward	
	1953	1954	1953	1954
Number of telegrams ..	24,036	22,894	23,735	22,831
„ „ despatches and savingrams	64,007	65,239	63,332	64,041

(No statistical record is kept of the official letters received from and despatched to addresses in this country.)

When necessary and possible, ordinary methods of communication are supplemented by use of the long-distance telephone, but there are obvious limitations on the usefulness of this device and it is reserved for very special occasions. It was, after all, a Colonial Office man who wrote:

Business is seldom really and usefully transacted otherwise than in writing.[1]

The Colonial Office works night and day, for its night is day in many of the territories with which it is in correspondence. In former times there was competition amongst the younger bachelors for the posts of Resident Clerk. There were two of these officers, who were given an allowance and were provided with free furnished quarters in a comfortable flat in the Downing Street building. With the in-creasing prevalence of marriage, the job became less popular and a rota system was introduced, officers serving as Resident Clerk for a week at a time. This arrangement still prevails, but the duties have changed. In the old days the Resident Clerk had to code or decode very urgent telegrams himself, but the volume of telegraphic corres-pondence is now so great, and the knowledge of codes and cyphers required is so specialised, that the code and cypher section have to work a shift system. The Resident Clerk's responsibility is to take action, or obtain directions, on any urgent matter which comes in on Sunday or after 6 p.m. on week-days. Saturday afternoons are covered by a Duty Officer.

THE LIBRARY

An indispensable central Office service is the Library. This com-prises a unique and comprehensive collection of books, other

[1] Sir Henry Taylor, *The Statesman.*

publications and maps concerning the Colonial territories, and is freely resorted to by students and research workers as well as by the various departments of the Office itself. It contains a Legal Section, where all the laws of all the territories are available for consultation; a Reference Section, where miscellaneous enquiries from the public are answered and 'briefs' for Office use prepared; and a Revision of Records Section which deals with the Office archives, the destruction of old routine correspondence and the transfer to the Public Record Office of papers which are to be permanently preserved. The annual *Colonial Office List* is prepared and edited in the Library.

When the Colonial Office left Downing Street in 1947, the Library, or most of it, had to be left behind, which was a great inconvenience. Eventually, however, the large space needed to accommodate the collection and staff was made available in Sanctuary Buildings, and the Ministry of Works provided excellent modern equipment. Although the Library must await the completion of the new building before attaining its full stature, it remains in the meantime an institution of which the Office is justly proud. Much of the credit for the notable development, despite all handicaps, of the Library in recent years belongs to the late Mr. A. B. Mitchell, who came from Saint Andrews University in 1947 to take up the post of Joint Librarian for the Colonial and Commonwealth Relations Offices. His untimely death early in 1954 was a great loss to the public service.

ASSOCIATED ORGANISATIONS

The headquarters organisation of the Colonial territories includes two institutions which, though not part of the Colonial Office, are closely linked to it. One is the Office of the Crown Agents for Oversea Governments and Administrations. This cumbrous but accurate title recently replaced the traditional name of Crown Agents for the Colonies. It does not make much difference: they are always called 'Crown Agents' either way, and have been so called since 1833.

The status of the Crown Agents is peculiar. There are two of them (there have at times been three and even four); they are appointed by the Secretary of State, who may select them from the Colonial Office, from the Oversea Service or indeed from any source he thinks fit. At present, one is a Colonial Office man, the other a retired Colonial Governor. The Crown Agents and their staff—a staff about as big as that of the Colonial Office itself—are not home civil servants but are employed on practically the same conditions as home civil servants, and the staff are recruited through the Civil Service examinations. The funds for the cost of running their office are provided by fees and commissions on the agency work that they do for their principals—that is to say the governments and other authorities who employ them—any surplus being distributed amongst the principals.

Their work is to carry out on behalf of their principals whatever business those principals may have to transact in the United Kingdom. Such business includes the procurement, inspection and shipping of stores for government purposes, the negotiation of contracts, the engagement of consulting engineers and other professional advisers, the designing of public works, the investment of funds, the issue of loans, the payment of government accounts, the disbursement of salaries and pensions to persons who are in this country, the booking of passages and the recruitment of certain kinds of staff, mainly in the subordinate and technical grades not covered by the Colonial Office recruitment machinery. It will be seen that this work, while extensive and multifarious, touches many things which must be of concern to the Colonial Office, and although the Colonial Office does not give directions to the Crown Agents, the two Offices work in very close partnership. For example, the Chief Engineer in the Crown Agents' Office is also Engineering Adviser to the Secretary of State. It will also be seen that the Crown Agents are not in any sense a trade or information agency, and their duties do not overlap with those of the trade commissioners or other representatives whom most of the larger Colonial governments now maintain in London.

The Crown Agents occupy a handsome building, which is their own property, at 4, Millbank. As with the Colonial Office, their staff has expanded along with the modern development of the Colonial territories, and they have recently had to acquire a number of adjacent and neighbouring buildings in order to accommodate their growing numbers.

Reference will be made to various activities of the Crown Agents later in the book. But one at least needs no introduction to the public, since it is known to every schoolboy and indeed all the world over, for the most amateur philatelist cannot be ignorant of the meaning of the initials 'C.A.' The production of postage stamps for the Colonial governments is one of the most colourful and responsible of the Crown Agents' duties, and the quality of the stamps produced is justly celebrated. The actual designs are usually prepared, or at any rate suggested, by the governments themselves, and require Royal approval. The function of the Crown Agents is to place the contracts, supervise the work and arrange the despatch of the articles to their destination. Currency notes are dealt with in the same way.

There are numerous other bodies more or less closely associated with the Colonial Office, but only two of them can be mentioned here. In former days, when Colonial governments were accountable to the United Kingdom Parliament in far more detail than they are to-day, their accounts were audited by the Exchequer and Audit

Department. In 1910 the responsibility was vested in the Colonial Audit Department, now called the Oversea Audit Department. This Department is the headquarters of the Oversea Audit Service. With certain exceptions, the auditing of the several government accounts is carried out by members of this Service, each territory having its own Audit Department, which is part of its own public service, but staffed in its higher grades by members of the Oversea Audit Service. The independence of the audit is secured by the general supervision of the Director-General of Oversea Audit, who is appointed by the Secretary of State, and by the fact that the postings of members of the Service are subject to the approval of the Secretary of State on the recommendation of the Director-General. Like the Crown Agents, the Director-General and his headquarters staff are not home civil servants but are employed on similar terms. The cost of the office is shared amongst the governments of the territories where the Oversea Audit service operates.

The other organisation referred to is the Oversea Nursing Association. Founded in 1896, this is an unofficial body, but it is regularly used as the channel of recruitment for the nursing branch of the Oversea Service which, by gracious permission of H.M. Queen Elizabeth the Queen Mother, is known as Queen Elizabeth's Oversea Nursing Service. The Colonial Office is represented on the Association's Executive Committee by the Chief Nursing Officer and a woman member of the Oversea Service Division.

PART FOUR

Aspects of
Colonial Administration

CHAPTER XI

Her Majesty's Oversea Civil Service

ORIGINS OF THE SERVICE

THE expression 'His (or Her) Majesty's Colonial Service' has been in use since at least the reign of William IV. In June, 1954, the Government announced that a new title—'Her Majesty's Oversea Civil Service'—would be introduced in October of that year. The main reason for this change was the fact that members of the Service are already employed and may in future be increasingly employed in countries which not only are not Colonies but may not even be within the responsibilities of the Colonial Office. Also, to an increasing extent, the civil services of the territories are becoming local services, staffed largely by local inhabitants, and the conception of an all-embracing Colonial Service has lost much of its relevance to modern conditions.

In the old Colonies of settlement, the Crown had traditionally reserved the right of 'patronage' in filling Governorships and other principal public offices, even though the remuneration of these posts was paid from the funds of the Colony. No doubt the system lent itself to abuse, as we can read, for example, in the pages of *Vanity Fair*, but there is no reason to suppose that most of these officials—many of whom were drawn from the local colonist or settler community—were otherwise than conscientious and efficient according to the standards of their time. However that may be, these were the body of people which came to be known as the Colonial Service. Their numbers grew as existing Colonies developed and more territories were added to the list. The same principle was followed: the posts were filled by persons selected by the Secretary of State, but they were paid from the revenues of the territories. The Secretary of State could select anybody he wished, but he usually tried to make suitable appointments, and it became a normal practice in filling the better paid posts to consider men who had gained experience and proved their worth in junior offices in the same or another territory. So, without there being any very definite rule or system, the Colonial Service began to be established as a Service extending over all the territories and offering prospects of promotion not limited to any one of them.

There was only one exception to this informal arrangement. When the competitive examination system was introduced for the Home and Indian civil services, it was made to apply also to the so-called Eastern Cadetships. These were the civil services (that is to say, the administrative class) of Ceylon, Hong Kong, the Straits Settlements and the Malay States. All appointments to these Cadetships were made from candidates who were successful in the examination, and the members of these civil services were to some extent regarded as interchangeable amongst the territories concerned. They formed, therefore, a sort of limited and self-contained Colonial Service within the wider whole. Apart from the Eastern Cadetships, recruitment from outside the territories themselves of candidates for first appointment was infrequent and spasmodic until after the end of the nineteenth century. Since the appointments were within the personal gift of the Secretary of State, such 'patronage' work as there was could conveniently be done by his Private Secretary and it was not regarded as the proper business of the Colonial Office as such.

EXPANSION AND UNIFICATION

In the period between 1900 and 1914, the newly developing African territories began to need staff on an increasing scale, and their requirements began to strain the resources of the Secretary of State's private office. In 1910 a young man named R. D. Furse was brought in as Assistant Private Secretary with recruitment as his special duty. During the next four years he gained experience which was invaluable to the Office when, in 1918, he returned—still in the capacity of a Private Secretary—to handle an unprecedented demand from overseas for staff of all kinds. With the help of a small team of assistants, Furse built up, in the post-war years, an efficient recruiting machine with a wide range of contacts in universities and other sources of supply both at home and in the Dominions, and with a large experience of the needs of the territories and the technique of selecting the right kind of people to supply those needs. All this was still done under the umbrella of 'patronage', and Furse and his staff were not permanent civil servants, nor was their organisation an official department of the Office. The arrangement had some advantages, but it had serious disadvantages, not only because the personal position of the staff was unsatisfactory, but because the patronage system was open to challenge as being archaic and liable to abuse.

As has already been mentioned, it was not until after the separation of the Offices in 1925 that this kind of problem received proper attention. In 1929, however, after some preliminary soundings, the whole system was brought under review by the Committee presided over by Sir Warren Fisher, and as a result of their recommendations and of consideration by the Colonial Office Conference of 1930, the Personnel Division was established, as already explained. At the same time, the existence of the Colonial Service as a 'unified' Service was formally recognised, and it was decided to create within it a series of functional unified Services—the Colonial Administrative Service, the Colonial Agricultural Service and so on.

The Personnel Division was organised at the outset in two sections. One dealt with recruitment and training and was presided over by Major (afterwards Sir Ralph) Furse who, with his assistants, became for the first time a part of the normal Office establishment. In order to safeguard the principle of open competition, recruitment was placed under the general supervision of a Colonial Service Appointments Board, appointed by the Secretary of State on the nomination of the First Civil Service Commissioner, who was himself to be *ex officio* Chairman of the Board.

The other section of the Division dealt with the Colonial civil servant after his admission to the Service. All questions of promotion, transfer, pensions and conditions of employment were handled on this side, and also establishment matters within the Colonial Office itself.

Before the setting up of the Personnel Division, promotions and transfers in the Colonial Service (as distinct from recruitment) had for some time been handled by permanent officials as part of the work of the General Department. The system was that all the annual confidential reports received from Governors on their officers were scrutinised, and those individuals whose reports were considered to justify it were 'noted'. Vacancies in senior posts were notified by the geographical departments to the Promotions Branch, and a list of possible candidates was prepared. The vacancies, with the lists and reports of the candidates, were then placed before a Promotions Committee consisting of the heads of the geographical departments and the General Department, under the presidency of one of the Assistant Under-Secretaries of State.

This arrangement had worked well enough while the Colonial Service was on a small scale, but it did not suit the conditions of 1930. The Warren Fisher Committee recommended that the Promotions Committee should be reconstituted at a higher level, and should consist of the Permanent and Assistant Under-Secretaries, with heads of departments and advisers attending as required, according to the place and nature of the vacancies under consideration. This procedure was observed for some years, but fell into disuse as it became increasingly clear that each vacancy needed more intensive and less formal discussion and more individual consideration than could be secured by the committee system.

The original lay-out of the Personnel (later called the Colonial Service) Division remained until after the second world war, except for the removal (as already mentioned) of Office Establishment questions from its scope. The separation, however, of recruitment work from the work connected with promotions and transfers was not wholly satisfactory. In 1950 the Division was therefore reorganised so as to include three 'Staffing Departments', in each of which recruitment, promotions and postings of officers in particular branches of the Service are dealt with. A fourth department handled all questions of conditions of employment; and a fifth all general questions of recruitment and training. In 1954 this last department was abolished and training matters divided amongst the staffing departments. In the same year the Division was rechristened the Oversea Service Division.

RECENT DEVELOPMENTS

The changes in Office machinery which have been very briefly summarised were, of course, only a reflection of developments in the Colonial Service itself, and these in their turn were the reflection of political, social and economic developments in the territories.

The policy of unification was adopted in 1930 to meet conditions in which—leaving aside some of the older West Indian and other Colonies—the territories were in effect governed and staffed in the higher posts by civil servants drawn for the most part from the United Kingdom. The object of the unification scheme was to attract recruits of the best quality, and, having attracted them, to deploy them to the best advantage. The logical development from this beginning might have been the establishment of fully unified functional services, directed from the Colonial Office and employed on standard conditions. Such a development would not however have been possible in practice, whatever might have been said for it from the point of view of logic and pure efficiency. The progress of the territories towards self-government meant not only that the position of civil servants in the machinery of administration was changing, but that the public service of each country was tending to become really as well as nominally a self-contained and separate organisation. Moreover, the effect of educational and economic advancement was to produce an increasing number of locally-recruited public servants ready and able to work alongside of, and often to replace, the officials recruited from outside.

This was recognised in a statement of policy (Col. No. 197) issued after much deliberation in 1946 which, while rejecting the idea of a 'Secretary of State's Service', laid down some positive principles for the organisation of the post-war Colonial Service, and announced the allocation of substantial funds under the Colonial Development and Welfare Act for training purposes, including special arrangements for enabling candidates from the territories themselves to qualify for the higher posts. There remained, however, a dilemma. The territories still needed staffs recruited from outside on a scale four or five times that of pre-war recruitment. At the same time, political changes in some of the more important territories created uncertainty as to the future. This affected the morale of serving officers and the attractiveness of the service to recruits. Close study was given by the Colonial Office, in consultation with the oversea governments, to the possibility of providing some kind of guarantee which would allay these misgivings. The situation was eased by the statesmanlike attitude adopted by the political leaders in the Gold Coast and Nigeria towards the so-called 'expatriate' officers in those countries; and eventually, in June, 1954, a further statement of policy (Col. No. 306) was issued announcing the merging of the unified branches of the Colonial Service into a new organisation to be known as Her Majesty's Oversea Civil Service, with provision for safeguarding the interests of its members in the event of future political changes in the territories.

Meanwhile the old idea of a fully unified Service, based on the United Kingdom, from which officers could be lent out to oversea governments which might want them, has received influential public support in this country and the Government have not ruled out the possibility of some future development along these lines. Any such new Service would presumably have to be relatively small and consist largely of 'experts' in various fields if it were to offer a genuine prospect of a continuous career.

RECRUITMENT AND TRAINING

The responsibilities of the Secretary of State towards the public services of the territories flow from his general responsibility for good government. The nomination of persons to the higher appointments is retained in his hands not in order that he may find 'jobs for the boys' but in order that these key posts may be filled by impartial selection from the widest possible field of the persons who are best qualified for the work. There is everything to be said for appointing candidates of local origin to any posts which they are qualified to fill. But in most territories and most branches of the service there are not yet and cannot be for a long time enough of such candidates to go round. In 1953 a total of 1,227 first appointments to the Colonial Service was made by the Secretary of State. Most of these came from the United Kingdom, a few from other Commonwealth countries and the Irish Republic. The total included 108 administrative officers,

62 agriculturalists, 252 engineers, architects and town planners, 222 education officers, 133 doctors and dentists, 47 police, 43 surveyors, 36 veterinary surgeons, 50 barristers and solicitors, 21 geologists, 14 forestry officers, as well as smaller numbers of candidates qualified in broadcasting, civil aviation, civil defence, co-operatives, customs, fisheries, industrial relations, social welfare, statistics and other professions and activities. The total number of appointments made in 1954 was 1,135; and rather more than that number of vacancies were listed as 'unfilled' at the end of the year.

This was an average year's recruitment, with no very exceptional features. In practically every branch of the service more candidates could have been taken if enough of suitable quality had come forward. This recruitment undertaken by the Colonial Office is all in response to requests from the oversea governments, with whom it rests to decide whether to ask the Secretary of State to find candidates from outside. Most of the important territories now have their own Public Service Commissions which skim the local cream in the first place. And this recruitment is almost entirely for permanent and pensionable posts of superior status offering the prospect of a career. There is also a large amount of recruitment in the United Kingdom for sub-professional posts and for posts to be filled on temporary contract; this is carried out, not by the Colonial Office but mainly by the Crown Agents. In some cases the London representatives of the territorial governments undertake a certain amount of independent recruitment, and this practice is tending to increase.

A vacancy notified to the Secretary of State by a Governor may be in one of two categories. It may be a senior post which would represent promotion to someone in the service, and the Governor may or may not have a recommendation to make for filling it. The procedure for dealing with such vacancies will be described presently. Here we are considering the other kind of vacancy—that for which it is necessary to look for candidates from outside the service. These vacancies, also, fall into two categories. There are the regular branches of the service, recruitment for which is always going on; and there are special vacancies for which someone with definite qualifications and experience fitting him for a particular post has to be found. The latter naturally have to be dealt with by special advertisement or enquiry according to the nature of the case.

In the regular branches, the need is to keep public interest alive and to make sure that the existence and requirements of the service are continuously brought to the notice of possible candidates and those who advise them in the choice of careers. This is done partly by running advertisement of current vacancies in professional journals and the general press, but even more by close and constant contact between the staffing departments of the Colonial Office and the established sources of supply, such as universities, training colleges and professional institutions. To such places, as well as to individual enquirers, literature is circulated about the Service generally and about particular vacancies. There is a comprehensive booklet describing appointments in Her Majesty's Oversea Civil Service, which is brought up to date every year and contains full information about the various branches of the Service, the salaries, terms of employment, etc., and the living conditions in the territories. There is also an attractive illustrated booklet called *A Career in the Oversea Service*, originally written by Mr. Kenneth Bradley in 1950, and recently revised.

When a prospective candidate writes to or calls upon the Colonial Office, he is given—as might be expected—an application form, in which he has to give full details about himself, his parentage, education, experience and so on, accompanied by testimonials and the names of referees. The Staffing Department then proceeds to collect information about him from his referees and others who know him, and when this is complete he is usually asked to call for an interview. The first interview may be followed by another or by appearance before a board—either the Oversea Service Appointments Board itself or, if the post in question is a professional or technical one, a specially constituted board containing experts in the subject. There is no written examination, but the enquiries made about the candidate and the searching nature of the interviews, render such an examination unnecessary and amply safeguard the principle of open competition.

The final recommendation for the selection of a candidate rests with the Oversea Service Appointments Board and is signified by the Chairman of the Board, who, as stated above, is the First Civil Service Commissioner. When this recommendation has been made and has been formally accepted by or on behalf of the Secretary of State, the candidate is then sent an official 'offer' of the appointment for which he has been selected. If he accepts the offer, and has been passed as physically fit by one of the Colonial Office's Consulting Physicians, he may then have to attend a course of study before his selection is finally confirmed.

There are, today, fairly elaborate training schemes for most branches of the Oversea Service. It would be impossible in this chapter to give details of them all, and some general remarks must suffice. Different branches have different requirements. In some—for example the medical branch—the candidate has acquired his professional qualification before selection and requires only some special instruction in the adaptation of his skill to tropical colonial conditions. In other branches, a more extensive kind of training is needed. The Agricultural Branch has for many years depended on a system of probationerships, for which candidates are selected after attaining a degree in agriculture or other approved branch of natural science. During the two years of the probationership, they take a special course of post-graduate studies, usually at Cambridge and the Imperial College of Tropical Agriculture in Trinidad. A probationership system is also in force for the Forest Branch and for some legal appointments.

Training for the Administrative Branch presents some special problems, to which great attention has been paid since the first 'Tropical African Services Course' was instituted in 1909. During the second world war an authoritative Committee under the Chairmanship of the late Duke of Devonshire, then Parliamentary Under-Secretary of State, drew up what became known as the Devonshire Scheme. The basis of this scheme was that administrative cadets should attend, before going overseas, a 'first course' at Oxford, Cambridge or London, and then, after an 'apprentice tour', should return for a 'second course' at one of those universities. The second course would not be confined to administrative officers but would be taken by officers of all branches.

The courses were duly instituted, and the programme was followed as far as practicable. Experience showed, however, that the scheme needed some important modifications, and a new system was introduced in 1954 which in effect confined the first course (Oversea Services Course A) to Oxford and Cambridge, because the number of candidates now being recruited made division amongst three universities uneconomical. The second course (Oversea Services Course B) has been made selective, and includes better provision for officers who belong to the territories themselves; it is also designed to come somewhat later in the officer's career than the Devonshire Second Course as originally planned.

SECRETARY OF STATE'S RESPONSIBILITY FOR SERVING OFFICERS

When the candidate's selection has been finally confirmed, with or without his having completed a course before reaching that stage, the Crown Agents are asked to arrange his passage and the Governor of his territory is told of his selection and is asked to give him a letter of appointment on his arrival. For the Secretary of State's part in the procedure is limited to selection. The post to which the officer is appointed is a post in the service of the government of the territory, paid for from the territory's funds and subject to the territory's laws and regulations. The constitutional power of appointing persons to posts in the public service is vested in the Governor as the local representative of the Crown.

This does not, however, mean that, once the officer has received his appointment from the Governor, the Colonial Office ceases to be concerned with him. Although the Secretary of State is not the officer's employer, he necessarily retains an interest in the people whom he has recruited. He is responsible for seeing that the conditions which he has offered are observed by the employing government. He reserves to himself the decision on such questions as the dismissal or disciplinary punishment of officers who have been selected by him, and such officers have a right of appeal to him if they have a grievance. When officers come on leave, it is the Colonial Office which looks after any business requiring official decisions, though practical matters such as the booking of passages and the issue of pay are dealt with by the Crown Agents. But perhaps the most important aspect of the Secretary of State's interest, and the thing which above all justifies the claim that Her Majesty's Oversea Civil Service is a Service, and not just a collection of civil servants, is to be found in the work of filling senior appointments and arranging transfers.

This work is based upon the two-fold responsibility of the Secretary of State: his responsibility to the territories for seeing that they get the best possible men and women in their key posts; and his responsibility to the people whom he has recruited into the service, for seeing that they get full and impartial consideration for any avenues of advancement that are legitimately open to them. Therefore, Governors are required by the regulations to refer all vacancies above a certain level (which may vary from place to place) to the Secretary of State. They may, of course, recommend someone in the service of the territory to fill the vacancy and such a recommendation will naturally carry weight. But it is understood that the Secretary of State may select someone else, in which case the Governor will appoint that someone to the vacancy.

It is the task of the Staffing Departments to deal with the vacancies as they come in, to make a list of the possible candidates, to analyse their qualifications for the particular post and, in consultation with the geographical departments and—when applicable—the Secretary of State's Advisers, to submit proposals for consideration by higher authority. In order to do this, the Staffing Department must have as intimate a knowledge as possible of the officers in the branches of the Service with which it deals. This knowledge is acquired in several ways. First, there is the information on record about the officer when he was originally selected for appointment to the Service. Secondly, there are the annual confidential reports rendered by Governors. These basic data are supplemented wherever practicable by personal interviews with officers on leave, by observations made by members of the Colonial Office when on tour, by discussions with Governors and senior officers about their staffs and, when necessary, by special enquiries about individuals in relation to a particular post. It is remarkable how often the result of this reviewing of the 'field' is to produce a clear conclusion as to the name to be submitted for approval. Of course errors of judgment can be made, but if so they are at least honest errors.

CONDITIONS OF SERVICE

Between 1930 and 1939 the Personnel Division was largely engaged in establishing some settled principles governing the employment of officers in the Colonial Service, and especially of those officers—termed 'European' or 'expatriate'—recruited from outside the territories and mainly from the United Kingdom. Absolute standardisation of terms was not practicable, but a good deal of broad uniformity was achieved over questions of remuneration, pensions for officers and their dependants, leave and passages, medical care and so forth. For the most part, the principles laid down before 1945 hold good, but there is now less uniformity than before in the local application of some of those principles, and the tendency must inevitably be away from rather than towards standardisation.

Fluctuations in local costs of living and other conditions have obliged the territorial governments in recent years to revise their salaries and terms of employment at more or less frequent intervals, and it is quite uncertain whether stability has yet been reached. These revisions are sometimes carried out by local commissions or committees, but more often the Colonial Office is asked to find one or more experienced and impartial persons from outside the territory to investigate and report, either by themselves or in association with local representatives. The Colonial Office helps not only by finding the investigators but by putting at their disposal its experience and knowledge of the problems which they are invited to tackle and of the ways in which similar problems have been dealt with in other territories.

One field of operations which has to be centralised to some extent, and which calls for a specialist staff, is that concerning pensions. Pensions are never a simple matter, and in the present context they are bound to be exceptionally complicated. An officer on retirement may have served in two, three or more territories, each with its own pension laws; perhaps also in the home civil service or some other public service. If in addition to all this he has become a Governor, there is a separate series of Acts of Parliament which apply to his case; for Governors' pensions are paid from the home Exchequer and not from territorial funds. Elaborate arrangements, based on a scheme started in 1928, exist for determining and sharing out the pension of an officer with 'mixed' service. To operate this scheme and generally to keep an eye on the whole complex pension system, including the many and various Widows' and Orphans' Pensions Schemes, is one of the larger tasks of the Oversea Service Division.

Another subject calling for central handling is discipline. The Colonial Regulations—which, as mentioned in Chapter VIII, have existed in various forms since 1837 as a code of rules laid down by the Secretary of State for the guidance of Governors—prescribe in detail the procedure which must be followed before any civil servant in the oversea territories can be dismissed or otherwise punished. Here again the advice of a staff with experience and knowledge of decisions previously taken in comparable circumstances is needed in order to ensure proper safeguarding of the respective interests of the public service and of the individual. In most cases reference to the Secretary of State's Legal Advisers is also involved.

Another general subject dealt with centrally in the Oversea Service Division is that of honours. Recommendations for the grant of honours to persons in the territories are initiated by the Governors, but it is the Secretary of State who decides which names out of those recommended are to be submitted to the Sovereign. The Chancery of the Order of St. Michael and St. George is located in the Colonial Office. This Order, originally founded in 1818 with special reference to Malta and the Ionian Islands (then under British protection), has for many years been available for the recognition of services to the Crown in connection with Commonwealth and foreign affairs. To-day the Foreign and Commonwealth Relations Offices, as well as the Colonial Office, have each a certain quota of appointments in the Order, and some also are available to the Prime Minister for the recognition of services not assignable to any one of the three Offices. The Permanent Under-Secretary in the Colonial Office is *ex officio* Secretary of the Order.

UNOFFICIAL ACTIVITIES

This chapter would be incomplete without reference to some important unofficial activities sponsored by the Colonial Office for the benefit of the Oversea Service.

The Corona Club was founded in 1900 by Mr. Joseph Chamberlain for the purpose of organising an annual dinner in London for past and present members of the Colonial Service, the Colonial Office and associated official bodies. The dinners have been held in unbroken succession (except for unavoidable intervals during the two world wars) ever since. The 1954 dinner—the last, presumably, to be called the 'Colonial Service' Dinner—was the 44th of the series. By tradition the Secretary of State for the time being presides: there have been only two occasions on which, in his unavoidable absence, the Parliamentary Under-Secretary of State took his place. There is only one speech, in which the Secretary of State proposes the health of the Club.

The Corona Club Dinner is a masculine affair, and no guests are admitted. A parallel organisation—the Women's Corona Club—was founded in 1937 for women members of the Colonial Service and for the wives of male officers. In 1950 this Club—which in 1953 changed its name to Women's Corona Society—expanded its activities far beyond the original idea of providing an annual social gathering. It aims now to help the wives of Oversea Service Officers with their educational and family problems; to arrange introductory courses and personal contacts for women going overseas for the first time; to extend hospitality and help to members from overseas, especially those who visit England for the first time; and generally to foster a tradition of voluntary social service and to act as a link between its oversea members and the voluntary organisations in the United Kingdom.

The name *Corona* has also been given to a monthly magazine started by the Colonial Office in 1949 as 'the Journal of His Majesty's Colonial Service.' *Corona* is published for the Colonial Office by H.M. Stationery Office and is edited by a retired officer of the Oversea Service. Its objects are to keep members of the Service in touch with events in other territories and at home, to provide a topical background to their work, and to give them a forum for the exchange of ideas, experiences and information. It also enables retired members of the Service, and any of the general public who are interested enough to buy or read it, to keep abreast of current developments in the oversea territories.

Finally, it would be fitting here to make some reference to the Rajah of Sarawak Fund. One of the most serious items of expenditure which has to be faced by an oversea civil servant whose home is in the United Kingdom is that of his children's education. In most cases it is unavoidable that they should be sent to boarding school at home, and the cost of education and maintenance for an officer with two or three children of school age is very heavy. Many territories indeed take this into account in fixing salaries and allowances, and some officers are able to obtain assistance by way of grants and scholarships. The Colonial Office makes it its business to see that oversea officers receive any benefits for which they may be eligible under United Kingdom legislation. There are, however, always hard cases, especially when the breadwinner's career is cut short by illness or death.

To meet such hard cases, H.H. the Rajah of Sarawak has established, by two successive benefactions, a capital fund, the income of which is administered by trustees, secretarial services being provided by the Colonial Office. Within the conditions laid down in the trust, the Oversea Service, or to their widows, towards the educational expenses of their children.

CHAPTER XII

Economic Development and Finance

GROWING MOMENTUM OF ASSISTANCE

AS was observed in Chapter II, the active stimulation of economic and social development in the Colonies by the Home Government is a growth of the last quarter of a century. Up till then, the prevailing doctrine was that Colonial Governments must be financially self-supporting, save in cases where the budget could not provide even the bare necessities of administration; in which case grants-in-aid, involving detailed control of the Colony's expenditure by the Home Government, were made on an annual computation of strict need. Commercial development was left to private enterprise: social development was limited by local financial resources. Those territories progressed which had easily developed resources; some of them, such as Malaya, attained considerable prosperity. But the rest lagged behind, there being no means of 'priming the pump'.

The enactment, in 1929, at a time of serious unemployment in Great Britain, of the Colonial Development Act first broke new ground by creating a Colonial Development Fund of £1,000,000 a year 'to aid and develop agriculture and industry in the Colonies thereby promoting commerce with and industry in the United Kingdom.' Admittedly this Act had many limitations. Colonial development even by then was not conceived as an end in itself but as a means of helping to alleviate unemployment at home. The structure of the Fund tended inevitably to a 'project by project' approach and did not permit any long-term planning. Moreover there was no provision for social development or scientific research as such. Nevertheless, it enabled many important developments to take place, for example the construction of the Lower Zambesi Bridge to provide an outlet for Nyasaland to Beira, and the opening up of the iron ore resources at Marampa in Sierra Leone. It was, too, a boon to some of the poorer Colonies in a host of schemes small in themselves but of great local importance. Most important, however, it did for the first time establish the principle of grants for development as distinct from deficiency grants-in-aid.

The next stage, which, as has been seen, followed from recommendations made by the Royal Commission on the West

Indies, was the enactment in 1940 of the first Colonial Development and Welfare Act which for the first time made money available for Colonial development, welfare and scientific research as ends in themselves. At this time, the British Commonwealth was in the early stages of a long and devastating war. As the war went on, it became more and more important to increase the production in the oversea territories both of the raw materials and foodstuffs needed by the Allied countries and of the essential foods needed by the populations of the territories themselves. The Colonial Office had to be expanded and adapted to inspire and to co-ordinate a vast all-round effort and to act as a link between the oversea territories and the British and allied organisations concerned with the control of trade and the procurement of supplies.

But in spite of immediate preoccupations, the future was not overlooked. It was realised that when (no one thought 'if') the war was won, the policy of development would have to go forward with increasing momentum. As much time and effort as could be spared was put into planning for the post-war years.

COLONIAL DEVELOPMENT AND WELFARE ACTS

The Colonial Development and Welfare Act of 1940 provided for a maximum expenditure of £5,000,000 a year for ten years on schemes of economic and social development, as well as £500,000 a year for research. Later, the currency of the Act was extended and the total funds increased, first to £120,000,000 and later to £140,000,000 for the ten-year period due to end on 31st March, 1956. A new Act passed early in 1955 provided for a further £80,000,000 which, with the unspent balance of £40,000,000 still remaining under the previous Act, made a total of £120,000,000 available up to 1960.

The purpose of the original provision was to enable the territorial governments to draw up balanced long-term development plans of their own, in the knowledge that substantial Exchequer assistance would be available for approved schemes which could not be fully financed from local resources. A request to the oversea governments to prepare ten-year plans was sent out by the Secretary of State in 1945, and the following years were largely taken up in the compilation, negotiation and final settlement of these plans. In this work the Secretary of State was assisted both by his permanent Advisers (including for a time the late Sir Frank Stockdale as Adviser on Development Planning) and also by a Colonial Economic and Development Council, which was appointed in 1946 and was dissolved, on the completion of its work, in 1951.

The development plans, which were not, of course, rigid and irrevocable but constantly reviewed and brought up to date, covered both economic and social services, for the two must needs go hand in hand. On the economic side, the plans were not intended to deal with what are usually termed 'commercial projects'. The emphasis in most territories was naturally on the improvement of agriculture and animal husbandry and on the opening up of communications. On the welfare side, health and educational services were in the fore-front. The scale of the plans varies very greatly. The Gold Coast plan is for expenditure of over £81 million, that of Tanganyika for over £24 million, that of British Guiana for £14½ million, that of Seychelles for £325,000.

A certain part of the funds was reserved for use by the Secretary of State on centrally organised schemes. From this source money has been found for higher education, the training of public officers, the promotion of broadcasting, topographical and geological surveys, the welfare of colonial students and other activities of value to the territories as a whole.

In 1948 there was also established the Colonial Development Corporation, which is 'charged with the duty of securing the investigation, formulation and carrying out of projects for developing resources of Colonial territories.' It has power to borrow up to £110 million from the Exchequer. The Corporation was created not to supplant but to supplement private commercial enterprise. Its purpose is complementary to that of the Colonial Development and Welfare Acts, which provide assistance in those fields of economic development which are a matter of government activity.

ECONOMIC ORGANISATION IN THE COLONIAL OFFICE

The new impetus given to economic development and the increasing need for co-ordinating Colonial economic policy with world economic policy, and in particular with that of the United Kingdom and the rest of the Sterling Area, has led to a considerable expansion in the administrative work of the Colonial Office on the economic side, which is now grouped in an Economic Division. The work of this division is closely integrated but four main aspects can be distinguished.

One important branch of the work is concerned with what the Colonies require from outside, for example financial assistance, technical advice and, especially during the war and in the years immediately following it, help in procuring necessary supplies of capital and consumer goods. Closely related with this branch of the work is the control of foreign exchange.

The second main branch of the work is concerned with what comes out of the Colonies, that is to say, the production and marketing of Colonial produce. Thirdly, there is work connected with commercial treaties, customs and tariff questions. Fourthly, there is scientific research.

The Office arrangements for dealing with these aspects of economic work are varied from time to time to correspond with fluctuations in the relative importance of different subjects. General questions of development policy are handled in an Economic General Department, which also has a wide field of activity in connection with the numerous international and inter-Commonwealth bodies which, under a variety of initials, survey, discuss and co-ordinate the economic problems of the world. In this part of the Office is provided the link between the British oversea territories and the American and other schemes for technical assistance. Here also is the Office link with the Colonial Development Corporation. A small staff of economists in this department reviews and analyses the trend of economic progress in the territories. Statistics are looked after by a separate department of the Economic Division under a Chief Statistician; its work, though largely on the economic side, is concerned also with demography and social services.

Questions of international trade, commercial treaties and trade agreements, tariffs and customs (including the General Agreement on Tariffs and Trade—G.A.T.T.) are now dealt with in a Commercial Relations and Supplies Department. With progressive relaxation of controls, the procurement of supplies is no longer the major problem for the Colonial Office which it was during and for some time after the war, but there is still a good deal of work in connection with Exchange Control, which affects the import programmes of the territories.

PRODUCTION AND MARKETING

The purpose of economic development is, in a word, trade. The peoples of the territories cannot improve or even maintain their standards of life except by producing goods which the rest of the world is prepared to buy and to exchange for the things that the territories cannot produce or make for themselves.

An important part, therefore, of the functions of the Colonial Office is to help the territories to help themselves by developing their trade. This means the provision of advice and assistance in various ways. In this matter as in others, the primary responsibility lies with the government of the territory to see that the resources of the country are developed and exploited by public or private enterprise for the benefit of the inhabitants. But to a greater or less extent most governments need to lean upon a central organisation which can help in answering, from a broader experience, the many questions which challenge the planner and administrator in relating the productive potentialities of a country to the needs of the possible markets for its products. It is useless to stimulate production of an article that is not wanted or cannot be sold at a profitable price. It is equally useless to stimulate demand for a product and then fail to supply it at a price which the consumer can pay.

The Colonial Office acts, then, as a central organisation for helping the oversea governments to determine what kinds of production should be encouraged and how that encouragement can best be given, and to assess the potential demands of the markets and the factors, such as quality and grading, which affect the marketability of products. The main part of this work falls upon two Production and Marketing Departments. The commodities with which this work is concerned can be divided into agricultural products (foodstuffs and others), and the products of fisheries, forests and mines. The main foodstuffs produced in the territories for export, as has been seen in the geographical chapters, include oilseeds and vegetable oils, sugar, cocoa, fruit, coffee and tea. Other agricultural produce includes cotton, fibres, tobacco and rubber. The markets for many of these products are affected by international considerations, sometimes through specific commodity agreements (for instance, sugar and, prospectively, tin), or by quota systems. Wherever such complications arise, it is the task of the Colonial Office to provide a link between the oversea producers and Governments and the Departments of the United Kingdom Government which are concerned with the external relations of this country. In the general stimulation of production, the improvement of quality and quantity, and the promotion of better marketing methods, the Secretary of State's Advisers on Agriculture, Animal Health, Forestry, Fisheries and Co-operation have important parts to play.

The mineral resources of the territories include bauxite, copper, diamonds, gold, iron ore, manganese, petroleum and tin. The work connected with these includes the provision of advice on questions of mineral royalties and mining taxation.

COMMUNICATIONS

Since the Colonial territories depend upon oversea trade, the provision of communications is vital to their interests. Roads and railways must be constructed and maintained to link the areas of production with the seaports. There must be harbours at which ships can be loaded and unloaded in safety; and there must be arrangements with the shipping companies to ensure that the ships come and go.

Before the era of Colonial Development and Welfare the provision of roads, railways and harbours depended upon the ability of the territories to meet the costs from revenue, either directly or by the servicing of loans. Some assistance was available, on conditions, under the Colonial Development Act of 1929, and the United Kingdom Government also helped, on occasion, by guaranteeing the interest on loans. In most territories, however, the development possible in these circumstances fell far short of the needs and potentialities of the country, and it is not surprising that a large part of the development plans which have been put into operation with assistance provided under the Colonial Development and Welfare Acts since 1940 has been devoted to the extension and improvement of internal communications and of ports and harbours. In practically all territories the roads, railways and harbours have been constructed and maintained by the government. The modern tendency, however, is to separate railway and harbour administration from direct management by government and to entrust it to statutory corporations.

The conveyance of goods about, out of and into a territory is, of course, only one of the essential functions which are performed by communications. The postal, telegraph and telephone services are a necessity for the conduct of business, the social progress of the community and the working of the government organisation. Ships, railways and road transport convey not only goods but mails and passengers. So, to an ever-increasing extent, do the civil aviation services, the modern development of which is perhaps the most revolutionary single factor in the Colonial world of to-day. Except for a few of the remote territories, such as St. Helena, Seychelles and the Falkland Islands, all the Colonial territories are now linked directly or indirectly with the United Kingdom and other parts of the world by main trunk-route air services; and in the larger territories there are also internal airlines run by private enterprise with government support. Places which a few years ago were far off the beaten track are to-day great international airline junctions and the scene of a large and growing commercial and tourist traffic.

In the Colonial Office, the work arising out of all this activity is centred in the Communications Department, which is not actually included in the Economic Division, though it can most conveniently be considered in this chapter. The department deals with what are barbarously called telecommunications, mails, stamp issues, international postal and telegraph matters, and also with shipping services, shipping agreements and motor transport legislation. The greater part of its work, however, is concerned with civil aviation and all the administrative, international, legal and technical questions involved in this field of activity.

FINANCE

The administration of the Colonial Development and Welfare

Acts is only a part, though an important part, of the financial work. The functions and activities of the Colonial Office in the financial sphere are unlike those of any other government department. The Colonial Office is neither a revenue-producing Department nor in the ordinary sense a spending Department. The total annual turnover of revenue and expenditure (including expenditure on development) in the territories with which the Office is concerned was in 1954 of the order of £400,000,000 (compared with about £60,000,000 at the beginning of the second world war). The great bulk of this revenue is obtained by local taxation imposed by the laws of the territories, and the expenditure is voted by the territorial legislatures. The Colonial Office is directly concerned only with that part of this expenditure which is financed from the United Kingdom either out of Colonial Development and Welfare Funds or out of grants in aid of administration made to territories which are unable, without such assistance, to balance their budgets. These grants, and certain other payments, are borne on the Colonial Services Vote. (It ought not to be necessary to mention, but perhaps it should be stated in case any reader should be under any misapprehension, that the United Kingdom does not impose any kind of taxation or tribute upon the Colonial territories.)

In the main, therefore, the financial work of the Colonial Office is supervisory; the degree of supervision varies in practice according to the political advancement and financial stability of particular territories from time to time, the general tendency being towards a progressive relaxation of control as territories become more self-sufficient. The kind of detailed financial control exercised in the old days, as described in Chapter VIII, has long since fallen into disuse.

This supervisory financial work is obviously bound up with the general political and administrative responsibilities of the Secretary of State, and is therefore primarily a matter for the several geographical departments of the Office, the role of the Finance Department being to supply advice and assistance when called upon.

It is indeed only in recent years that the Colonial Office has felt the need to have a Finance Department as such. The actual disbursement of money voted by Parliament by way of salaries, office expenses, grants to oversea governments and so forth, the preparation of Estimates and the necessary bookkeeping connected with these transactions has always been and still is dealt with in an Accounts Department (or Branch, as it is now called) under a high-ranking Executive Officer, known as the Accountant. (For a time this post was designated Chief Accountant, but this no longer obtains.) The Accounts Branch is concerned with the correct application of policy decisions, but these decisions, and the necessary negotiations leading to them, were, until the end of the second world war, matters for whichever department of the Office happened to be involved. This arrangement was suitable to days in which administration was less complex than today, but the dispersal of responsibility became inconvenient both to the Colonial Office and to the Treasury as United Kingdom funds became more deeply committed.

The Finance Department is now the main channel of correspondence and discussion with the Treasury on all matters involving United Kingdom finance in relation to the Colonial territories. Such matters include, of course, business connected with the Colonial Development and Welfare Vote, but also provisions made in the Colonial Services Vote for grants in aid of oversea governments and various institutions and authorities. The Finance Department also deals with and co-ordinates proposals put forward by the oversea governments, for raising loans on the London Market or from the International Bank, and its work covers, too, a variety of general financial subjects, such as currency, banking and taxation.

The Accounts Branch which, as already stated, handles the actual financial transactions, including the administration of the Vote for the Colonial Office itself, is part of the Finance Department.

ADVISORY AND RESEARCH SERVICES

It is obvious that many of the subjects dealt with in the Economic Division call for the application of the best available scientific and professional advice. In general, some distinction can be drawn between questions on which advice is needed for the formation of policy or the solution of immediate practical problems, and those which call for research or fundamental investigation.

The first organised arrangement for securing advice on any economic aspect of Colonial policy was the constitution, in 1929, of the Colonial Advisory Council of Agriculture and Animal Health. Its functions were enlarged in 1943 to include forestry. A Fisheries Advisory Committee was constituted in 1943, and an Advisory Committee on Co-operation in 1947. To these, as to the many other standing advisory bodies associated with the Colonial Office, the foremost experts in the subjects concerned generously contribute the weight of their wisdom and experience.

In their early stages these Councils and Committees dealt with all aspects of their subject. As time went on, the fields covered became too great to be satisfactorily handled by single bodies, and a separate series of Committees was established to deal with research matters and specialised aspects of the work. The general bodies mentioned above are usually presided over by a Minister, but the specialist and research bodies are usually presided over by an expert in the subject, or sometimes by a senior official of the Colonial Office. The range of these special bodies is very wide. In addition to those concerned with social services, which will be considered later, there is a Committee for Colonial Agricultural, Animal Health and Forestry Research (with a professional Secretary), founded in 1945; a Colonial Economic Research Committee, founded in 1947; and an Advisory Committee on Colonial Geology and Mineral Resources, constituted in 1949. Other bodies deal with such varied subjects as the mechanisation of agriculture; insecticides, fungicides and herbicides; and the scientific investigations in the Falkland Islands Dependencies.

Another important organisation is the Colonial Products Council, which exercises a general oversight over a Colonial Products Laboratory. The purpose of this organisation is to consider how, by the application of research, greater use can be made of the plant and animal products of the territories, and to advise on what raw materials produced overseas are of most use to the manufacturing industries and on the scientific work needed for the development of these products. The laboratory, which is under a Director of Colonial Products Research, carries out tests of raw materials and supplies information about them to industrial concerns.

All these research activities, together with those on the social service side, which will be mentioned in the next chapter, come under the general aegis of a Colonial Research Council which is presided over by a Minister and consists of the Chairmen of the various specialised research committees. The Council advises the Secretary of State on research policy generally, and in particular on the allocation of Colonial Development and Welfare Research Funds amongst the various branches of research, and co-ordinates the work of the specialist bodies. The administrative work in the Colonial Office·is dealt with by the Research Department, the head of which is Secretary to the Council.

Much of the actual research work overseas is carried out by governments or by official organisations. The staffs engaged in this work constitute what used to be called the Colonial Research Service and is now the Research Branch of H.M. Oversea Civil Service.

The provision of advice on geological surveys is dealt with in a separate specialist Directorate, the Head of which is Adviser to the Secretary of State on all geological survey matters. The Directorate of Colonial (Geodetic and Topographical) Surveys is likewise a separate specialist organisation, the Director of which is also the Secretary of State's Adviser on his subject. This organisation is notable as being the only part of the Office which carries out direct operations on a large scale in the oversea territories. It is responsible, in general terms, for the mapping of the territories, both for general geographical purposes and for various special needs. The field staff, working in collaboration with the territorial survey departments, employs both ground survey techniques and photography. In the latter it is helped by the Royal Air Force and by commercial air services. The work overseas is directed from the headquarters at Tolworth, in Surrey, where the resulting maps are prepared and produced.

Advice on engineering matters generally is given by the Engineer-in-Chief at the Crown Agents' Office; and the Secretary of State enjoys the services of a distinguished consultant as part-time Adviser on Drainage and Irrigation.

CHAPTER XIII

Social Development

HEALTH

ECONOMIC development is a means to an end, or rather, as Lord
Lugard pointed out many years ago, to a double end. The world
needs the things that the oversea territories can produce. The territories must do their part in supplying the needs of other members of
the world community; and it is on the proceeds of their production
that they must rely to make themselves self-supporting and to improve
the welfare and standard of living of their peoples. But social services do not only follow from economic prosperity: they are needed
beforehand in order that economic prosperity may be made possible.
Without a basic minimum of health, educational and other welfare
services a people starting from primitive conditions cannot within
any reasonable time generate the necessary momentum to enable itself
to overcome its handicap. And so, from the inauguration of the
'forward policy' in 1940 onwards, development and welfare have
gone together.

Before 1940, the role of the Colonial Office was to supply advice
and guidance, but, apart from the very limited assistance available
under the 1929 Colonial Development Act, what could be done
depended upon the resources of the territories themselves. The passing
of the Colonial Development and Welfare Acts enabled financial
assistance to be given for educational and health services, housing,
water supplies, broadcasting and numerous other activities in the
realm of social welfare. The administrative and advisory machinery of
the Colonial Office itself was expanded so that the Office could play
its part in the general effort. Some aspects of the work were already
being dealt with and there were foundations on which to build; but
the rapid social development of the territories brought into
prominence many new questions to which the Office had never before
had occasion to pay much attention.

Amongst the old-established subjects medicine and public health
claim first mention. Serious interest in tropical medicine dates at
least from the beginning of this century when the Schools at London
and Liverpool were founded with the active support of the Colonial
Office. Quite naturally, that interest was chiefly inspired by concern
for the health of British officials, missionaries, traders, soldiers and

sailors whose callings took them to the 'white man's grave'. The government medical officers first appointed to serve in the oversea territories were sent out with the primary purpose of looking after their European brethren. But the study of the causes and cures of tropical diseases necessarily brought the doctors into touch with the indigenous populations who soon became the object of both professional interest and humane concern. From early days in West Africa and also, as time went on, in East Africa, Malaya and elsewhere, the conception became established of a state medical service whose members were civil servants paid a salary by government and charged with the care of the health—so far as their numbers and resources would allow—of the general population. Recognition of the importance of health services became a firm tradition both in the Colonial Office and in the territorial administrations. In maintaining and strengthening this tradition the Secretary of State's Advisory Committee of medical experts gave powerful support. This was reinforced by the appointment to the Office of a Chief Medical Adviser in 1926.

It is not often possible to define phases in the constantly evolving pattern of relationship between the Colonial Office and the oversea territories. But in the medical sphere as in others the picture today is different from that of, say, twenty years ago. The formative stage of policy, in which the Colonial Office was for a long time deeply concerned, has passed. General principles are now established. The territorial medical departments proceed under their own steam. Yet this does not mean less, but more, work at the centre. The advice needed may be more specific and less general, but it is still needed. The Secretary of State's advisers (now consisting of a Chief Medical Officer, a Deputy, a Principal Medical Officer, a Director of Colonial Medical Research, a part-time Consultant on Tuberculosis, and a Chief Nursing Officer) not only have much to do at headquarters but must spend much time in touring the territories and discussing problems on the spot. (A valuable reinforcement was for some years provided by the Nuffield Foundation in financing visits to oversea territories by eminent consultants in various specialities.) The medical advisory staff also have to take part, on behalf of the territories, in the activities of the World Health Organisation and other general bodies.

The Colonial Advisory Medical Committee remains in being for general purposes, but research matters have been dealt with since 1945 in the Colonial Medical Research Committee, which is appointed by and advisory to the Secretary of State jointly with the Medical Research Council. A specialist body called the Tsetse Fly and Trypanosomiasis Committee advises on the many problems connected

F

with the human and animal manifestations of the disease commonly known as sleeping sickness. Another body appointed by the Secretary of State and serviced by the Colonial Office is the Managing Committee of the Bureau of Hygiene and Tropical Diseases. The Office is closely associated with, though not responsible for, the work of such societies as the British Empire Leprosy Relief Association and the British Empire Society for the Blind; it also takes an active interest in the doings of the London and Liverpool Schools of Tropical Medicine and of the Tropical Diseases Hospital in London, which, under the National Health Service, is a self-contained unit forming part of the University College Hospital group.

The work of the Consulting Physicians to the Colonial Office should be mentioned here. Before the term 'medical adviser' acquired its modern sense, the Colonial Office employed under that title distinguished private practitioners with tropical experience, for the purpose of examining candidates for appointment and officers on leave. There were generally two in London and one each at Edinburgh, Liverpool, Belfast and Dublin. The system still obtains, except that the doctors are now called Consulting Physicians and one of the London men is a whole-time officer with rooms in the Colonial Office building. The Consulting Physicians not only carry out an essential official function but are able to give much valued personal help to oversea officers who are in need of medical care when they come to this country.

EDUCATION

Next to health in order of traditional importance comes education. Until comparatively lately the provision of education in the oversea territories was largely left to private enterprise and missionary endeavour. In Tropical Africa especially, it was the missionary societies who laid the foundations of the modern educational services. In the 1920s, governments began to take a hand, both by giving financial support to the mission schools and by setting up State educational institutions. Inspiration, guidance and co-ordination in promoting progressive educational developments at first in Africa and from 1929 onwards in all the territories were provided by an Advisory Committee. This Committee had two distinguished educationists as joint Secretaries, who were paid from funds contributed by the Colonial governments.

In 1940, as part of the new Development and Welfare machinery, an Educational Adviser was appointed to the Office staff. Later, he was provided with a deputy and a team of assistants—one a woman and one an expert in technical education.

Although, up to the outbreak of the second world war, the main problem in most territories was to establish the groundwork of primary and secondary education, it was always recognised that provision for higher education must be made as soon as the conditions necessary for success had been created. Between 1943 and 1945 three important Commissions were at work. As a result of their labours, and with the help of funds provided under the Colonial Development and Welfare Acts, it was decided to set up University Colleges in the West Indies, West Africa, and East Africa (later, also, in Central Africa) and a University in Malaya. (Universities already existed in Malta and Hong Kong.) These Universities and University Colleges are autonomous bodies, enjoying academic freedom as in this country. In this effort the powerful co-operation of the British Universities was secured, and an Inter-University Council and a Colonial University Grants Advisory Committee were set up. These bodies are concerned with Colonial Universities and University Colleges: a separate advisory body deals with the problems of technical education and the Colonial Colleges of Arts, Science and Technology which have so far been set up in West and East Africa.

At the other end of the educational scale is what is variously known as Mass Education, Fundamental Education and Community Development. Much attention has been given during and since the war to the problems of illiteracy and popular ignorance both in the African territories and in other Colonies, notably in Jamaica. Development has been stimulated and assisted not only by the Colonial Office but also by U.N.E.S.C.O. A Mass Education Sub-Committee of the Advisory Committee on Education in the Colonies was constituted as a separate advisory body in 1949. In 1953 it was merged in a new Committee as recorded in the next section.

SOCIAL WELFARE

One of the difficulties with which the Colonial Office has had to contend within the last quarter-century of rapid social development is that of sorting out a complex collection of related activities into a workable system of division of labour. Inevitably there has been much trial and some error, but at least the need for flexibility has been kept in mind.

It became clear early in the late war that there were a number of fields of social welfare which were becoming important (or, it would perhaps be better to say, were becoming acknowledged to be important) but fell outside the scope of existing machinery.

The accepted organisation of government departments was not equipped to deal with such problems as the provision of youth services or the creation and development of positive measures to counteract the effects of detribalisation and drift away from the countryside to towns and seaports. In 1937, the Secretary of State had set up a Committee on Penal Administration. This body went into the subject of juvenile delinquency, and produced a report in which it pointed out that the study of the treatment of offenders could not be divorced from an examination of the general social background. It was then decided, in 1943, to set up a Social Welfare Advisory Committee to help the Colonial Office and Colonial Governments in dealing with the social welfare problems of urban and rural communities and the training of social workers. Penal administration questions were entrusted to a sub-committee of this body, which, in 1952, was separated and constituted the Advisory Committee on the Treatment of Offenders in the Colonies. The Social Welfare Committee produced a basic document of guidance on policy in which stress was laid on the importance of positive and constructive as well as of purely remedial action and on the need to integrate in a coherent scheme both official efforts and the often excellent but unco-ordinated work of religious and other voluntary organisations. A full-time Social Welfare Adviser was added to the Office staff in 1947. In 1953 it was agreed that a rearrangement of advisory services and terms of reference would be advantageous, and the Social Welfare Committee was amalgamated with the Mass Education (Community Development) Committee under the title of the Advisory Committee on Social Development in the Colonies. In August, 1954, the Colonial Office convened at Ashridge a conference of civil servants from a wide range of territories and representing many aspects of social service work. The purpose of the conference was to exchange ideas and experience on social development generally.

The social no less than the natural sciences rest upon the foundation of research. The task of advising on research in this field in relation to the oversea territories was entrusted in 1944 to a Colonial Social Science Research Council. Standing Committees on Anthropology and Sociology, History and Administration, Law (including Land Tenure), Linguistics and the training of research staffs have been set up under the aegis of the Council. The Colonial Office also has a Local Government Advisory Panel, a Native Law Advisory Panel and an Adviser on Housing and Building Research. The subject of local government organisation is one of particular interest and importance in a large number of the territories under modern conditions. It has been the policy of successive Secretaries of State to foster the development of local government institutions wherever possible as a training ground and a basis for the development of sound and responsible democratic government at the centre. In this they have had most valuable co-operation from local authorities in the United Kingdom, who have been generous both in accepting

Colonial staffs for training and in sparing their own officers to go out and advise. Special attention has been paid to this subject by the African Studies Branch of the Colonial Office; but the problem is by no means confined to Africa, and the Secretary of State welcomed the assistance of the Royal Institute of Public Administration in organising a large-scale conference covering all territories, which was held at Cambridge in 1955.

LABOUR

The remaining major sphere of social services is that affecting labour and industrial relations. Though there are some exceptions, such as Hong Kong and Singapore, the economy of most of the territories is based on agriculture conducted very largely by peasant farmers. In some places, recent years have seen a rapid development of small-scale secondary industries, but it is broadly true that, except in the mines of Africa and Malaya and some other places, there is no great amount of full-time paid employment apart from transport and public utilities, which are usually run by government. On the other hand, there is a great deal of part-time and seasonal employment, and the whole picture is very complex.

During the last twenty-five years, labour questions have demanded and received increasing attention by the Colonial governments and in the Colonial Office. Development has been along two complementary lines: one is the enactment of legislation, in forms suitable to current local circumstances, for the regulation of working conditions and the protection of the interests of workers; such legislation is often based upon the conventions produced by the International Labour Office. The other line of development is the creation of supervisory machinery for handling the practical problems of relationship between employers and employed.

An early step in the provision of a central organisation was the appointment of a Labour Adviser to the Secretary of State in 1938. Later a second post was added, and for a time there was a third, occupied by a woman Assistant Adviser. A Colonial Labour Advisory Committee, including representatives of the Trades Union Congress, the British Employers' Confederation and the Overseas Employers Federation, as well as other experts, was set up in 1941.

Successive Secretaries of State, with the help of their official and unofficial advisers, have been active in promoting the development of healthy trade unionism in the oversea territories. Guidance has been given from the centre about legislation providing for the proper conduct of trade unions, for the establishment of wage-fixing, conciliation and arbitration machinery, for workmen's compensation, for the inspection of labour conditions, and for the carrying out of obligations accepted under International Labour Conventions.

At the same time, the territories have been encouraged and supported in creating efficient labour departments. The Trades Union Congress has helped very greatly both by finding experienced trade union officials to join the oversea labour departments in an executive or advisory capacity, and by training and counselling the local leaders of the emerging trade unions in the territories themselves.

It would be too much to expect that industrial troubles can be entirely avoided in all the territories at all times. Disputes do occur, leading sometimes to strikes, accompanied occasionally by outbreaks of violence and disorder. These troubles have to be dealt with when they arise; that they are less frequent and less serious than they might otherwise be is due to the patient work of many people, both official and unofficial, in the territories themselves and in this country. And this does not mean only the people immediately concerned with labour questions, but all the people whose work has been touched upon in this and the previous chapter, as well as those charged with responsibility for general administration. For industrial relations cannot be considered apart from the social and economic background, nor can social progress and economic development be separated from one another.

What is happening to-day in the British oversea territories can fairly be described as a social revolution. It was bound to come, and he would be a bold prophet who would undertake to predict the end of it. The question which faced the British and Colonial governments in the years between the wars was whether the revolution should be left to work itself out by the interplay of natural forces or whether some effort should be made to guide and control it. The crucial decision of 1939-40 was to intervene positively with the powerful tool of financial assistance on a significant scale. This made it possible to forestall discontent by keeping achievement in step with aspiration, and to ensure that the developments which must in any event come about should as far as possible be in directions most advantageous to the best interests of the peoples concerned and of the Commonwealth as a whole.

CHAPTER XIV

Laws and Constitutions

THE LEGAL ADVISERS

A LAYMAN must approach the subject of the Legal Division's work in the Colonial Office with humility and diffidence. But no one, however lacking in legal training, can serve for any time in the Office or in the oversea territories without realising the fundamental importance of law in the whole system of government. The British conception of government is indeed based upon the rule of law and every act of administration is the law in action.

From the earliest days of British colonisation, authority to make laws was conferred upon the Crown's representative in the new settlements, and provision was made for some body of citizens to be associated with him in the enactment of legislation. I quote from the Colonial Regulations of 1843:

> In every Colony belonging to the Crown there is a local Legislature authorised to make laws for the peace, order and good government of the Colony, such laws not being repugnant to the laws of England.
> In every Colony the Governor is a component and indispensable member and branch of the local Legislature.
> In all Colonies laws are in some cases passed with suspending clauses; that is, although assented to by the Governor, they do not come into operation or take effect in the Colony, until they shall have been specially confirmed and finally enacted by Her Majesty.
> No law can be passed in any Colony which The Queen may not subsequently disallow. . . . .

These passages give the clue to one of the original and essential functions of the Colonial Office, namely the examination of legislation enacted in the territories. The enactment of laws is the business of the local Legislature, however constituted. But the Crown has to be advised whether the laws so enacted are or are not repugnant to an Act of Parliament, or to an Order in Council or other instrument issued under an Act of Parliament, since any legislation so repugnant is void. If the laws in question have been reserved for the Royal assent, the Crown must be advised that assent should or should not be given. When a law has been assented to by the Governor, the Crown must be advised whether or not the power of disallowance should be exercised; for this power exists, though in fact it is very rarely used. The Minister responsible for advising the Crown in all these matters is the Secretary of State, and he must clearly have expert assistance in deciding what advice to tender.

It is not surprising, therefore, that the office of Legal Adviser is one of respectable antiquity. In fact it dates from 1867, though between 1870 and 1911 the post was designated Legal Assistant Under-Secretary of State. A second legal post was created in 1897, a third in 1930 and a fourth in 1935. After the second world war, the work was entirely reorganised, and in 1949 the legal advisory staff were constituted a Legal Department (subsequently divided into two departments known collectively as the Legal Division). The main effect of this change was to empower the officers concerned to take administrative action on behalf of the Secretary of State in addition to acting in a strictly advisory capacity. This made for efficiency and economy by enabling the legal staff to assume direct responsibility for certain kinds of administrative and executive work of a legal or quasi-legal nature. The present professional establishment of the Division consists of the Legal Adviser, three Assistant Legal Advisers (equivalent in rank to Assistant Secretaries) and eight other officers. One or two of these posts are usually filled by retired legal members of the Oversea Service; and serving members of that Service are often attached to the Division as supernumeraries to give their help and enlarge their own experience.

When the Colonial and Dominion Offices were separated in 1925, the Legal Adviser and his assistants continued to serve the two offices jointly, and this is still the position. For convenience, some of the professional officers work in the Commonwealth Relations Office and concentrate upon the questions that arise in that Office.

CONSTITUTIONS

One function of the Legal Division has already been touched upon, namely the examination of the laws (usually called Ordinances) enacted by the oversea Legislatures, and the tendering of advice on the action which the Secretary of State may be called upon to take in each case. All except the smallest territories now have their own competent legal advisers who are responsible for the actual drafting of the legislation, but the Legal Division often has to take part in preliminary consultations between the Secretary of State and Governors before the introduction of a Bill, in addition to giving advice when the Bill comes home after enactment by the local Legislature.

There are, however, other forms of legislation in which the Colonial Office plays a more positive part. The United Kingdom Parliament has power to legislate for the dependent territories, and from time to time Bills are presented to Parliament affecting particular territories or the territories generally. The Colonial Office Legal Adviser is naturally associated closely with Parliamentary Counsel in the drafting of such Bills.

With a few exceptions (including Bahamas, Barbados and Bermuda), the Crown has general power to legislate for the territories by Order in Council. Such Orders may cover a wide variety of subjects, but perhaps the most important are those which embody the constitutions of the territories. The drafting of constitutions, until lately a relatively minor activity of the legal advisory staff, has in these days of rapid political development become a large section of the work, calling for special knowledge and experience; and this in great part accounts for the very considerable expansion of the staff since 1945. Whether or not it is a good thing, practically all the oversea territories—unlike the Mother Country herself—have written constitutions. Some have endured for centuries, but most, framed to meet temporary conditions, become out of date and have to be changed at intervals which tend to be more frequent as the pace of progress increases; and nearly every change requires some kind of legal action.

The substance and timing of constitutional changes are matters of administrative policy, and as such are dealt with in the geographical departments in the first instance. These changes do not come about fortuitously or automatically, but are the product of much careful thought and often of protracted negotiation. The sense that the existing constitution in a particular territory has become out of harmony with current conditions may grow up gradually, or the need for change may be forced upon the public attention by some crisis in the territory's affairs. What follows will depend upon circumstances. Sometimes the issue can be settled by informal discussions and confirmed by an exchange of despatches between the Governor and the Secretary of State. Sometimes a local Committee or Commission is appointed to consider the matter and make a report: a notable example of this technique is the report of the all-African Commission under Sir Henley Coussey which planned the constitution of the Gold Coast in 1949. Sometimes an independent Commission may be appointed by the Secretary of State and sent out to the territory to study the question in consultation with local leaders: an example of this is the British Guiana Constitution Commission of 1950-51 under the Chairmanship of Sir John Waddington. Sometimes—as in 1953-54 in the case of Nigeria—a formal conference of interested parties may be convened by the Secretary of State himself.

F₊

The general trend of change is, naturally, in the direction of fuller local self-government. Although the details vary from place to place, the pattern of development is fairly well marked. Executive Councils, originally composed of officials, have unofficial members added to them by stages. Provision may be made for some of these to be elected, or submitted to the Governor for nomination, by the Legislative Council. When experience has been gained, some of these unofficial members may be assigned portfolios covering certain government departments. This may develop into the formal appointment of Ministers and to the establishment of a rule or convention that the Governor normally acts on ministerial advice, though retaining reserved powers for dealing with matters involving public order, public faith and good government. At a very advanced stage the official members of Executive Council may (as in the Gold Coast to-day) disappear from the scene, leaving the day-to-day government of the country to be carried on by a Prime Minister and Cabinet responsible to the Legislature.

In the Legislative Council or Assembly, members would at the early stage be chosen by the Governor; later, provision would be made for some to be elected, and the proportion of elected to nominated members would probably be increased from time to time. The constitution may specify the scope of the franchise, and in territories inhabited by more than one race it may lay down the number of seats to be assigned to persons of different races.

When a change of any kind which involves an amendment of existing constitutional instruments has been decided upon in principle, it falls to the constitutional lawyers to translate the decision into the appropriate action. The Legal Division carries out this work in consultation with the Law Officers of the territory concerned.

Though for historical reasons the pattern and form of the constitutional instruments varies from territory to territory, there are normally three complementary instruments. First there is usually an Order in Council, which may be called the basic document. This makes provision for the government of the territory and lays down in general terms the composition and powers of the Executive and Legislative Councils, the procedure with regard to legislation, the establishment of Courts of Justice (unless this is provided for in local legislation), and whatever else is necessary. Secondly, there are Letters Patent constituting the office of Governor and defining his powers and duties as the representative of the Crown. Thirdly there are Royal Instructions, which lay down the procedure to be followed by the Governor in the exercise of his powers and duties. In addition to these instruments, there are often local ordinances embodying some features of the constitution.

H.M. OVERSEA JUDICIARY

The oversea territories have inherited the British tradition of judicial independence. Provision is made everywhere for Courts of Justice with Judges usually appointed on the instructions of the Sovereign. (In one or two of the very smallest Colonies the Governor acts when required as Judge; but this does not invalidate the principle, for appeal lies from his judgment, as from that of any other Judge, to the Queen in Privy Council.) The Colonial Office is not, therefore, as a rule directly concerned with the day-to-day administration of justice in the territories or called upon to intervene in questions which come before the local Courts. The Secretary of State is, however, responsible for advising the Crown on the appointment of Judges.

Judges are not, of course, civil servants, though for convenience they usually serve under the same pension, leave and other regulations as civil servants. Once appointed, they are (as has been officially stated) as secure in the tenure of their offices as their judicial brethren in the United Kingdom, being removable only after an elaborate procedure including reference to the Judicial Committee of the Privy Council. It is, however, an established convention that Judges retire on reaching the age of 62 (65 in the case of Justices of Appeal), unless granted a special extension; and naturally a Judge who became physically or mentally incapable of service before reaching that age would tender his resignation. Nor are Judges immune from the risk (slight though it may be) of abolition of office.

Vacancies in judicial posts may occasionally be filled by direct selection from lawyers in private practice at the Bar of the territory concerned or (rarely) that of the United Kingdom or some other Commonwealth country or territory. When territories reach an advanced stage of social development, there is a natural tendency for judicial like other senior posts to be filled by people of local origin, whether directly recruited from the ranks of the profession or promoted from junior offices. The need to safeguard judicial independence by preserving these appointments from political influence has not been overlooked in framing constitutions which provide for self-government. In the last constitution devised for Ceylon under the Colonial Office, an independent Judicial Services Commission was set up to deal with appointments to judicial office; and similar arrangements have been incorporated in the latest constitution for the Gold Coast.

Most judicial posts in most territories, however, have been and continue to be filled by officers of what was known as the Colonial Legal Service until the change in the title of the Colonial Service in 1954. The junior ranks of this branch of the Oversea Service consist of barristers and solicitors employed as Magistrates or Crown Counsel or in other capacities requiring a legal qualification. From these posts they may be selected by the Secretary of State for promotion to posts of Law Officer (Attorney-General or Solicitor-General) and other senior offices as well as for appointments as Puisne Judges, Chief Justices or Judges of Appeal. There is in practice a good deal of transfer on promotion, since the establishments of senior posts in most territories are small and the advantages of selection from a wide field are evident in a service where general professional experience is more important than local knowledge, and where complete detachment from local politics or controversies is desirable.

The Secretary of State must, therefore, look to his Legal Adviser, working in collaboration with the Oversea Service Division, to have a comprehensive and intimate knowledge of the personalities in the legal branch of the Service, of their qualifications, experience and merits, in order that he may satisfactorily discharge the responsible duty of advising the Sovereign on appointments.

The Legal Adviser is also concerned with questions of recruitment and with assisting students from the oversea territories who wish to be called to the Bar in England. Large numbers of such students come to this country, mostly with the intention of going into private practice in their own territories, though some go into government service. There is still, also, a considerable demand for the recruitment of legal staff from the United Kingdom through the Colonial Office machinery—50 places were filled in 1953—and a probationership scheme has been introduced to help in creating a supply of good candidates who can be considered for employment in any territory where they may be wanted.

DISCIPLINARY CASES, APPEALS AND PETITIONS

There is an immense variety of subjects arising in the ordinary course of Colonial Office business on which legal advice is required. There are, to begin with, questions connected with the employment of officers in the public services. Numbers of appeals and petitions are received, addressed to the Secretary of State or sometimes to the Sovereign, from public servants in the territories who consider themselves aggrieved or claim that the government which employs them has not carried out its proper obligations towards them. All such appeals and petitions—many of which are extremely voluminous and complicated, often pathetic and sometimes not untinged with comedy—are very seriously considered in the Colonial Office and almost invariably call for legal advice. This independent examination is carried out in spite of the rule that all petitions and appeals must be forwarded through the Governor. Naturally, the Governor himself considers the case first, and if he thinks the grievance legitimate he will deal with it. The petitions which come forward are those which the Governor considers to be without substance. Usually the Secretary of State finds no reason to disagree; but occasionally some new point emerges from the examination of the case in the Colonial Office and leads the Secretary of State to suggest to the Governor that the matter should be further considered.

Another body of legal work arises out of the Secretary of State's responsibilities towards the higher ranks of the public services overseas. The Colonial Regulations prescribe a detailed procedure for the investigation of disciplinary charges against officers above a certain level, which varies in different territories but covers all those who have been selected for their appointments by the Secretary of State. (Even below this level, any appeal from an officer against a Governor's decision has to be sent to the Secretary of State.) The charges have to be dealt with by a properly constituted tribunal and the officer concerned must have full knowledge of everything alleged against him and full opportunity of calling and cross-examining witnesses and presenting his case. The findings of the tribunal are considered by the Governor in Council, and any recommendation which he may make for the dismissal or other punishment of the officer is subject to the approval of the Secretary of State.

Though the number of disciplinary cases which come before the Office is certainly no larger than might reasonably be expected in relation to the size of the Service, it is enough to keep up a steady flow of work. In the nature of things, the cases are rarely clear-cut and straightforward, and the issues which they raise are of profound importance not only to the individuals concerned, whose livelihood may be at stake, but to the whole Oversea Service which looks to the Secretary of State as its guarantor against injustice. The Secretary of State does not, of course, attempt to retry the cases. But he has a duty to satisfy himself that the investigation was conducted with complete fairness, that the conclusion reached by the tribunal was not inconsistent with the evidence, and that the recommended penalty is reasonable in the light of the circumstances of the case and the practice and tradition of the Service. This means that the usually voluminous documents have to be carefully studied by one or more of the legal staff. Sometimes protracted correspondence ensues before a case can be finally closed.

MISCELLANEOUS LEGAL WORK

Another section of work is concerned with the application of United Kingdom legislation to the oversea territories. A United Kingdom statute may apply to a territory in two different ways. It may *as part of the law of the U.K.* apply in respect of a territory.

For example, under the Colonial Probates Act, 1892, probate of a will obtained in a Colony may be resealed in this country and thereby acquire legal validity here, if the Act has been applied to the Colony. Secondly, an Act may apply *as part of the law of the Colony itself*. A good example of this is the Emergency Powers (Defence) Act, 1939, which empowered Governors to make defence regulations, just as defence regulations in the United Kingdom were made by the King in Council under the same Act. Some Acts apply in both senses; thus the Indian and Colonial Divorce Jurisdiction Act, 1926, empowers the Courts of a Colony to which the Act has been extended to grant decrees of divorce to persons domiciled in this country. It operates in both ways because it gives jurisdiction to the local Court and also ensures the recognition under the law of this country of decrees granted under the Act.

The application of these Acts gives rise to a good deal of legal and executive work over a wide range of subjects, such as nationality and naturalisation, visiting forces, maintenance orders, copyright, extradition and removal of prisoners. (Under the Colonial Prisoners Removal Act, convicted persons of British origin may be removed from oversea territories to this country if their health would be endangered by serving long sentences in the tropics or for other reasons.) The executive work, and that which arises out of the conferment of certain powers and duties upon the Secretary of State by Colonial laws, is now centred in the Legal Division: formerly it used to be looked after in the General Department.

A rather special piece of work which is larger and more continuous than the layman might suppose is that connected with the Prize Courts and Prize Law. The clearing up of prize cases arising out of the first world war was not completed until after the beginning of the second, which, in its turn, left a long legacy for the future.

In addition to all these specific functions, the Legal Advisers are constantly called upon for opinions or advice whenever anything with a legal aspect crops up on any Office file. A list of the possible subjects would be a list of all activities which come within the orbit of modern government. The questions may concern international or ecclesiastical law; the laws governing trade or taxation, finance or currency; the interests of individuals in connection with matrimonial or lunacy laws, contractual obligations, relations of debtor and creditor; the laws affecting freedom of speech and the freedom of the Press; in short almost anything and everything.

CHAPTER XV

International Relations, Defence and Security

EXTERNAL AFFAIRS

so long as Her Majesty's Government in the United Kingdom retain any responsibility in respect of an oversea territory, they must keep in their hands the ultimate control of the territory's foreign relations and must seek to ensure that arrangements are made for its defence against external aggression and the preservation of the peace within its boundaries.

Whatever degree of internal self-government the territories whose affairs are dealt with in the Colonial Office may possess or have achieved, they all have this in common: they can have no direct diplomatic relations or enter into any treaty with, or make war upon, any other State. All such transactions between States are carried out by Her Majesty's Government in the United Kingdom. This is the legal position, but it is not, of course, suggested that the views of the oversea governments on matters affecting their interests are not freely sought by Her Majesty's Government, or that they do not have opportunities of representing their case in international counsels.

The heading 'external affairs' includes a good deal of routine business connected with passports, visas, consular representation and so forth. In the Colonial Office this work is done in the General Department. Under this heading, too, comes a large body of economic and financial work concerning trade agreements, exchange control, Commonwealth Economic Conferences, American and other foreign technical assistance and all kinds of activities dealt with by the numerous international organs whose titles make wholesale drafts upon an inadequate alphabet. These matters are handled, according to their subjects, in the Economic Division and Social Service Departments.

The International Relations Department, a modern addition to the Colonial Office organisation, is concerned with the broader aspects of international affairs as touching the oversea territories for which Britain is responsible, and in particular with the relationship of the United Kingdom, as a 'colonial' power, with the United Nations.

For good or ill, 'colonialism', which used to be taken for granted, has become a major factor in international politics. There is no lack of critics who—some for creditable and others for more dubious reasons—seek to establish the theory that it is a bad thing for any nation to have dependent territories and that any nation which has them is accountable to the rest of the world for its administration of them. This theory cannot be accepted in any sense which would diminish the authority of the United Kingdom Government in handling its relations with colonial territories. Nor does it find any support in the text of the Charter of the United Nations. Nevertheless it is now recognised that regard must be paid to international opinion and to opinion in individual foreign countries in shaping and above all in presenting colonial policies. An important function of the International Relations Department is to keep in touch with the development of such opinion and advise on how account should be taken of it in the work of the Colonial Office.

So far as the United Kingdom is concerned, it has long been accepted that the British Government regards itself as a trustee for the interests of the Colonial peoples and as committed to lead them forward to self-government. When the League of Nations was set up after the first world war, the principle of trusteeship was embodied in the mandates conferred upon the United Kingdom and other Powers for the administration of the former German Colonies. This caused no difficulty, for British colonial policy was already in line with what was formally laid down in the mandates. The transition from mandate to what is now explicitly called 'trusteeship' under the United Nations made no practical difference.

INTERNATIONAL CO-OPERATION

The Colonial Office takes an active part in the work of the British representatives in the United Nations and a member of the Office staff is stationed in New York as Counsellor (Colonial Affairs) with the United Kingdom delegation. An important section of the delegation's work consists of the presentation of reports on the Trust Territories to the Trusteeship Council, with the consequent debates and correspondence. There is also much work arising out of the interest of the General Assembly in non-self-governing territories generally, as well as Trust Territories in particular. Although the 'colonial' Powers are in no sense accountable to the United Nations for their administration of any but the Trust Territories, they have undertaken, under the United Nations Charter, to transmit regular information about economic, social and educational conditions in the territories for which they are responsible. This information is collated by the United Nations Secretariat and examined by a committee appointed by the General Assembly.

The activities of the various technical Commissions and Specialised

Agencies of the United Nations provide a further body of work which falls to the International Relations Department. An important development in recent years has been the creation of forms of associate membership in the Specialised Agencies whereby colonial territories or groups of territories may take part in the technical work of these organisations and gain useful experience in international affairs. It is a function of the Colonial Office to ensure that these associate members receive the best introduction and guidance in their first participation in these activities. There is other work, too, which is not connected with the United Nations. There has been in recent years a growing development of co-operation between Britain and other colonial Powers over practical problems of common interest, especially in Africa. Close relations exist between the British Colonial Office and the corresponding organisations of the French, Belgian and Portuguese governments, and all take part in a formal Commission for Technical Co-operation in Africa South of the Sahara. Similarly the part played by the United Kingdom in the Caribbean and South Pacific Commissions is of primary concern to the Colonial Office.

Special importance is attached to liaison with the United States Government, and a representative of the Colonial Office is regularly posted as Colonial Attaché at Her Majesty's Embassy in Washington.

One of the cares of the Colonial Office is to see that the oversea territories themselves take as full a share as possible in the international activities which the United Kingdom conducts on their behalf. The British delegation to the United Nations has on several occasions included distinguished members of one or another of the oversea peoples. At Commonwealth economic and financial conferences it is the regular practice for oversea representatives to be attached to the United Kingdom team in an advisory capacity.

DEFENCE

The general principle governing the defence arrangements of the oversea territories is that the ultimate responsibility rests with Her Majesty's Government in the United Kingdom, but the territories make such contribution as they can according to their means and resources.

The Governor of a Colony or Protectorate is usually styled 'Commander-in-Chief', but this titular office gives him no actual command over Her Majesty's forces, except in Gibraltar, where the Governor is also Fortress Commander.

Most territories have some kind of volunteer defence force, which is raised, organised and paid for locally under local law. In some places service is compulsory. These forces are trained and armed in accordance with general policy laid down by the Secretary of State in consultation with the Service Departments, and the assistance of British officers and instructors is made available to them as necessary. Many of these forces provided oversea contingents which rendered distinguished service during both world wars. In most territories, also, the police are trained in the use of arms and can be mobilised when required as a military force; but the modern tendency is against making use of this provision in practice. It is found that the police have their own work to do in the case of emergency and are better left to do it.

Regular local forces exist in the larger territories. The Royal West African Frontier Force covers the four West African territories and the King's African Rifles perform a similar service for East Africa and Nyasaland. The King's African Rifles provide a contingent for service in Mauritius. At one time these two forces were directed from the Colonial Office, where an Inspector-General was stationed; and officers and non-commissioned officers were provided by secondment from the British Army. During the second world war these forces were greatly expanded (by voluntary enlistment) and taken over by the War Office. They provided important contingents for active service outside their own territories and made notable contributions to the conduct of the war in Italian East Africa and Burma. In May, 1945, the number of Africans serving in regular military units was estimated at 374,000. Since the war the African forces, on a much reduced scale, have remained under War Office administration; the Colonial Office and Colonial governments are consulted on questions of finance.

The possible revival of the old West India Regiment, also under War Office administration, is now being closely examined. In South-East Asia the Malay Regiment is administered by the War Office for the Government of the Federation of Malaya, and units of a Federation Army are in process of being raised.

Some of the oversea territories are geographically in key positions and play a part in the general pattern of Western defence and strategy; for example, Gibraltar, Malta, Cyprus, Singapore, and the West Indian islands in which bases were leased to the United States during the late war.

Nevertheless, it is the exception for permanent garrisons of United Kingdom troops to be kept up in the oversea territories in time of peace. Assistance from this source has to be called on, however, when there is a threat of external aggression against a particular territory or when internal disturbances occur on a scale with which the local security forces cannot deal. Thus, Hong Kong has been, and is,

strongly garrisoned in view of the civil wars and subsequent developments in China and Korea. Substantial British forces have been sent
to deal with the disturbances in Malaya and Kenya, supplemented
in the former case by contingents from East Africa and Fiji, as well
as by Gurkhas. Troops were despatched to British Guiana when the
political crisis developed there in 1953, and were still there at the
time of writing (1955).

The Colonial Office has, therefore, to be in constant touch with
the Ministry of Defence, the Service Departments and the Chiefs of
Staff. It has to see that the defence interests and needs—actual and
potential—of the territories are kept in view. It has to take part in
discussions about what military assistance can be provided for the
territories, having regard to other commitments, and what the territories can be expected to do for themselves or to contribute to the
common stock. It has to make sure, by consultation with Governors,
that when Ministers have to take decisions they have all relevant
considerations before them; and, when decisions have been taken, it
has to communicate and expound them to the oversea governments.
Naturally, most of the day-to-day work and negotiation take place
in London; but from time to time regional conferences are held to
consider financial arrangements in a particular area, and on such
occasions the Colonial Office takes part along with the representatives
of the territorial governments and the fighting Services.

INTERNAL SECURITY

Bound up with the question of military defence are the arrangements for obtaining intelligence about subversive elements and for
taking counter-action. To give any details of the organisation dealing
with these matters would obviously be impossible. It must suffice
to say that the organisation exists.

The task of counter-action is not made easier by the fact that the
ill-disposed often use the well-meaning as their unconscious agents.
It is not always simple to draw a line between activities that are
legitimate and those that are definitely harmful to the true interests
of the oversea peoples. Parliamentary and public opinion is rightly
watchful against any tendency to employ measures which could be
regarded as contrary to the principles of freedom of speech and freedom of the Press. On the other hand, the Secretary of State has a
responsibility for protecting the oversea peoples from attempts to
subvert loyalty, trade on ignorance and lead them into courses
which can only bring grief and disaster upon them.

This leads to the question of internal security in the territories,
which is the business of the police. Every territory has its own police
force which, like other branches of the public service, is employed

under local laws and regulations and paid from local funds. The history of these police forces is an interesting study, and even more interesting is their modern development.

For reasons which I have discussed more fully in another book[1] most of the Colonial police forces were originally modelled upon the Royal Irish Constabulary and were organised as semi-military forces, trained in arms and capable of undertaking quasi-military operations. Unlike the police forces of Great Britain, which are organised on a regional basis, these Colonial police forces were part of the machinery of the central government. At the same time, they inherited also the special British police tradition, under which the constable, as an independent officer of the Crown, exercises, on behalf of his fellow-citizens, the citizen's duty of preserving the King's or Queen's Peace by preventing crime if he can, and, if he cannot prevent crime, by bringing the law-breaker before the courts of justice.

During the last forty or fifty years there has been an increasingly noticeable shift of emphasis. Instead of being regarded as a sort of soldier who also has some civilian duties, the policeman is now thought of as primarily a civilian who retains some residual military functions. His training, which in most territories had been formerly almost entirely of a military character, is now mainly concerned with the special techniques of police work in its various branches. He normally goes about his daily duty unarmed, and is taught to rely upon gaining the confidence and support of the public by the service he renders to them.

All the police forces of the territories are now developing along some such lines, though each has its own problems and characteristics. It is a process which has largely been engendered within the forces by the precept and example of enlightened and far-seeing officers. But it has lately been confirmed and encouraged by positive action in the Colonial Office.

Except in regard to recruitment and training of police officers the Colonial Office had very little concern with police questions before the second world war. In the unsettled conditions which prevailed after that war, however, much concern was felt by responsible authorities about the adequacy of internal security arrangements in the oversea territories. It was clear that conditions in many places were favourable to an increase of crime and of breaches of the peace arising from industrial disputes or inter-racial clashes, in addition to the activities of subversive elements. The idea, which had been canvassed before the war, of setting up some central co-ordinating authority was therefore revived, and in 1948 the Secretary of State appointed an experienced English police officer as Police Adviser.

[1] *The Colonial Police.*

His job, like that of other Advisers in the Colonial Office, was to provide the Secretary of State and his staff with expert advice on questions within his special sphere, and to go round the territories, discussing local problems on the spot and giving advice and help to the local governments. In 1950 the title of the office was changed to Inspector-General of Colonial Police, and a Deputy Inspector-General was appointed not long after. Both posts are now held by senior officers drawn from the Colonial Police Service.

The work of these officers has done much to inspire and to support the efforts of the local Police Commissioners to bring their forces up to date and improve their organisation. Two Conferences of Commissioners have been held (in 1951 and 1954) and have helped forward the cause. The training facilities generously made available by the Police College, the Metropolitan Police and other British police forces have also made a notable contribution.

Meanwhile, the constitutional position of the police in relation to the development of self-government in the territories has raised a problem to which serious thought has been given. The solution which is being worked out, and embodied as opportunity offers in new constitutional documents, is to establish a conception of the police as the instrument of the law and the servants of the public; and to safeguard their independence of political pressure in some such way as the independence of the judiciary is safeguarded.

[NOTE.—While this book was in proof, it was decided to strengthen the office organisation for dealing with the subjects discussed in this chapter by creating two new departments—one for police matters and one for intelligence services.]

CHAPTER XVI

Information Services

A MODERN NECESSITY

INFORMATION work in the Colonial Office has a double purpose. One side of it is to tell people outside the territories about the territories; the other is to tell people in the territories about the world outside. The interests of the territories are deeply involved in both sides of the work. It is important to these places that public opinion in the United Kingdom and other countries should be well informed about them; it is also important to them that their own peoples should be well informed about world affairs and especially about the aims and policies of the United Kingdom. It is important, too, to the United Kingdom both that the peoples of the territories should understand and support British policy, and that other countries should have an accurate appreciation of what the British have achieved and are trying to achieve in the colonial field.

Although, therefore, we sometimes hear criticism of government 'public relations' (and such activities can certainly be overdone), the Colonial Office would be failing in its duty if it did not take some trouble to supply these needs.

Until after the first world war, no organisation existed in the Office or was felt to be needed for any kind of information service, except that provided by the Library. When Sir Winston Churchill came from the War Office as Secretary of State in 1921, and the addition of the Middle East Department at the same time brought the doings of the Office more into the public eye than previously, he arranged for the Press Officer of the War Office to act also for the Colonial Office. The convenience of having a specialist to act as a link between the Press and the Office was soon proved by experience, and a Press Officer was a regular member of the establishment during the years between the wars.

When the new policy of development and welfare was set on foot in 1939-40, the need for some more extensive form of public information service became apparent. During the war, considerable developments took place. The Colonial Office collaborated closely with the Ministry of Information and made full use of its machinery for disseminating information both in and about the oversea territories in the interests of the Allied war effort. The potentialities of various publicity media—posters, pamphlets, films, broadcasting, lectures, feature articles for the Press and so forth—were studied and experience was gained.

After the war, it became clear that these services would have to go on in peace-time, although the Ministry of Information, which had existed purely for war purposes, was wound up, and replaced by the Central Office of Information, which has more restricted functions. The isolation of the oversea territories from the world of public affairs was a thing of the past. Colonial questions were attracting keen interest in Parliament and in international quarters. The peoples of the territories were emerging from the status of wards to that of partners who demanded and deserved to be taken into confidence and given material to make up their own minds instead of having their minds made up for them. Accordingly, information services, in all their aspects, came to be regarded as an important section of Colonial Office work. The staff was expanded and reorganised, some of it being taken over from the Ministry of Information, and a senior administrative officer was appointed as Director of Information Services. (This title was dropped in 1953.)

RELATIONS WITH THE PRESS

The work of supplying information about the territories to the home and oversea public falls into two parts: communication of news through the Press and communication of background information through other media.

Relations between the Colonial Office and the British Press are close and generally cordial. The Press Section of the Information Department is staffed by professional journalists who are constantly available to Fleet Street, answering enquiries directly or putting enquirers in touch with those who can help them. In contrast to earlier days, when it was often an effort to persuade the Press to take an interest in Colonial affairs, the oversea territories have to-day, for good or ill, become 'news', and there are few issues of any national newspaper or of the serious weeklies in which some happening in one or other of the territories does not receive prominence. A very few important daily papers now have a special member of their staff who devotes his attention to these matters, which of course is a welcome arrangement from the Colonial Office point of view, but there is no general body of 'Colonial' correspondents similar to the body of diplomatic correspondents with which the Foreign Office is in daily touch. It is however becoming increasingly common for papers to send representatives out to territories which are in the news, either to produce background articles or to cover particular events;

and in most such cases the Colonial Office is asked to help with introductions and facilities.

BACKGROUND INFORMATION FOR HOME PUBLIC

When the Information Services were expanded after the war, it was decided that the time had come for an intensive effort to inform the British public about the peoples and problems of the territories for which the United Kingdom is responsible. As a culmination of long planning, in which the Colonial Office was helped by its Honorary Adviser on Information Services (Mr. Gervas Huxley) and many other official and unofficial collaborators, a 'Colonial Month' was held in London in June, 1949. The campaign was inaugurated by His late Majesty King George VI who, with his Queen, visited the Colonial Office in Church House to perform the opening ceremony. The Gold Coast Police furnished an impressive bodyguard and a representative from each territory was introduced to Their Majesties.

The principal feature of the Month was the showing in Oxford Street of a comprehensive Exhibition, *Focus on Colonial Progress*, produced for the Colonial Office by the Central Office of Information. This was visited by over half a million people during the time that it was open, its popularity proving to be so great that its 'run' was extended to five months. Many other exhibitions and displays were organised by voluntary organisations, missionary societies and business houses; and the flags of the territories were flown *en masse* at the Crown Agents' building and on the old Westminster Hospital building which then still occupied the site earmarked for the future Colonial Office.

During the following years, the campaign inaugurated in London was carried into other parts of the country. A smaller, travelling version of the Exhibition was constructed, and arrangements were made for it to be shown in as many cities and provincial centres as could provide the necessary accommodation and facilities. Beginning at Southampton in May, 1950, the Exhibition went on to Bristol, Cardiff, Liverpool, Glasgow, Birmingham and Newcastle. During the Festival of Britain in 1951, it was staged at the Imperial Institute in London, where an important display of traditional art from the Colonies was also presented. After this the Exhibition went on a second tour, visiting Leicester, Edinburgh, Manchester, Leeds and Middlesbrough. It returned to the Imperial Institute during the Coronation celebrations, and made a final appearance at Hastings in March, 1954. In its original and touring forms, the Exhibition was seen by nearly 1½ million people. During its visit to each centre, local Colonial Weeks were arranged with appropriate lectures and film displays, and there was invariable and enthusiastic co-operation from civic authorities, educational organisations and chambers of commerce.

The Exhibition was a short-term, intensive effort, designed to arouse and stimulate public interest. Continuous work for spreading information about the oversea territories consists mainly in the production of literature and visual material, some addressed to the general public, some to the student of colonial affairs, and some designed specially for school children. The literature includes a comprehensive annual report made by the Secretary of State to Parliament, and also annual or biennial reports on the several territories. These last, which are compiled on a set pattern by the local governments, are now issued in a more attractive form than in the past and contain illustrations; some of them are printed and produced —sometimes very handsomely produced—in the territories themselves. The Oversea Service magazine *Corona* has already been mentioned in Chapter XI. The serious student is also catered for by various periodical publications—a series of Economic Surveys, a bi-monthly Digest of Statistics, and various occasional reference papers. On a more ambitious scale is the *Corona Library*, a series of first-class books by distinguished authors on individual territories, published by H.M. Stationery Office in collaboration with the Colonial Office and Central Office of Information. The aim of the series is 'to fill the place between official Blue Books on the one hand and the writings of occasional visitors on the other, to be authoritative and readable, and to give a vivid yet accurate picture.' At the time of writing, volumes on Hong Kong and Sierra Leone have been published and one on Nyasaland is nearing publication.

In a lighter vein, and prepared in the hope that they will be particularly useful to schools, are booklets, picture sets and posters, illustrating many aspects of life and progress in the oversea territories. These are produced by the Central Office of Information for the Colonial Office and are on sale to educational authorities and the public. Films (16 and 35 mm.) are available on hire from the Central Film Library. All these publications and facilities are described in detail in a catalogue called *The Colonies: A Guide to Material and Information Services available to Schools and the Public.*

The Imperial Institute in South Kensington has played an increasingly important part in this work of providing background information for the home public. The exhibition galleries there, which are maintained by the oversea governments and have been much improved of late years, together with the cinema theatre and special shows, provide a wealth of interest and instruction for the general visitor and the organised school party. The Institute is also responsible for running lecture services both for schools and for adult audiences throughout the country; and it has an extensive lending library of film strips and lantern slides.

Another essential medium for the dissemination of information is radio and television. The B.B.C. has always been fully alive to the importance of including news and features about the oversea territories in its broadcasts. Not only do the territories receive attention in the sound programmes, but a good deal of newsreel material is shown on television.

The cinema film is also an essential medium. During the war, a Colonial Film Unit was established at the Ministry of Information, mainly with the purpose of making films specially adapted to the needs of audiences in the territories and aimed at helping them directly or indirectly to assist the war effort. Some of the films produced by the unit were suitable for showing as documentaries to audiences at home and in allied countries. As time went on, the work of the Unit—which was carried on for a time after the war by the Central Office of Information and eventually taken over (in a much restricted form) by the Colonial Office itself—was concentrated on the development and training of local units to operate in the territories themselves as organisations of the oversea governments.

Before the official Crown Film Unit was abolished in 1952 it made several excellent documentary films for the Colonial Office. One of these, *Daybreak in Udi*, made by the Unit on location in Nigeria, achieved world-wide recognition.

Generally speaking, however, the films available for commercial showing in this country have been made by the film companies in the ordinary course of their business, the co-operation of the Colonial Office and the oversea governments being freely sought and given. An early example of a commercially produced film illustrating the life and problems of an oversea territory was *Men of Two Worlds*. Several others of varying merit have since appeared, as well as travel and documentary films of which some outstanding specimens were included in the *March of Time* series offered by the Rank organisation.

Such, in broad outline, are the main activities of the Information Department in telling the public about the oversea territories. There is much more that could be said, but only one further aspect of the work can be mentioned here. This is the organisation which has been run for many years by Sir William McLean for providing notes and memoranda for the information and use of Members of both Houses of Parliament who take an active interest in Colonial affairs.

BACKGROUND INFORMATION FOR OVERSEA PUBLIC

It is now time to turn to the other side of the Department's work—

the provision of information for the public in the territories themselves. Most territories, indeed, now have their own public information or public relations departments, some of them very highly organised and efficiently equipped. These are essentially organs of the local governments, and their main task is to interpret the policies and aims of those governments to the public of the territory. They can and do act also as a channel for the distribution of information about the aims and policies of Her Majesty's Government in the United Kingdom and about Commonwealth and world affairs in general. The material for this has, however, to be supplied from this end, and experience has shown that if it is to be fully and effectively used the home government must have some organisation of its own on the spot. Accordingly, it was decided in 1954 to make financial provision for establishing United Kingdom Information Offices, attached to the Colonial Office, in certain main centres, namely Nigeria, the Gold Coast and the West Indies.

The reason for developing activity in this field is not far to seek. As the peoples of the territories become inevitably more involved in world politics, they become the targets of propaganda from various quarters. Some of this propaganda is friendly and intended to be helpful; some is deliberately aimed at creating strife and embarrassment. The British people owe it to themselves and to the peoples for whom they are responsible to take active and positive steps to see that those peoples receive every help to form a balanced judgment based on accurate presentation of facts.

Within its own specialised range of functions, the British Council is an essential agency in carrying out this task, and reference will be made later to its work. In the distribution of political and general information, the Colonial Office, working through the local information departments and through its own oversea information offices when these are established, makes use of all available media, within the rather severe limitations of the financial resources placed at its disposal. So far as visual media (posters, picture sets and film strips) and literature are concerned, advantage is taken of the work produced by the Central Office of Information for general oversea consumption. The chief item specially produced for the Colonial Office is an illustrated magazine called *To-day*. This contains a minimum of letterpress (the main English edition being supplemented by editions in various vernacular languages) and consists mostly of coloured and monochrome photographs illustrating topical events and depicting typical aspects of the way of life both in Britain and in the oversea territories. *To-day* is in great demand by educational institutions, community centres and public reading rooms in the territories.

A special weekly newsreel, *British News,* is distributed to the territories. This is made up of selected items from the commercial British newsreels, supplemented by items received from the oversea film units. A special series of films about British life and institutions is produced under the joint sponsorship of the Foreign Office, Commonwealth Relations Office and Colonial Office; and arrangements are made from time to time to secure distribution rights in selected British commercial documentaries.

Sound broadcasting has made great progress in the territories, though they have so far been denied the blessings of television. The number of listeners is now estimated at more than three million. Most of the governments operate the broadcasting service directly; in a few it is run by a public corporation and in a few by private enterprise. The considerable modern development in this field has been helped by financial grants totalling over £1 million under the Colonial Development and Welfare Acts, and the B.B.C. have co-operated generously by providing and training staff, by giving expert advice, and by seconding liaison officers to the Colonial Office Information Department. In 1953 the B.B.C. lent one of their senior engineers to act as the Secretary of State's Adviser on broadcasting engineering problems. This officer has since visited all but a few of the territories.

It would clearly have been pointless to develop the transmitting side of broadcasting without regard to facilities for listening. Many territories have organised arrangements for community receivers to be operated in village halls and other centres where the public meet together. Home listening is a more difficult problem in most places, but it has to some extent been solved by commercial enterprise having designed and placed on the market certain types of dry battery receiving sets (of which the 'saucepan special' is an outstanding example) at prices within the reach of a wide public.

The programme material offered to listeners in the territories is entirely arranged by the authorities operating the services and is largely produced locally to suit local conditions. Extensive use is, however, made of material provided by the B.B.C. either by relay or in the form of recordings. Co-operation with the B.B.C. Oversea Services is among the activities of the Information Department. The services include several programmes specially produced for the Colonies, such as *Calling West Africa* and *Calling the West Indies*. In the building up of this side of the Corporation's work an important part was played by the late Mr. Grenfell Williams.

THE BRITISH COUNCIL

The British Council, as is well known, was formed shortly before the second world war in order to publicise British achievements in the social and cultural field and to provide a positive answer to the intensive 'cultural propaganda' then being put out by other Powers, notably Germany and Italy. Its sphere of operations included Malta, Cyprus and Palestine because of their geographical position and not by virtue of their being territories administered under the Colonial Office.

During the war, when people came to realise the importance of the 'projection of Britain' to the colonial and other territories, it became apparent that in the British Council there existed a ready-made organisation which only needed to be developed and expanded along its own established lines to suit admirably the purpose in view. Arrangements were set on foot which resulted eventually in the establishment of British Council representatives in nearly all the important territories.

Although the British Council technically works on an agency basis for the Colonial Office, and is financed for the purpose by a Parliamentary vote, it has the advantage of being an independent chartered body specifically debarred from participation in political affairs. It is therefore accepted by the public in the territories on its own merits for the services which it renders, and official and un-official leaders alike have paid tribute to the great value of its work. That work takes various forms, according to local conditions. Its underlying purpose is the same throughout, namely to promote better understanding and friendship between the British and oversea peoples. In order to achieve this purpose, the Council carries on numerous activities which are in themselves of benefit to the peoples of the territories. It may, for instance, encourage and help musical, dramatic, literary or artistic societies by providing them with suitable British material. It may arrange for British experts in various subjects to conduct lecture tours or run courses, and generally it is likely to take a leading part in adult education movements: a much appreciated contribution to these movements is the provision of study boxes containing lecture notes, visual material, etc., on a wide range of subjects. The Council may maintain premises which constitute a meeting-place for members of all races to come together in pursuit of common interests. British Council centres normally include in their equipment a library available to the public; in some places the Council has inaugurated general public library services, but this is not now regarded as within its terms of reference. It can and does, however, advise local libraries in the selection of books and help with the training of staff. Council representatives are much concerned with the 'briefing' of students and visitors going to the United Kingdom and with putting them in touch with those who can help them here. The important work of the Council at this end in looking after the oversea sojourner in this country is complementary to these local activities and will be noticed in the next chapter.

ASSISTANCE TO LOCAL INFORMATION SERVICES

This chapter has so far been concerned with the work done directly or through agencies by the Information Department of the Colonial Office in furtherance of its dual purpose. The department has a supplementary but important function, namely to assist the territories in building up their own information services. Some reference has been made already to the work of the Colonial Film Unit in this field, and also to the important contribution which the Office and the B.B.C. have made towards the development of local broadcasting. More generally, the department is always at the disposal of the territorial information and public relations officers and is ready to give them any advice, introductions or facilities which they may want.

Amongst its other activities in this direction, the Information Department has run, since 1949, a series of regular courses for senior locally-born officers of the territorial government information services. Up to 1954, twenty such officers had attended these courses, which included appropriate lectures, discussions and visits as well as opportunities of gaining first-hand experience by working alongside the regular members of the department. In 1951, a conference of Colonial Public Relations Officers was held for the first time at the Colonial Office. Representatives of 21 territories attended, and the success of the gathering justified the hope that similar conferences would be arranged in future from time to time.

In some oversea territories there are well-established and well-produced newspapers, but much of the Colonial Press is of recent development and is handicapped by small circulations, poor equipment and lack of experienced editors and writers. The independence of the Press is one of the safeguards of democracy, and is as fully respected in the oversea territories as in the United Kingdom, provided that the laws against seditious or subversive activities are observed. Where, however, Press standards are low, it is recognised to be in the public interest—and therefore a matter of proper concern to government—that facilities should be afforded for improving those standards.

Official help may take various forms. One form is the provision of news items and background material which editors can use at their discretion. Another form is the offer of facilities for oversea journalists to visit the United Kingdom for organised tours in the course of which they can study British institutions and make contact with their professional brethren and with men and women in public and private life. Such tours are regularly arranged by the Central Office of Information on behalf of the Colonial Office, as mentioned in the next chapter. Between 1949 and 1951, the Colonial Office made available a number of scholarships to enable Colonial journalists to attend, along with United Kingdom students, a series of professional courses in journalism arranged in London by the Regent Street Polytechnic.

MISCELLANEOUS DUTIES
OF INFORMATION DEPARTMENT

I have listed only a selection of the multifarious duties of the Information Department. The work includes many activities which do not easily lend themselves to analysis or description: the preparation of 'briefs' and memoranda for the use of Ministers or for the information of other departments or governments; the 'vetting' of books, articles, film or broadcast scripts submitted to the Office for verification or criticism; the compilation or editing of material prepared in the Office or by oversea governments for official publication; and the daily answering of enquiries of all kinds, some easily dealt with, others requiring extensive research.

Before the Information Department existed to deal centrally with enquiries, they had to be handled by whichever department or officer happened to be concerned. Telephone enquiries often presented a problem to the switchboard operator, and it was perhaps excusable that a question about Jerusalem artichokes should be put through to the Palestine Department.

There used to be some large rooms in the Downing Street building, in which several Principals and Assistant Principals worked together. One day a telephone enquiry came through to which the man addressed did not know the answer. Unwilling to let the Office down by admitting his ignorance, he asked the client to hold on, went to another desk and rang up the information bureau of a famous store which guaranteed to supply any information requested. The bureau asked him to hang on in his turn while they got him the answer; and in a few moments came through on a third telephone in the same room: 'Would the Colonial Office kindly tell them . . .?'

CHAPTER XVII

Students and Visitors from Overseas

A GROWING MOVEMENT

THIRTY years ago, Colonial Office concern with visitors to this country from the oversea territories was almost entirely limited to the occasional stranded seaman who turned up asking for help and was invariably passed on to such a charitable organisation as the British Sailors' Society. A handful of students—mostly from the West Indies, Malaya, Ceylon and the coast of West Africa—came to this country for higher education, but the Colonial Office had no responsibility for them. There was a Director of Colonial Scholars—usually one of the Crown Agents—who looked after the financial affairs of scholarship holders and gave them any other help they might need; and some of the oversea governments retained the services of retired officers to keep a general eye on their students here.

By the beginning of the second world war, the student population had begun to reach appreciable numbers, and some thought was given to setting up a proper organisation to deal with its problems. One problem was the finding of places at universities and colleges for the increasing number of applicants. The would-be students needed help, and the educational institutions often wanted information to enable them to select the most suitable candidates. Another problem was accommodation, especially in London and other centres where students are not lodged in college. A scheme was in fact drawn up for establishing a Colonial student centre, where these problems could be dealt with, but the war prevented anything coming of this. Meanwhile the Social Service Department of the Colonial Office did what it could, with the help of the Victoria League and other voluntary organisations interested in the welfare of oversea students.

In 1941 an entirely new set of problems was created by a government decision to recruit substantial numbers of workers from the West Indies and elsewhere for employment here in war factories, in timber production and on the land. Arrangements for the housing and welfare of these workers had to be improvised and the Colonial Office was called upon to collaborate actively with the Ministry of Labour and other home departments in looking after their special needs. In 1943 a separate Welfare Department was set up to deal with all matters affecting Colonial people in this country, whether students, workers or Service personnel. Under war conditions, many things which are normally left to voluntary effort and private enterprise had to be handled directly by government, and for some years the Colonial Office found itself responsible for the actual running of hostels and welfare services in various parts of the country. The evacuation to Great Britain, and later to Northern Ireland, of virtually the whole civil population of Gibraltar added to the work.

ASSISTANCE TO STUDENTS

After the war, the workers, evacuees and Servicemen and women were gradually sorted out and returned to their homes. The student population however was still growing, as a result both of educational developments in the territories overseas and of the launching of large new scholarship schemes for Colonial ex-Servicemen and women and for the training of Colonial people for higher posts in their home countries. Whereas in 1939 there were only 300 Colonial students in this country, there were 1,000 in 1946 and nearly 8,000 at the beginning of 1954, about a quarter of whom were holders of government scholarships of different kinds and the rest private students. Some of the private students prefer to be entirely independent, but many wish to take advantage of whatever organised arrangements there may be for welfare and general assistance.

Developments on this scale went far beyond what could be handled in a small Colonial Office department, and two important steps were taken between 1946 and 1950. The first was to ask the governments of the territories from which most students came to take a more direct part in looking after their students. As a result, all the governments with important interests in this field were persuaded to appoint and pay for liaison officers of their own. These officers—who might be retired civil servants or younger people seconded for the purpose from the territory concerned—were attached to and housed in the Welfare (now called Students) Department of the Office, and worked under the general direction of the head of that department, who had also taken over the title and functions of Director of Colonial Scholars. The work of the liaison officers was to keep in personal touch with the students and help them with their individual problems in a more effective way than was possible for Colonial Office officials with little or no knowledge of these young people's home background.

The placing of students in universities and other institutions continued to be dealt with centrally in the Students Department, which also retained responsibility for the administration of government scholarships. This arrangement has worked well, but it is gradually being superseded by development arising from political

G

progress in the territories. As the territories move forward towards self-government, it is natural and inevitable that they should wish to be more closely identified with the arrangements for the higher education of their students overseas, many of whom are destined to take a leading part in the future political and social life of their countries. The present trend, therefore, which has been fully encouraged by the Colonial Office, is for the oversea governments to set up 'students units' of their own within the framework of their Commissioners' offices in London. During 1954 the setting up of such units was carried out or decided upon by the Governments of the Federation of Malaya and Singapore; the Gold Coast; Sierra Leone and the Gambia; Uganda; and Nigeria. The units will absorb the liaison officers and take over some at least of the Students Department's responsibilities for scholarship administration, payment of fees and allowances, and negotiation with certain institutions (but not at present with Universities) for the placing of students.

THE BRITISH COUNCIL AND STUDENT WELFARE

The other major decision to which reference has been made was to invite the British Council to take over, from the beginning of 1950, responsibility for the reception and accommodation of colonial students in this country, and for the arrangement of general welfare services for their benefit.

The British Council already possessed an organisation and a fund of experience which gave a secure basis for development. Financed by a special grant made under the Colonial Development and Welfare Act, the Council has set up comprehensive and efficient arrangements for looking after these students. All students known to be arriving in this country are met and given any help they may need in settling down. In the year 1952–53, 2,730 students from British colonial territories were met on arrival and transit accommodation was arranged for 1,455. As far as possible the Council's oversea representatives 'brief' the intending students in advance and help them to avoid the distressing and pathetic experiences which have sometimes marred the introduction of these young people to the mother country.

The Council took over the hostels formerly run by the Colonial Office and made various changes in the arrangements. At the time of writing, the Council runs two hostels for men and one for women in London, and smaller hostels at Edinburgh and Newcastle. The Council also co-operates with the Universities and voluntary societies who maintain hostels for students generally.

It is necessary to have some basic hostel accommodation to provide for students who are in transit or on temporary visits, or who need time to accustom themselves to a strange environment. It has never been thought, however, that special hostels should be the main solution of the student housing problem. The bulk of the students prefer and are encouraged to live either with their colleagues from this and other countries in academic halls of residence, or with British families and in private lodgings. The British Council keeps up and is constantly extending a list of inspected and recommended lodgings where students can find accommodation at fair rates and without difficulties due to colour prejudice. Thanks to the Council's efforts and to the good quality of the students themselves, such prejudice, while by no means wholly eliminated, is now far less common than in the past.

During the year 1952–53, the Council accommodated 451 Colonial students in its own residences, and found accommodation for 190 in University residences and for 880 in lodgings.

In addition to these special services, the Council's general organisation for oversea students provides many facilities and amenities of which the Colonial students can take advantage. Vacation courses, week-end courses, surveys and study visits are made available. Introductions are given to societies such as the Rotary and Inner Wheel Clubs and also to private hospitality. Many social activities are carried on at the Council's student centres both in London and in other parts of the United Kingdom.

While the direct work of looking after the welfare of students is thus carried out by the British Council and many voluntary agencies, and not by the Colonial Office itself, the Office keeps in touch with what is going on and exercises general supervision. Since the British Council's activities are financed from public funds, the Office is necessarily in close and constant consultation with the Council. But on the broader aspects of student welfare, the principal machinery consists of a Consultative Committee over which the Parliamentary Under-Secretary of State presides. This includes representatives of the student Unions and associations as well as of the Colonial Office, the academic authorities, the British Council and the political parties. It provides a forum where policy can be discussed, complaints ventilated and representations made.

VISITORS FROM OVERSEAS

The arrangements just described refer to students, that is to say men and women who come to this country for academic, professional or technical training covering periods of months or years. There are also large and increasing numbers of people who come here, either on their own account or under organised arrangements, on shorter visits in order to see something of Britain and British life either in general or in some special aspect in which they are interested. The value of such visits, both to the oversea territories and to this country, is clearly very great. There is no substitute for personal observation and contact.

Amongst organised schemes, one of the most interesting and widely appreciated is that run by the Commonwealth Parliamentary Association, reference to which, and to the other activities of the association, was made in Chapter II. For organised visits and tours outside the parliamentary and legislative circle, the official agencies are the Government Hospitality organisation, the Central Office of Information and the British Council. Any important entertaining of oversea visitors is a matter for the Government Hospitality Fund. The organisation arranges on behalf of the Colonial Office for receptions, luncheons and dinners at Lancaster House or elsewhere for visitors from the oversea territories, who may be distinguished individuals or delegates to a conference. Sometimes the Office makes larger calls upon the organisation, as for instance in connection with the invitation of oversea guests to the Festival of Britain in 1951 and the Coronation in 1953. On such occasions, Government Hospitality helps with the booking of hotel accommodation, the arrangement of sightseeing and the general welfare of the visitors.

In recent years it has become a regular thing to arrange for parties of influential people from one territory or from a group of territories to come here for organised tours in which instruction and entertainment are judiciously blended. The request for facilities and the selection of visitors are matters for the oversea governments concerned; sometimes they act on their own initiative, sometimes in response to an invitation from the Colonial Office. The kinds of party for which regular arrangements exist include journalists, school teachers and trade unionists. These are looked after by the Central Office of Information. Since 1948, 102 journalists and others have visited Britain under this scheme, including a special party of 25 journalists from 21 territories which covered the Coronation celebrations in 1953. Other parties which come to study British institutions generally or particular subjects such as local government or social services, together with the individual visitors who come in great variety with all sorts of special interests, are looked after by the British Council, their expenses mostly being paid either by themselves or by the governments of their territories.

MIGRANT WORKERS

This chapter has so far been concerned with the people who come to the United Kingdom from overseas in search of instruction, enlightenment or recreation. There is also an important class of persons who come here in search of a livelihood.

Before the second world war, this class consisted almost entirely of merchant seamen, a certain number of whom, having come to British ports in the course of their work, were attracted to settle down and make their homes here. Some of them continued to go to sea; others abandoned or were abandoned by the seafaring profession and turned to other kinds of employment. As time went on, small but appreciable communities of such settlers were established in such ports as London, Liverpool and Cardiff. During the war, their numbers were considerably augmented, and in some places their presence gave rise to social problems which called for careful and sympathetic handling by local authorities and government departments.

The Colonial Office was naturally concerned in these matters ,but it is the accepted view that the Office is not directly responsible for questions relating to persons from the oversea territories who become resident in this country. Such people are British subjects (or protected persons). They share citizenship with the native of the United Kingdom, and if they choose to make their homes here they are in exactly the same position as other citizens. They are under the same obligations and entitled to the same participation in the benefits provided by the State. At the same time, it is mere common sense to recognise that their integration into the national community does raise problems needing special thought and attention. It is, therefore, also accepted that the Colonial Office should concern itself with general questions such as colour discrimination, and should co-operate freely with the Home Office, Ministry of Labour, National Assistance Board, local authorities and others with whom the actual executive responsibility lies.

This has become the more necessary during recent years because of the influx of immigrants seeking work. A small proportion of them are stowaways, but these are not enough to create any serious problem. The great majority are respectable people who have paid their fares to come here by air or sea, though often they have used up their available resources to do so. Most of them come from the West Indies, and especially from Jamaica, whose government has appointed a liaison officer to look after the welfare of Jamaican immigrants. Some were in this country as Servicemen or munition workers during the war, and decided that they preferred conditions here to those they found on their return home. Others, without previous experience, have been attracted by what they have heard about prospects in Britain in a time of full employment and about the British social services.

By the end of 1953 the annual rate of immigration was about 2,000, and it went very much higher in 1954. The coloured resident population in Great Britain which, before the second world war, was estimated at from 15,000 to 20,000, is now probably about four times as large, including perhaps as many as 30,000 West Indians. This is not an important figure in relation to the total population of the country, but of course there are particular places where the concentration of some thousands of people of non-European race may create a special problem. Amongst the immigrants, as in any other collection of human beings, there are some failures and some bad lots, but most of them so far have found employment and settled down satisfactorily.

CHAPTER XVIII

Past, Present and Future

THE work of the Colonial Office, as it has developed in scope and variety on an ever-widening scale from small beginnings to the present day, comprises in itself (as Mr. Pickwick said of the word 'politics') a difficult study of no inconsiderable magnitude. Plainly, within the limits of a single volume, anything like a thorough treatment of any aspect of the work has been impossible. There have been many omissions and doubtless many errors of proportion. But I hope that a broad outline, for it can be no more, has emerged.

One thing at least can be said with some certainty, and that is that this book must in many respects soon be out of date. To the historian of the future, our present situation will be seen not only to be the inevitable result of past developments but to be the prelude to consequential events which will seem as inevitable to him as they are obscure and uncertain to our vision. Yet even we can discern certain present trends and portents which may enable us, without undue presumption or indiscretion, to attempt some estimate of things to come.

The state of the British dependent territories has often been pictured as a ladder, at the top of which is 'Dominion status' or independence; and the territories have been conceived as standing upon different rungs of the ladder, moving from time to time to a higher (sometimes indeed back to a lower) rung. Like all analogies, this breaks down if pressed too far. There is not in fact one ladder or one set of rungs, nor is there one platform at the top to which all can climb. Some territories clearly have the potential capacity to become independent states in the family of nations; but some out of these have grave and difficult problems of internal integration to solve before that capacity can be realised. Other territories can hardly look forward to sovereign independence on their own account, owing to their small size or geographical situation, but may be in a position to combine with others to form a national or federal state. Others again would seem, so far as anyone can now foresee, to be destined to remain attached to the United Kingdom in some degree of dependence.

Self-government, therefore, in all cases is the proclaimed goal, but the term is obviously not in all cases synonymous with sovereign independence. The British Commonwealth is an adaptable and flexible organisation, resting rather upon the spirit than the letter, and new forms of association and relationship will no doubt be worked out as time goes on. Meanwhile it is clear that even if some of the territories whose affairs are now dealt with in the Colonial Office become independent sovereign states in the fairly near future, the Office will still have immense continuing responsibilities for as long as any planner can usefully look ahead. There can be no doubt that these responsibilities will be fully sufficient to engage the attention of a full-scale separate Ministry, and it is difficult to see any prospect of reverting to the pre-1925 arrangement under which a single Secretary of State and body of officials had to deal with the affairs of the whole Commonwealth (excepting India).

The Colonial Office is certainly likely, therefore, to continue in existence, whether or not it retains its present historic title. It is a long time since that title was strictly accurate. The Secretary of State is in fact Secretary of State for the affairs of most (but not all) of the Colonies, and also of Protectorates, Protected States and Trust Territories. No one could contemplate using such a rigmarole in practice, and no one has yet thought of a generally correct and acceptable word to cover all the different kinds of territory. The oldest territories (from the point of view of connection with the British Crown) are Colonies, and although 'colonialism' has become a word of ill repute in some international circles, the status of British Colony is greatly prized by many of Her Majesty's possessions. There is no ground of convenience or of principle for varying the ancient and honourable titles of the Secretary of State and his Office.[1]

Those titles have already survived many changes in the work and functions of the Office, not least during the thirty years since the self-governing Dominions passed out of its responsibilities. In 1925 the function of the Office could be broadly described as the supervision of administration. Except in the few Colonies of original settlement with their ancient constitutional privileges, the administration of the territories was in the hands of Governors and officials exercising powers delegated to them by His Majesty's Government in the United Kingdom. Almost all matters of importance—and some matters of very little importance—were in principle and to a large extent in practice subject to the approval or decision of the Secretary of State. Quite often, administrative questions which arose at this end were decided in the Office and the Governor concerned was merely informed of the decision.

Such a conception of the functions of the Office would seem

[1] The change in the title of the Colonial Service in 1954 was explained at the beginning of Chapter XI.

fantastic to-day, and it would not be an exaggeration to say that very few of the questions which used to come up for the Secretary of State's decision in 1925 now come before the Office at all, whereas most of the questions which now have to be considered in the Office were not even thought of in 1925. A general responsibility for the supervision of administration indeed remains, but essentially the main work of the Office now could best be described as the conduct of relationships. The territories are no longer considered as places which are being administered by agents on behalf of Her Majesty's Government but as political entities standing in a special relation to the United Kingdom. As has been shown in this book, the special relation takes different forms in different contexts. The point, however, is that the conduct of business between any territory and the United Kingdom is now approached in a spirit of bilateral negotiation and not of unilateral direction. Even when the United Kingdom has the last word, it does not pronounce it without hearing and considering the view of the other party.

In the old days, the Secretary of State looked exclusively to the Governor to express any point of view that had to be expressed on behalf of a territory. This is still an important part of the Governor's functions, but the more politically advanced a territory becomes the more the Secretary of State must take account of the point of view of the Ministers and other leaders who represent local public opinion. It is quite common now for delegations from territories to visit the Colonial Office and confer directly with the Secretary of State. The Governor is always kept in the picture, but he does not necessarily take an active part in the negotiations.

Conversely, it is now quite usual for Secretaries of State and other Ministers to visit territories and conduct negotiations or give decisions on the spot. Such a procedure would have been unthinkable a few years ago. Parliamentary Under-Secretaries had often visited the territories, but rarely, if ever, had a Secretary of State in office done so. When Mr. Oliver Stanley (Secretary of State 1942–45) set a new fashion by visiting personally East and West Africa and the West Indies, there were many misgivings about this innovation. It was suggested that the authority of Governors would be weakened, and that the Secretary of State would be embarrassed by demands for snap decisions on matters which called for detailed consideration, and would lose prestige if he temporised. Happily the advantages of personal contact were found to outweigh any possible disadvantages, and it is now recognised as an important part of the Secretary of State's job that he should visit in person or by deputy, as occasion requires and parliamentary duties allow, the territories under his charge. His senior officials and advisers, too, must spend much of their time in oversea visits, either in attendance on Ministers or on their own account. A list of official visits made during 1954, which was an average year in this connexion, is given in Appendix V.

The Colonial Office has adapted itself and will go on adapting itself to a new pattern of relationship in which formal conferences or informal discussions with unofficial as well as with official leaders have largely taken the place of long, analytical despatches as the media by which differences are resolved and conclusions reached. If experience proves the need for more new methods and new machinery, no doubt the need will be supplied. One can, for instance, envisage the possible development of a system under which some oversea governments might exchange accredited representatives with Her Majesty's Government in the United Kingdom.

Paradoxically, while the indirect administrative responsibilities of the Office in regard to the government of the territories have diminished, its own direct administrative and executive responsibilities have greatly increased, especially during the past fifteen years. In 1925 the Office had practically no direct administrative functions at all. To-day it has many. To begin with, it is entrusted with the management of the large funds provided by Parliament for Colonial development and welfare. Most of these funds are eventually passed on to oversea governments, but substantial amounts are retained to finance schemes which are administered centrally—which is to say, by the Colonial Office. An example of such schemes can be found in the organisation of training courses for officers of the Oversea Service. Other examples can be found amongst the various research projects carried out under the auspices of the Colonial Research Council. It is the Office policy to take advantage, wherever it can, of the most generous co-operation and facilities offered by academic institutions, and by such organisations as the British Council and the Imperial Institute, to get the actual work done by the people best qualified to do it. But the administrative and financial responsibility rests upon the Office, and there are some kinds of work—for instance the running of political conferences—which the Office cannot delegate to others but must handle directly.

The Colonial Office, again, has acquired new and direct administrative responsibilities for operating information services, both in this country and overseas, and for the work done on its behalf in this field by the British Council and the Central Office of Information. Another important field of responsibility is that connected with the education of oversea students. Although much of the personal welfare work is now undertaken by officials of the oversea governments, the Colonial Office retains important functions which it discharges either directly or through the agency of the British Council.

Leaving aside, however, these formal and identifiable spheres of action, it will be apparent from what has been said in this book that the Office to-day, while preserving the traditional forms and conventions, is in fact running a comprehensive and far-reaching organisation for providing material and technical assistance, expert advice and qualified staffs for the oversea territories. This raises a problem to which much thought has been given and it is right that it should be stated, though it would not be appropriate in this book to argue for or against any possible solution.

The advisory and staffing organisation is not a separate and definable thing. It has grown up inside the Colonial Office by *ad hoc* expansion here and there as circumstances required. It is thoroughly mixed up with the general Office organisation and (except for the fact that, by arrangement with the Commonwealth Relations Office, the South Africa High Commission Territories have access to it) it has no functions in relation to anything outside the political responsibilities of the Secretary of State.

So long as the range of those responsibilities broadly coincides with that of the geographical areas which need the kind of advice and assistance which the Colonial Office has been organised to supply, all is well. Up to now, this has been the position. The only territory (apart from the special cases of Iraq, Trans-Jordan and Palestine) which has gone out of the political sphere of the Colonial Office since 1925 is Ceylon, and Ceylon by 1948 was making little use of Colonial Office services and was well able to arrange for meeting its own needs in so far as these were not supplied from its own resources.

There are, however, to-day other territories which are well on the way to political autonomy at least in their domestic affairs, but which will for a very long time to come need staff and services from outside. This is fully acknowledged by their own responsible leaders. It can be assumed that the United Kingdom will remain the obvious main source of supply and that the British government will continue to be ready and anxious to give all the help it can. Clearly, however, it cannot so confidently be assumed that the present form of organisation will necessarily remain the most suitable under all new conditions that may come about. New means may have to be devised for some separation of the dual functions now combined in the Colonial Office, so that questions of practical assistance to oversea territories may be dealt with apart from questions of political relationship.

A pointer towards a new kind of approach may be seen in the foundation, under the joint auspices of the Colonial Office and the University, of Queen Elizabeth House at Oxford. The House is designed as a centre for encouraging and facilitating the study and discussion of administrative, political, economic and social questions 'with special but not exclusive reference to those territories overseas for which Her Majesty's Government in the United Kingdom are responsible'. It is clearly possible that, as this institution develops, the facilities which it offers may enable the Colonial Office to divest itself of some of its present work, leaving it to be carried on in the academic and politically neutral atmosphere of the House.

But it would be improper to pursue such speculations too far. This book is not an essay on Colonial policy or administration, nor a history, though in order to present an intelligible cross-section of the continually developing and changing story of this great Office of State as it stands in 1955, some examination of the past has been necessary.

The circumstance that the task should have fallen to be performed at this of all moments of time may be regarded as fortuitous or providential, according to the way one looks at things. In either case it is singularly appropriate, not merely because 1954 marked the century of the Office's independent existence, but because the intensive effort of the last third of that century is now moving up to its climax.

At such a watershed of history the Colonial Office could ask for no more fitting motto for itself and for its fellow workers in the Queen's service overseas than that of the knightly order with which this Office and that service are specially associated:

AUSPICIUM MELIORIS ÆVI.

Appendices

The Colonial Territories, Area and Population

	Area (square miles)				Population (1952 mid-year estimate)
ALL TERRITORIES	1,960,000[1]				77,000,000
EAST AND CENTRAL AFRICA					
Somaliland Protectorate ...	68,000				640,000
Kenya	224,960	(including water		5,230)	5,761,000
Uganda	93,981	(,,	,,	13,689)	5,262,000
Tanganyika	362,688	(,,	,,	19,982)	7,943,000
Zanzibar and Pemba ...	1,020				272,000
Northern Rhodesia ...	288,130	(,,	,,	3,000)	1,977,000
Nyasaland	49,177	(,,	,,	11,600)	2,460,000
WEST AFRICA					
Gambia	4,003				278,000
Gold Coast (excluding Togoland)	78,802				4,068,000[2]
Togoland	13,041				410,000
Nigeria (excluding Cameroons)	339,169				30,000,000[2]
Cameroons	34,081				1,500,000[2]
Sierra Leone	27,925				2,000,000
EASTERN GROUP					
Federation of Malaya ...	50,690				5,706,000[2]
Singapore ([3])	224				1,121,000[2]
Christmas Island ...	62				1,800[2]
Cocos-Keeling Islands	5				605[2]
Brunei	2,226				50,000
North Borneo	29,387				355,000[2]
Sarawak	47,071				592,000[2]
Hong Kong	391				2,250,000[2]
MEDITERRANEAN					
Cyprus	3,572				506,000[2]
Gibraltar	2¼				24,000
Malta and Gozo	122				315,000
WEST INDIES GROUP					
Barbados	166				216,000
British Guiana	83,000				459,000[2]
British Honduras	8,866				72,000
Jamaica ([3])	4,411				1,460,000
Cayman Islands ...	100				7,600
Turks and Caicos Islands	166				6,600

WEST INDIES GROUP—*continued*

	Area (*square miles*)	*Population* (1952 *mid-year* *estimate*)
Leeward Islands:		
Antigua	171	48,000
Montserrat	32	13,400
St. Christopher, Nevis		
and Anguilla	153	51,000
Virgin Islands	67	7,300
Trinidad and Tobago ...	1,980	664,000
Windward Islands:		
Dominica	305	56,000
Grenada	133	81,000
St. Lucia	238	82,000
St. Vincent	150	71,000
WESTERN PACIFIC GROUP		
Fiji	7,040	307,000
British Solomon Islands ...	11,500	99,000
Gilbert and Ellice Islands...	369	38,000
New Hebrides	5,700	53,000
Pitcairn	2	125
Tonga	269	50,000
ATLANTIC AND INDIAN OCEAN		
Bahamas	4,404	83,000
Bermuda	21	38,500
Falkland Islands ([3]) ...	4,618	2,300
St. Helena ([3])	47	4,900[2]
Ascension	34	170
Tristan da Cunha ...	38	281
Aden Colony and Perim ...	80	130,000
Aden Protectorate ...	112,000	650,000[2]
Mauritius and Dependen-		
cies	809	523,000
Seychelles	156	37,000

[1] Excluding area of Falkland Islands Dependencies.
[2] 1953 mid-year estimate.
[3] Excluding Dependencies.

APPENDIX II
Distribution of Work in the Office

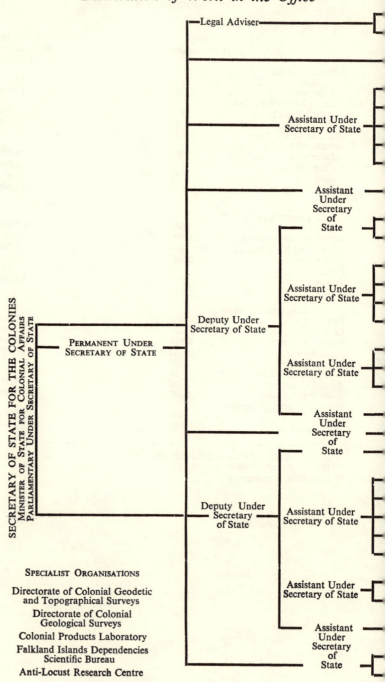

Legal Adviser

Assistant Under Secretary of State

Assistant Under Secretary of State

Deputy Under Secretary of State

Assistant Under Secretary of State

Assistant Under Secretary of State

Assistant Under Secretary of State

Assistant Under Secretary of State

SECRETARY OF STATE FOR THE COLONIES
MINISTER OF STATE FOR COLONIAL AFFAIRS
PARLIAMENTARY UNDER SECRETARY OF STATE

PERMANENT UNDER SECRETARY OF STATE

Deputy Under Secretary of State

Assistant Under Secretary of State

Assistant Under Secretary of State

Assistant Under Secretary of State

SPECIALIST ORGANISATIONS

Directorate of Colonial Geodetic and Topographical Surveys

Directorate of Colonial Geological Surveys

Colonial Products Laboratory

Falkland Islands Dependencies Scientific Bureau

Anti-Locust Research Centre

Principal Advisers and Consultants

Agricultural Adviser.
Secretary for Colonial Agricultural Research.
Adviser on Animal Health.
Adviser on Co-operation.
Adviser on Drainage and Irrigation.
Education Adviser.
Engineer-in-Chief, Crown Agents (Engineering Advice).
Fisheries Adviser.
Forestry Adviser.
Labour Adviser.
Chief Medical Officer.
Director of Colonial Medical Research.
Consultant on Tuberculosis.
Chief Nursing Officer.
Consulting Physicians.
Inspector General of Colonial Police.
Chief Security Officer.
Security Intelligence Adviser.
Adviser on Social Welfare.
Surveys Adviser and Director of Geodetic and Topographic Surveys.
Geological Adviser and Director of Colonial Surveys.
Director of Colonial Products Research and Officer-in-charge, Colonial Insecticides Research.
Colonial Building Research Officer and Housing Adviser.
Colonial Road Research Liaison Officer.
Colonial Pest Infestation Liaison Officer.

Advisory Councils and Committees

Advisory Committee on Colonial Colleges of Arts, Science and Technology.
Advisory Committee on Co-operation in the Colonies.
Advisory Committee on Education in the Colonies.
Advisory Committee on Colonial Geology and Mineral Resources.
Advisory Committee on Social Development in the Colonies.
Advisory Committee on Treatment of Offenders in the Colonies.
Colonial Advisory Council for Agriculture, Animal Health and Forestry.
Colonial Advisory Medical Committee.
Colonial Agriculture, Animal Health and Forestry Research Committee.
Colonial Agricultural Machinery Advisory Committee.
Colonial Economic Research Committee.
Colonial Fisheries Advisory Committee.
Colonial Housing and Town Planning Advisory Panel.
Colonial Insecticides, Fungicides and Herbicides Committee.
Colonial Labour Advisory Committee.
Colonial Local Government Advisory Panel.
Colonial Medical Research Committee.
Colonial Native Law Advisory Panel.
Colonial Products Council.
Colonial Research Council.

Colonial Social Science Research Council.
Consultative Committee on Welfare of Colonial Students in the United Kingdom.
Falkland Islands Dependencies Scientific Committee.
Inter-University Council.
Colonial University Grants Advisory Committee.
Managing Committee, Bureau of Hygiene and Tropical Diseases.
Tsetse Fly and Trypanosomiasis Committee.
Advisory Committee on Anti-locust Research.

In addition the Library Association have set up a Committee to advise the Secretary of State on library services in the Colonies; and likewise the Archaeological and Historical Advisory Committee of the British Academy offers advice on matters within its competence relating to the Colonial territories.

Official and Other Organisations Closely Associated with the Colonial Office

Crown Agents for Oversea Governments and Administrations.
Oversea Audit Department.
Colonial Income Tax Office.
Colonial Development Corporation.
British Caribbean Currency Board.
East African Currency Board.
West African Currency Board.
Imperial Institute.
British Council.
Bureau of Hygiene and Tropical Diseases.
British Empire Society for the Blind.
Overseas Nursing Association.

Colonial Government Agencies

The Bahamas Government Information Bureau, 29, New Bond Street, London, W.1.
The Bermuda Travel Information Office, Regent House, 89, Kingsway, London, W.C.2.
Cyprus Government Office, 15, Victoria Street, London, S.W.1.
The East African Office, Grand Buildings, Trafalgar Square, London, W.C.2.
The Gold Coast Office, 13, Belgrave Square, London, S.W.1.
Hong Kong Government Office, Grand Buildings, Trafalgar Square, London, W.C.2.
The Office of the Commissioner for Malaya in the U.K., Malaya House, Trafalgar Square, London, S.W.1.
The Commissioner-General, Malta Government Office, 39, St. James's Street, London, S.W.1.
The Secretary, Mauritius House, 16, Upper Montagu Street, London, W.1.
Nigerian Commissioner in London, 5, Buckingham Gate, London, S.W.1.
Commissioner for the Western Region of Nigeria, 18, Grosvenor Gardens, London, S.W.1.
Office of the Trade Commissioner for the British West Indies, British Guiana and British Honduras, 40, Norfolk Street, Strand, London, W.C.2.

APPENDIX IV

Ministers and Principol Civil Servants, 1925-1955

SECRETARIES OF STATE

1925 L. S. Amery.
1929 Sidney Webb (afterwards Lord Passfield).
1931 (Aug.) J. H. Thomas.
1931 (Nov.) Sir P. Cunliffe-Lister (afterwards Viscount Swinton).
1935 (June) Malcolm MacDonald.
1935 (Nov.) J. H. Thomas.
1936 W. Ormsby-Gore (afterwards Lord Harlech).
1938 Malcolm MacDonald.
1940 Lord Lloyd.
1941 Lord Moyne.
1942 (Feb.) Viscount Cranborne (afterwards Marquess of Salisbury).
1942 (Nov.) Oliver Stanley.
1945 G. H. Hall (afterwards Viscount Hall).
1946 A. Creech Jones.
1950 James Griffiths.
1951 Oliver Lyttelton (afterwards Viscount Chandos).
1954 A. Lennox-Boyd.

MINISTERS OF STATE

1948 Earl of Listowel.
1950 J. Dugdale.
1951 A. Lennox-Boyd.
1952 Henry Hopkinson.

UNDER-SECRETARIES OF STATE

Permanent
1925 Sir Samuel Wilson.
1933 Sir John Maffey (afterwards Lord Rugby).
1937 Sir Cosmo Parkinson.
1939 Sir George Gater.
1940 Sir Cosmo Parkinson.
1942 Sir George Gater.
1947 Sir Thomas Lloyd.

Parliamentary
1925 W. Ormsby-Gore (afterwards Lord Harlech).
1929 (June) W. Lunn.
1929 (Dec.) Dr. T. Drummond Shiels (afterwards Sir Drummond Shiels).
1931 Sir Robert Hamilton.
1932 Earl of Plymouth.
1936 Earl de la Warr.
1937 Marquess of Dufferin and Ava.
1940 G. H. Hall (afterwards Viscount Hall).
1942 Harold Macmillan.
1943 Duke of Devonshire.

1945 A. Creech Jones.
1946 Ivor Thomas (afterwards I. Bulmer-Thomas).
1947 D. Rees-Williams (afterwards Lord Ogmore).
1950 F. T. Cook.
1951 Earl of Munster.
1954 Lord Lloyd.

Deputy
1931 Sir John Shuckburgh.
1942 Sir William Battershill.
1945 Sir Arthur Dawe.
1947 { Sir Sydney Caine.
      Sir Charles Jeffries.
1948 Sir Hilton Poynton.

Visits to Oversea Territories by Administrative Officers and Advisers in 1954

Permanent Under-Secretary of State: Singapore, Malaya, North Borneo, Sarawak, Uganda and Hong Kong.

Deputy Under-Secretary of State: Nigeria, Gold Coast, Sierra Leone and Gambia.

Assistant Under-Secretaries of State:
   (1) Uganda, Tanganyika, Kenya and Zanzibar.
   (2) Kenya, Uganda, Nyasaland and Tanganyika.
   (3) Hong Kong, Brunei, North Borneo, Sarawak and Federation of Malaya.
   (4) Singapore, Sarawak, Federation of Malaya and North Borneo.
   (5) Leeward Islands, Bermuda, British Guiana, British Honduras, Barbados, Jamaica, Trinidad and Windward Islands.
   (6) Nigeria and Gold Coast.

Assistant Secretaries:
   (1) Barbados, British Guiana, Bermuda, Windward Islands, Leeward Islands, Trinidad, Jamaica and British Honduras.
   (2) Aden, Northern Rhodesia and Nyasaland.
   (3) Kenya.
   (4) British Guiana, Jamaica, Leeward Islands and Windward Islands.
   (5) Malta and Cyprus.
   (6) Mauritius.
   (7) Nigeria and Gold Coast.

Chief Information Officer: Cyprus.

Chief Statistician: Trinidad, Barbados and Jamaica.

Advisers:
   (1) Gibraltar, Nigeria, Gold Coast, Gambia and Sierra Leone.
   (2) Federation of Malaya, Singapore, Hong Kong, North Borneo, Sarawak, Brunei and Fiji.
   (3) Fiji, Solomon Islands, Tanganyika, Mauritius and Uganda.
   (4) Nigeria, Gold Coast, Gambia, Sierra Leone and Federation of Malaya.
   (5) Kenya, Uganda, Tanganyika, Northern Rhodesia, Nyasaland, Zanzibar, St. Helena and Mauritius.
   (6) Northern Rhodesia, Nyasaland, Nigeria, Sierra Leone, Gold Coast, Kenya, Somaliland and Tanganyika.
   (7) Tanganyika, Uganda, Kenya and Trinidad.
   (8) Tanganyika, Kenya, Uganda, Gold Coast, Sierra Leone, Northern Rhodesia, Nyasaland, Jamaica, British Honduras, Leeward Islands, Windward Islands, Barbados, British Guiana, Trinidad, North Borneo, Singapore and Malaya.
   (9) Northern Rhodesia, Tanganyika and Nyasaland.
  (10) Cyprus, Fiji, Aden, Hong Kong and Somaliland.
  (11) Nyasaland, Northern Rhodesia, Zanzibar, Seychelles, Mauritius and Uganda.
  (12) Gambia, Gold Coast, Sierra Leone, Nigeria and Malta.

(13) Singapore, Malaya, North Borneo, Sarawak, Kenya, Uganda, Tanganyika and Zanzibar.
(14) Nigeria, Somaliland and Kenya.
(15) Nyasaland, Malaya, Singapore and Sarawak.
(16) Cyprus, Jamaica, Nigeria, Gold Coast, Trinidad and British Guiana.

Deputy Advisers:
    (1) Kenya, Uganda, Nyasaland, Federation of Malaya, North Borneo, Sarawak and Singapore.
    (2) Bahamas, Jamaica, British Honduras, Leeward Islands, Barbados, Windward Islands, Trinidad, British Guiana and Gibraltar.
    (3) Gold Coast, Gambia, Nigeria, Northern Rhodesia and Uganda.

Assistant Advisers:
    (1) Northern Rhodesia and Nyasaland.
    (2) Gibraltar.
    (3) British Honduras, British Guiana, Trinidad and Jamaica.
    (4) Gold Coast and Nigeria.
    (5) Gibraltar.

Principals:
    (1) Kenya and Uganda.
    (2) Windward Islands, Leeward Islands and Barbados.
    (3) Uganda.
    (4) Windward Islands, Jamaica, Trinidad, Bermuda and Bahamas.
    (5) Gold Coast, British Guiana and Trinidad.
    (6) Singapore, Sarawak, Malaya, Hong Kong and North Borneo.
    (7) Nigeria, Sierra Leone and Gold Coast.
    (8) Trinidad.
    (9) Gibraltar.
    (10) Nigeria.
    (11) Nyasaland and Somaliland.
    (12) Uganda, Tanganyika, Nyasaland, Kenya and Malta.

Senior Legal Assistant: Uganda and Malta.

Assistant Principal: Uganda and Mauritius.

APPENDIX VI

Bibliographical Note

Not many books have been devoted wholly to the work or history of the Colonial Office.

The Colonial Office: a History by Henry L. Hall (Longmans, Green & Co., 1937) deals mainly with the nineteenth century.

The Dominions and Colonial Offices by Sir George V. Fiddes in the Whitehall Series (Putnam, 1926) carries the story up to the separation of the two Offices.

The Colonial Office from Within by Sir Cosmo Parkinson (Faber, 1947) describes in some detail the work of the Office as seen by one who served there from 1909 to 1945 and rose to be Permanent Under-Secretary of State.

Numerous references to the Office are to be found in the literature of Colonial history and in the biographies of persons who have served in the Office as Ministers or civil servants. Amongst those writings which include first-hand observation of the Office since 1925, special mention may be made of *I Remember* by Earl Swinton (Hutchinson, 1948); *My Political Life* (Vol. II, War and Peace, 1914–1929) by L. S. Amery (Hutchinson, 1953); and *Colonial Civil Servant* by Sir Alan Burns (Allen and Unwin, 1949).

In *The Colonial Empire and its Civil Service* (Cambridge University Press, 1938) and *Partners for Progress* (Harrap, 1949), I have described the work and organisation of the Office with special reference to the handling of personnel matters.

INDEX

217

The places named on this map are the chief centres of Colonial administration, and do not include the small island dependencies of the Colonies themselves.

BERMUDA

BAHAMAS

BR. HONDURAS   JAMAICA
LEEWARD IS
WINDWARD IS
BARBADOS
TRINIDAD &
TOBAGO

BRITISH
GUIANA

GIBRALTAR
MALTA

GAMBIA
NIGERIA

SIERRA
LEONE
GOLD COAST
TOGOLAND
CAMEROONS
SOM

UGANDA

TANGANYIKA

NORTHERN
RHODESIA

ST. HELENA

BECHUANALAND
PROTECTORATE

ATLANTIC OCEAN

FALKLAND IS

N
W   E
S